pyt 3   26/6/07

Sport and Cr..

Can sport help to create an environment that dissuades young people from crime? How can we better measure the effect of sport-led initiatives against crime?

Around the world, a number of different sport-led initiatives have aimed to reduce youth crime and anti-social behaviour. *Sport and Crime Reduction* examines real world case studies set up with the aim of reducing levels of crime in the community, and provides a timely evaluation of these projects. The book explores:

- The rationale behind sport-led initiatives
- The successes and failures of the programmes
- Conclusions for 'best practice' in programme design and evaluation
- Practical difficulties with programme design and evaluation
- Synergies with sport development, social inclusion and other local government objectives
- The influence of the political context on programmes, evidence and policy
- Eight detailed evaluations of contrasting programmes.

This unique evidence base for the assessment of sport programmes aimed at crime reduction should be read by students and professionals in sport development, local government, youth and community work, criminology, the youth justice system and leisure policy.

Geoff Nichols is Senior Lecturer in Leisure Management at the Sheffield University Management School.

Sport and Crime Reduction

The role of sports in tackling youth crime

Geoff Nichols

 Routledge
Taylor & Francis Group

LONDON AND NEW YORK

First published 2007 by Routledge
2 Park Square, Milton Park, Abingdon, Oxon OX14 4RN

Simultaneously published in the USA and Canada by Routledge
270 Madison Avenue, New York, NY 10016

Routledge is an imprint of the Taylor & Francis Group, an informa business

© 2007 Geoff Nichols

Typeset in Goudy by
GreenGate Publishing Services, Tonbridge, Kent

Printed and bound in Great Britain by
Antony Rowe Ltd, Chippenham, Wiltshire

British Library Cataloguing in Publication Data
A catalogue record for this book is available from the British Library

Library of Congress Cataloging in Publication Data
Nichols, Geoff, 1955–
Sport and crime reduction: the role of sports in tackling youth crime/Geoff
Nichols.
p. cm.
Includes bibliographical references and index.
ISBN 978–0-415–39647–9 (alk. paper) – ISBN 978–0-415–39648–6 (pbk: alk.
paper)
I. Title.
HC79.E5N474 2007
364.4'–dc22
2006037496

ISBN-10: 0–415–39647–6 (hbk)
ISBN-10: 0–415–39648–4 (pbk)
ISBN-10: 0–203–08915–4 (ebk)

ISBN-13: 978–0-415–39647–9 (hbk)
ISBN-13: 978–0-415–39648–6 (pbk)
ISBN-13: 978–0-203–08915–6 (ebk)

Contents

Illustrations

Figures

Tables

Acronyms

BCU   Basic Command Unit
CSLA   Community Sports Leader Award
ISSP   Intensive Supervision and Surveillance Programme
OGRS   Offender Group Reconviction Store
OI   Offender Index
PNC   Police National Computer
TOC   Theory of Change
WYSC   West Yorkshire Sports Counselling
WYSCA   West Yorkshire Sports Counselling Association
YIP   Youth Inclusion Programme
YJB   Youth Justice Board
YOT   Youth Offending Team

Acknowledgements

The author is grateful to:

The Operations Director of Fairbridge and the editor of the *Journal of Park and Recreation Administration*, for permission to include extracts from Astbury, R., Knight, B. and Nichols, G. (2005) 'The contribution of sport related interventions to the long-term development of disaffected young people: an evaluation of the Fairbridge Program', *Journal of Park and Recreation Administration*, fall 2005, 23 (3), 82–98.

The National Youth Agency, for permission to include extracts from Nichols, G. (2004) 'The theoretical contribution of adventure education to those of criminology and youth work, in understanding the prevention of youth crime', *Youth and Policy*, 84, 39–54.

Taylor and Francis, for permission to include extracts from Nichols, G. (2004) 'Crime and punishment and sports development', *Leisure Studies*, 23 (2), 177–194, and Nichols, G. (1999) 'Is risk a valuable component of outdoor adventure programmes for young offenders undergoing drug rehabilitation?' *The Journal of Youth Studies*, 2 (1), 101–16. The publisher's website is: http://www.tandf.co. uk/journals/.

Blackwell publishing, for permission to include extracts from Nichols, G. and Crow, I. (2004) 'Measuring the impact of crime reduction interventions involving sports activities for young people', *The Howard Journal of Criminal Justice*, 43 (3), 267–83, and Nichols, G. (1999) 'Developing a rationale for sports counselling projects', *The Howard Journal of Criminal Justice*, 38 (2), 198–208.

The editor of Vista, for permission to include extracts from:
Nichols, G. (2003) 'Kirklees splash: balancing objectives of crime reduction and sports development', *Vista*, 8 (1), 26–30.
Nichols, G. (2001) 'The use and limitations of reconviction rate analysis to evaluate an outdoor pursuits programme for probationers', *Vista*, 6 (3), 280–8.
Nichols, G. (2001) 'The difficulties of justifying local authority sports and leisure programmes for young people with reference to an objective of crime reduction', *Vista*, 6 (2), 152–63.

Nichols, G. (1998) 'Would you like to step outside for a moment? – a considera-tion of the place of outdoor adventurous activities in programmes to change offending behaviour', *Vista*, 4 (1), 37–49.
Nichols, G. and Taylor, P. (1997) 'A case study of competitive tendering of sports counselling services', *Vista*, 3 (1), 36–46.

The former trustees of the West Yorkshire Sports Counselling Association, for permission to include extracts from Nichols, G. and Taylor, P. (1996) *West Yorkshire Sports Counselling, Final Evaluation Report*, Halifax: West Yorkshire Sports Counselling Association.

The managing director of the Clontarf Foundation, Gerard Neesham, for permis-sion to use the Foundation as a case study, drawing on its annual report. More details of the Foundation can be found on its website: www.clontarffootball.com.

Russell House Publishing Ltd, for permission to include extracts from Nichols, G. (2004) 'A model of the process of personal development through the medium of outdoor adventure', and, 'Research methods in outdoor education'. In Barnes, P. and Sharp, B. (eds) *The RHP Companion to Outdoor Education*. Lyme Regis: Russell House Publishing, pp. 26–33 and 34–42. The publisher's website is www.russellhouse.co.uk.

1 Introduction

Who the book is aimed at

This book is primarily aimed at four audiences. For managers of programmes that use sports activity as a way of reducing youth crime it offers practical examples of programmes and the methods of evaluating them. These managers include those working in local authority sports and leisure departments, those in the youth service, and in the Youth Justice Boards and Probation Service. The case studies highlight characteristics of a range of programmes, showing how and why they 'worked', in terms of reducing crime, and what might have been improved. They show how programme design will vary depending on the target group of participants and the causal link between the programme and crime reduction. These factors also influence the approach taken to evaluation. A further influence on evaluation is the political context, including the value judgements surrounding such programmes and the value of sport, and the preferences of policy makers for different types of evidence.

For programme managers working in local government the book shows how there may be synergy between programme objectives of crime reduction and sports development. Understanding the process by which sports activity may be an effective medium for crime reduction programmes has implications for programmes using other media, such as arts.

For policy makers the book also gives examples of programmes, and evidence of success. It will help policy makers to decide whether to support a particular programme, and to chose between programmes; by considering the plausibility of the programme manager's account of the causal relationship between the programme and crime reduction – in other words, by asking exactly how sport is being used to reduce youth crime. The book will help policy makers understand the amount and type of evidence that it is reasonable to expect and that it is important to build evaluation into programme design, and also to recognise that some types of programme are inherently more difficult to evaluate than others. There is a balance to be struck between demanding information that gives a high degree of certainty that a programme has been effective or not, and relying on the lessons from similar programmes. Inevitably, there is never perfect information about every programme, and policy makers will need to balance the information available with their own judgement. Hopefully this book will inform that judgement.

The book is also aimed at researchers considering approaches to evaluation. For this audience it shows how the selection of evaluation methods will be dependent on practical considerations of the type of programme and the resources available. However, for this audience the discussion is placed in the context of research methodology: assumptions about how one gains valid knowledge about the world, and the nature of the world. This is important for academic research. However, as these positions are based just on assumptions, and these may be contradictory, one also has to appreciate the position of 'evidence' within the battle for status between researchers. One person's 'evidence' will be another person's myth, derived from methods and assumptions that are perceived to be invalid.

Lastly, for students in leisure studies and criminology, the book places the examples in the policy context of the use of sport to promote crime reduction – and more generally, the justifications for the public subsidy of sport and leisure. Crime reduction, and more generally the maintenance of an ordered society, has been an implicit, or explicit, justification of publicly funded leisure since the Industrial Revolution. The demand for public accountability, through evidence of programme effectiveness, has always been clouded by value judgements since the prevalence of the 'rational recreation movement', in which regulated physical activity was regarded as good for the moral and physical development of, predominantly, young men. As for the other audiences the book is aimed at, it helps students critically evaluate the role of evidence in the justification of public policy and how this relates both to the practicalities of the research situation and the value judgements of key stakeholders.

Thus, different audiences may wish to pick and choose different parts of the book. However, an overall aim is to provide a bridge between the practical and the academic. For example, while programme managers may find the nuances of philosophical debates about the nature of the world and the creation of valid knowledge somewhat esoteric, they may help them appreciate some debates between academic evaluators on valid ways to approach programme evaluation. Similarly, the practicalities of programme design may not be of paramount importance to students, but reading the case studies should give a useful insight into the work of practitioners, especially if student research projects include programme evaluation. Of course, the audiences overlap, and may do further once they have used this book.

The book structure

Chapters Two to Six provide the theoretical background. Chapter Two considers the traditional rationale for sport and the value judgements that have continued to influence public policy. Laying them bare is a first step towards critical programme evaluation. Chapter Three develops a model of how programmes have a long-term impact, based on a synthesis of approaches from criminology, youth work and adventure education. This model was used as a starting point in researching three of the case study programmes: Summit, Sportaction and Splash (Nichols, 2004a). Its development drew on experience of the West Yorkshire Sports Counselling and the Haffoty Wen case studies. Chapter Four deals with the question of what is valid 'evidence' and how the judgement of validity may be contested, and is a consequence of philosophical assumptions. This is important because the benefits of publicly subsidised sport in achieving social objectives, such as crime reduction, have increasingly to be justified within a regime of 'evidence-led policy' (Coalter, 2006). Chapter Five describes the policy context: the importance of crime reduction as a political objective, and the emphasis on policy justified by evidence. The funding situation of local government means that many programmes are short-term. This may distort the priorities of programme managers; assuring next year's funding becoming a more important objective than the overall programme effectiveness. Short-term funding limits the ability of programmes to contribute to the long-term development of young people. Chapter Six is a key chapter because it builds a general model of how and why programmes might work to reduce youth crime. This model is then related to the subsequent case study examples.

Chapters Seven to Fourteen are case studies of specific programmes. They illustrate the different types described in Chapter Six, and show different approaches to evaluation. These are not all recent – one is taken from research in 1996 – but are selected because they illustrate the themes of the book. The logical order to read the case studies is the order in which they appear – and cross referencing is based on this. However, readers may prefer to dip into cases representing the type of programme they are most interested in. The cases give a lot of detail of the research methods – both those that worked, those that did not, and those that were rejected. This is to help readers who are concerned with the practical problems of evaluation, and to make the point that evaluation is far from straightforward; the notion of 'valid evidence' is contentious and so, therefore, is the ideal of 'evidence-led policy'. The detail is also to give practical hints to programme managers about what worked and why. A further reason for selecting these cases is that I have been closely involved in all of them, so am able to report on details that might not be obvious in research reports. Where possible I have supplemented these with details and commentary on national evaluations.

Chapters Fifteen to Eighteen build on the case studies. Chapter Fifteen reviews how the general model in Chapter Six can inform the design and evaluation of programmes. The choice of approach to evaluation is also influenced by the preferences of key policy stakeholders, and what it is practical to achieve; given resources, expertise, and the influence of changing funding sources and associated objectives on the development of local authority run programmes. It also considers the synergy between crime reduction and sports development objectives. Chapter Sixteen examines how the choice of approach to evaluation is influenced by academic theory, the values of key stakeholders, policy makers and politicians, and what it is practical to achieve.

However, even the best-evaluated programmes, which appear to be successful, may fail to maintain support because of factors beyond their control. Chapter Seventeen goes back to review the role of sport and Chapter Eighteen concludes by drawing together the main themes of the book – the implications for programme managers, policy makers and researchers.

Defining terms

'Youth', 'sport' and 'crime' are all contentious things to define. All are social constructs. Youth is taken to mean a transition between childhood and adulthood, approximately between the ages of 15 and 25. More important than age is the fact that the major task facing people in this transition is the definition and redefinition of an independent self-identity (Hendry *et al.*, 1993: 31–57). This provides the focal point for the model of pro-social personal growth, outlined in Chapter Three, as one mechanism of crime reduction. Some of the case study participants in this book were younger than 15 and some were older than 25.

Another important transition coinciding with 'youth' is the extent to which young people are treated differently by the law. This reflects a balance in the criminal justice system between applying a welfare principle, which considers the longer-term development of the individual and social retribution/punishment (Gibson, 2000) (although this balance itself is also affected by public opinion, media coverage of high profile cases and political pragmatism – discussed in Chapter Five). Hence the existence of Youth Courts, Youth Offending Teams (YOTs) and the Youth Justice Board (YJB), established under the 1998 Crime and Disorder Act. These organisations deal with people from the ages of 10 to 17 – the period of transition between childhood and the age of 'criminal majority'.

Young people are also important as a category as they have traditionally been seen as a threat, built up by the media, and hence the 'problem' of youth crime may well exceed the reality (Muncie, 1999: Chapter 1). Further, 'youth crime' is a high profile political issue, in the sense that political parties have to be seen to 'do something' about it, and they tend to compete for the policies that will appeal to the small proportion of floating voters who determine the outcome of UK elections (Bateman and Pitts, 2005).

Sport is an equally emotive subject. Sport involves physical activity with some form of gross bodily movement, or fine psycho-motor skills. So bowls, darts and pool would qualify, as well as football. It will normally have a competitive dimension, but sports taken part in by oneself, such as weight training, jogging and recreational walking, may also be included, as would mountaineering and rock climbing. There is a general trend away from team sports and towards individual participation (Coalter, 1999) so to ignore this type of sport would rule out many activities. Sport will normally take place within a structure of rules, but again this would not apply to weight training or jogging, or fell running as an individual. A useful defining characteristic is that the pursuit of the sport could potentially constitute what Stebbins (1997: 117) has termed 'serious leisure' – 'systematic pursuit of an amateur, hobbyist, or volunteer activity that participants find so substantial and interesting that, in the typical case, they launch themselves on a career centred on acquiring and expressing its special skills, knowledge and experience'. So it is clear how one can progress through levels of skill and experience in the sport, even if one is participating only as an individual. This illustrates that how one defines sport generally depends on what one wants to do with the definition!

One could restrict crime to illegal acts, irrespective of whether one is caught doing them, and if one is subsequently convicted. This seems straightforward, but it still leaves out the situation where there is a perception by one group that another is offending, but no crime is actually being committed. This reflects the perception of the 'problem' of youth crime, as noted above. This is relevant to some of the programmes in this book, where areas may be targeted where it is perceived there is a problem, though this may not necessarily be supported by any other evidence. It may be just one generation (normally the older one) perceiving a problem with another one hanging around in a public space. The difficulties of defining crime make it harder to measure if a programme has reduced it. Individual records will record only convictions – a small proportion of the crimes actually committed. Perceptions of a reduction may become as important as reality. If one is studying programmes aimed at crime reduction one does not actually have to define crime – one can regard a programme as relevant if the manager says that crime reduction is an objective. This was the approach taken in a study of a diverse range of local authority programmes (Nichols and Booth, 1999a).

This raises the point of what constitutes a 'programme'? One tends to think of it as a structured sequence of events in which an individual takes an active part. It aims to have a particular effect on a participant. However, for purposes of this book it is useful to extend this to any means by which youth crime might be reduced. One means might be through deterrence – in a survey of local authority officers (Nichols and Booth, 1999a) some mentioned CCTV cameras, and one of the case studies reported here involved providing a physical 'presence' in parks to reduce vandalism.

The main argument of the book

The book argues that an understanding of the role of sport in programmes to reduce youth crime requires an understanding of how such programmes have a positive impact. It is not sufficient to make generalisations about the benefits of sport per se. Chapter Six presents a typology of programmes based on a combination of the 'risk' level of the participants and the mechanism by which they might 'work'.

Briefly, the typology's categorisation of risk level of participant uses Brantingham and Faust's (1976) categorisation of programmes as primary, secondary and tertiary. Primary reduction is directed at the modification of the criminological conditions that are likely to give rise to offending. Sports programmes of this type would operate at the level of attempting to improve the community and reduce neighbourhood disadvantage. Programmes directed towards secondary reduction focus on the early identification of, and intervention in, the lives of those in circumstances likely to lead to crime. Sports programmes that operate in this way would try to target 'at risk' groups of young people. Tertiary programmes work with those who have already been identified as offenders, and they seek to prevent recidivism. Sports programmes of this kind are likely to take referrals from a criminal justice agency such as a YOT. Of course, these are pure types, and some programmes may operate in more than one manner.

Programmes can also be categorised by mechanism, and three main ones are proposed: diversion, deterrence and pro-social development. Diversion involves diverting the person from a place or at a time when they might otherwise be involved in crime. It could also include a diversion from boredom, and thus a reduction in the likelihood that they would get involved in crime. Thus, in the summer Splash programmes, supported by Youth Justice, the place and time the programme was run would be important, and also the fact that it was run in the school holidays when young people would otherwise be bored. The mechanism of deterrence works when the person thinks they are more likely to be caught if they commit an offence. For example, people attending a programme run on school premises are less likely to throw a brick through the window. So this mechanism is place and time specific. Pro-social development, the process described in Chapter Three, involves self-development, facilitated by parallel increases in self-esteem, locus of control and cognitive skills, directed by pro-social values. It is the mechanism typical of programmes working with identified offenders, relatively intensively, over a period of up to a year or more.

The programme typology arising from this combination of risk level of participant and mechanism has implications for programme design, the role of sport in this, and the approaches to evaluation. Programme design and evaluation must start from a plausible 'theory of change' – that is, a theory about how and why a programme will work with young people to reduce crime.

However, some programmes are inherently more difficult to relate to crime reduction than others and all evaluation has to make the best job it can, given limited resources. Nearly all evaluations can be criticised for not doing a perfect job, even within their own theoretical framework, and all can be criticised by those holding different methodological assumptions. Therefore, who (academics, policy makers, practitioners) considers what (programme evidence and evaluations) to be valid evidence is strongly affected by value judgements, as is the use of sport itself. However, the task of this book is not only to show where these are relevant, but also to plot a way through practical issues of programme design and evaluation.

2 Value judgements and some traditional rationales for sport

This chapter first considers value judgements associated with the role of sport in crime reduction programmes. These are a reflection of the nineteenth century 'rational recreation movement'. These value judgements are important because they influence policy makers' views and public opinion on the value of sport per se. The chapter then reviews some of the evidence for the value of sport as contributing to physical fitness, self-esteem, locus of control, legitimate excitement and as a 'hook' to attract involvement. This is necessary, but not sufficient. It could be argued that to start from a consideration of the role of sport in crime reduction programmes is to be led by the value judgements, outlined above, that sport is necessarily 'good' or, at least, to start from a misplaced focus on sport, rather than on the role it plays in any mechanism of crime reduction. For any one of these apparent benefits of sports participation one has to ask, 'what is the relation to crime reduction?'. So this initial review of the role of sport is followed in Chapter Three by consideration of approaches from criminological theory, youth work and adventure education to understanding how and why crime reduction programmes 'work'.

The influence of traditional values

Public policy has been considerably influenced by value judgements of politicians, practitioners and public opinion. This is not only the case for programmes aimed at preventing people at risk of becoming involved in crime actually committing it – 'secondary prevention' in the categorisation of Brantingham and Faust (1976) – but also for programmes aimed at preventing known offenders re-offending – 'tertiary prevention'. Value judgements are more influential on work with young people because the work of the youth courts is distinguished from work with older offenders by the need to balance retribution and preventing further crime, with the welfare principle of considering what is best for the long-term development of the young person (Gordon *et al.*, 1999).

Policy within public sector leisure provision in the UK has been considerably influenced by the legacy of the 'rational recreation movement' of the mid-nineteenth century. This involved the diffusion and promotion of modern sport, which had been codified through the public school system, to the mass of the population, who had recently experienced the transition to an urban industrial environment. This diffusion was inspired partly by the philanthropic aims of ex-public schoolboys and partly by fear of the new vast urban proletariat (Holt, 1990: 136–148). It led directly to the first Act of Parliament permitting local authority expenditure on recreation facilities, the Baths and Wash-houses Act 1846, and a succession of other permissive acts (Torkildsen, 2000: 256). These values, that sport and recreation have a general beneficial impact on both society and the individual, informed the 1960 Wolfenden Report, which led to the establishment of the Sports Council. Robins has maintained that they persist today in advocates of sports programmes aimed at reducing youth crime, who 'are often propelled by a sort of aggressive optimism which acts as a defence against the helplessness felt when confronting the destructive nihilism of criminalised youth' (Robins, 1996: 26).

Conversely, public opinion can react strongly against the idea that programmes for known offenders appear to be rewarding offending behaviour. This was illustrated by the press response to the publication of a Home Office report (Taylor *et al.*, 1999) on physically demanding programmes for offenders. The headlines in local and national newspapers on 19 October 1999, the day following the publication of the research report, included: 'No evidence that action holidays cure offenders' (*Daily Telegraph*); 'Report questions value of holidays for hooligans' (*Independent*); 'Offenders' course could be a waste' (*London Metro*); and 'Course for tearaways may be a waste' (*Sheffield Star*). There is an interaction between public opinion and the media. The policy context at the time was influenced by well-publicised cases of offenders who had re-offended following intensive one-to-one interventions, including time spent abroad. This led to a Home Office policy prohibiting funding of any programme that involved travel abroad, irrespective of any evidence for or against its efficacy.

In understanding the balance between the two competing value-led positions – retribution and welfare versus rehabilitation – a distinction can be drawn between secondary and tertiary interventions. In secondary interventions public opinion is not likely to be led by known offenders appearing to be rewarded with additional sports and leisure opportunities – rather, the argument that 'sport keeps them out of trouble' may prevail. In contrast, the press responses cited above were to tertiary programmes, directed towards known offenders.

Value judgements are relevant in understanding the reactions of politicians and policy makers to the type of programmes that are the subject of this book, but value judgements about the methods used to evaluate programmes also influence views on the validity of research 'evidence' by the public, press, politicians and academics. Although academics claim to take the debate to the level of methodology, methodological positions are themselves based on assumptions, not facts – as discussed further in Chapter Four.

Some traditional rationales for sport

Sport's contribution to physical fitness

There is clear evidence that sufficient sports participation will improve physical and mental health. However, even if a programme succeeds in increasing an individual's participation significantly, this still leaves the question of how this is related to crime reduction.

In a study of 10,000 young people in Scotland, Hendry *et al.* (1993: 72) found a strong relationship between participation in sport and perceived physical and mental health in male subjects. This was especially significant for males involved in team sports though it was not significant for females. Hendry concluded that: 'a considerable body of empirical evidence now exists to support the idea that an active leisure life can improve overall self-esteem and mental and physical health. Put simply, leisure has a big part to play in helping young people to make healthy and successful adjustments in this phase of their life.'

The Department for Culture, Media and Sport/Strategy Unit (2002: 49) review of the health benefits of sport included four estimates of the amount of participation required to have a positive impact on health. The UK estimate was '30 minutes of moderate intensity activity five times or more a week' – which only 32 per cent of adults in England report undertaking. The most extensive longitudinal study of users of local authority sports facilities in the UK (Roberts and Brodie, 1992) concluded that while those who took part in sport three times a week experienced improved strength and self-assessment of health, it did not improve cardiovascular health or freedom from illness. Those who participated, but for less than three times a week, benefited only in self-assessments of health – they thought they were healthier, but were not. The study was conducted in Northern Ireland, significant because of the extremely high number of sports centres in relation to the population – and led to the conclusion that the mere presence of these facilities will not have a significant impact on health. This study concluded that sport has a niche in improving health, but that this is only part of activities that contribute to a more healthy life style, such as good diet and reducing smoking. The relation between sports participation and improved health is not unambiguous – there are costs associated with sports-related injuries. The economic benefits of reduced healthcare on the health system, attained through sports participation do not outweigh the costs of sports injuries until people are over age 45 (Nicholl *et al.*, 1994). While this is a neat analysis, it would not be sensible to restrict sports promotion for health benefits only to the over-45s.

Clearly, while sports participation can contribute to physical and mental health, for any programme with this objective the first difficulty is in actually improving the participation rate of the targeted group by a significant amount. Even if this is achieved, in the context of a crime reduction programme, as has often been pointed out, it may just result in criminals who can run faster! So, promotion of physical and mental health by itself does not necessarily have a positive impact on crime reduction.

Sport's contribution to increased self-esteem and sense of control over one's life

Increased physical fitness as a consequence of sports participation is associated with enhanced self-esteem (Trujillo, 1983). Sporting achievement may also offer a means of improving self-esteem. Self-esteem is especially important for adolescents, for whom a central concern is establishing their own sense of self-identity through social relations (Hendry *et al.*, 1993: 31–57). In their review of theoretical links between sport and juvenile delinquency Purdy and Richards (1983) identified a set of studies that understood achievement in sport as giving individuals self-esteem that they were not able to obtain from educational achievement or from other sources of social status. As Fletcher (1992: 60) identified while conducting research into amateur boxing, the sport can be a way of maintaining status and respect amongst peers without actually having to fight on the streets. A boxer he interviewed explained this: 'It changes you, you don't have to fight, you're not really bothered ... You don't need it any more.' Sporting achievements may help to alleviate tensions between social expectations and the individual's ability to achieve them. However, by definition, status from excellent sporting achievement is attainable only by a few and there may be difficulties of readjustment when an individual loses the capability to perform sport at an exceptional level.

Enhanced self-esteem was reported as a significant benefit to participants in the Solent Sports Counselling Project (Sports Council Research Unit, North West, 1990: 66–67) that worked with probationers, though this conclusion relied on interviews rather than longitudinal measurements of change and the direct relation to sports participation was not clear. This evaluation of Solent Sports Counselling reported that: 'This aspect of the project was considered to outweigh all the other benefits that might occur.' A later study of Sport Solent clients also concluded that, 'after six months 67 per cent reported improvements in general health and well being' (McCormack, 2000: 275), though this was based on self-reporting methods for a limited number of participants.

Self-esteem is linked to the concept of 'locus of control', which describes the extent to which individuals feel control over their experiences, or feel powerless to influence outcomes that are primarily determined by external forces. Locus of control is measured on an internal-external scale. It has been refined to differentiate between three 'spheres of influence' (Paulus, 1983). These are: personal efficacy – control over non-social environment, for example personal sporting achievement; interpersonal control – control over personal relationships; and socio-political control – control over social and political events and institutions. This differentiation can explain why an individual may feel that they have a considerable influence in one sphere of influence, for example personal achievement in sport, but little influence over another, such as influence over government policy. Paulus (1983) found a significant positive relationship between sporting achievement and high 'internal' locus of control, although, as noted above, the capacity for sports participation in general to increase locus of control would therefore be limited by the competitive nature of the sport; only a certain proportion can 'win'.

Participants in predominantly individual sports are more likely to have a higher internal locus of control in the personal efficacy sphere, while those who play team sports are more likely to have a high internal locus of control in the interpersonal sphere. Paulus's work implies that sports participation and achievement can increase locus of control, and this sense of increased personal efficacy can be generalised to other spheres of life, though to varying degrees. However, we need a more precise understanding of the extent to which a sense of control is transferred from one setting to another. And, as in an increase in personal fitness, might it just result in a more competent criminal? Greater control over personal relationships could just result in a more competent fraudster.

Emler's studies of self-esteem (2001) found that measures of self-esteem tended to produce results similar to measures of locus of control, self-efficacy and neuroticism. This suggests these attributes are all related or all reflect the same underlying quality. Thus, the same people tend to have high self-esteem, believe they have control over their own lives, believe they have the capabilities to achieve what they want, and are unlikely to be insecure, guilt ridden and miserable. The relationship between self-esteem and locus of control may be important for understanding why increased self-esteem might lead to a reduction in crime. It would seem likely that increased self-esteem would lead to increased internal locus of control. However, the relationship is not likely to be that simple; if an individual achieved a more realistic view of their locus of control, this might help them to recognise where apparent failure was not a true reflection of their own capabilities and therefore was less threatening to their self-esteem. For example, failure to obtain employment or educational qualifications might not have such a detrimental effect on self-esteem if the individual concerned realised that they were significantly disadvantaged in the job or education markets. On the other hand, an individual who had experienced educational or social failure may have tried to protect their self-esteem by attributing their 'failure' to a system over which they had little control. In this instance they might underestimate their locus of control. A combination of increased self-esteem and realistic expectations of locus of control could allow the individual to be more selectively pro-active where they felt that they would gain the rewards of their own efforts. This result was apparent in Maruna's (2001) interviews comparing long-term offenders who desisted with those who continued to offend. Detailed content analysis of 65 interviews showed that desisters had an optimistic perception of personal control over their destiny; they felt much more in charge. In contrast, persisters had a fatalistic attitude; they felt they could not escape from offending and were constrained by circumstances beyond their control. Thus, an increase in self-esteem and locus of control could help individuals 'take control' over their own lives.

Increased internal locus of control can be related to one of the sets of theories identified by Purdy and Richards (1983), explaining a link between sports participation and juvenile delinquency. These theories linked non-delinquent behaviour to a belief that the social system would deliver just rewards – sports participation presumably being a metaphor for this. Conversely, delinquency was related to a belief in the injustice of the system. However, an increased internal locus of control could increase a belief that the system was unjust, if it resulted in the individual attributing apparent failure to social forces that were beyond their control. It could reinforce a belief that illegal acts were justified by an unjust system: one thinks of Robin Hood, taking from the rich; or violent protests at World Trade meetings. Thus, the relationship between locus of control and crime is also unclear.

Similarly, Emler (2001) challenged assumptions that increased self-esteem is a good thing in its own right, or can lead to other benefits. He emphasised the need to understand the mechanisms by which self-esteem is linked to other outcomes, such as reduced crime. If one wants to reduce crime and thinks that increased self-esteem has a role in this, one has to be precise about what that role is. An implication of Emler's analysis is that in some cases a reduction in self-esteem might be valuable, for example in reducing reckless behaviour led by the 'bravado' of youth. So different individuals, or perhaps groups involved in different types of offences, will need to be treated differently.

Sport's contribution to new peers and role models

Another set of theories, identified by Purdy and Richards (1983: 185), place importance on role models in understanding the relation between sports participation and juvenile delinquency: 'While delinquents may be learning delinquent behaviours and values from their peers, athletes are being socialised by values and behaviours more aligned with the conventional values and behaviours of society.' An example would be the potentially positive role model provided by a sports coach or a boxing trainer. Purdy and Richards considered that the length of contact between the role model and participant is important. This conclusion is probably related to their emphasis on relations within sporting contexts. However, it is likely that a role model in a shorter, but more intensely significant experience, such as a three-week Outward Bound course, will have a correspondingly more significant impact on the participant. Evaluations of the Solent Sports Counselling Project (Sports Council Research Unit, North West, 1990: 68) and of the West Yorkshire Sports Counselling Project (Nichols and Taylor, 1996: 90) both emphasised the importance of the sports leaders in the projects as positive role models for the participants.

However, peers may provide positive or negative role models. An amateur boxer in Sheffield described his sparring partners: '[you are] with the professionals here, you're sparring with top class people ... these are the best – no mistake. They are world class. Naz, he's going to be a world champion' (Fletcher 1992: 77). (In 1992 'Prince Nassem' was the rising star of British boxing.) Sports leaders on the West Yorkshire Sports Counselling project felt that the opportunity to meet a new peer group was important for participants as it could help them break out of a way of life in which petty crime is intrinsic, through providing alternative norms of behaviour. On the other hand, sports leaders recognised that, whatever happens to the participant on the project, 'you can't get a person to drop all their old friends' (Nichols and Taylor 1996: 69). Examples of negative role models are provided in Collison's (1996) analysis of young males' search for a sense of self identity through drugs and crime, and the media abound in negative role models provided by sports 'stars' – discussed below. (Naz may have been a young man's role model in 1992; in 2006 he was convicted of reckless driving in an incident in which he caused severe damage to another motorist.)

The role of sport in providing legitimate excitement

It has been argued, especially in relation to programmes designed to reduce offending behaviour, that risk in legitimate activities such as sport, could be an effective substitute for risk in illegal ones. This understanding of the motivations for crime was implied by Lyng's (1993) concept of 'edgework'. Drawing on Katz's (1988) interviews with criminals, Lyng concluded that they seek situations where the outcome is unpredictable but they will have to draw on all their resources of willpower and determination to achieve a successful outcome. 'The goal is to transport yourself and your victim to the limits of an ordered reality and then use to use your transcendent power as a hardman to control the ensuing chaos.' Katz's sample appears to have been taken from criminals with a well established criminal career, so his findings may be less relevant to programmes at the secondary level of intervention.

Roberts (1992: 11) has also remarked that: 'One underlying reason for much delinquency and all other riotous incidents is that such activities can be exceptionally good fun for the perpetrators. It can be exhilarating to be chased by police vehicles. Pitched battles with the police can be particularly rousing ...'. However, it is not clear what evidence Roberts had to make this assertion, and it is unlikely to be from personal experience. Roberts was not hopeful that the relevant young people would be 'deflected by socially approved recreation'. Earlier, Rosenthal had developed a similar thesis, that physical activity involving risk is physically and mentally invigorating, and produces a state of well-being and elation. He claimed to have supported this by a study of 120 juvenile offenders, 60 of whom were sent to Outward Bound schools and 60 of whom were sent to conventional training schools. A one-year follow-up indicated that only 20 per cent of the Outward Bound group had reoffended compared to 42 per cent of the boys in conventional schools (Rosenthal, 1982). However, it is not conclusive that the combination of physical activities and risk, involved in many of the Outward Bound activities, was responsible for this difference in reoffending rates.

Sport as a hook to gain involvement

While the excitement offered by particular sporting activities may or may not be a direct substitute for that gained by illegal means, the apparent thrills of some activities contributed to their effectiveness as a 'hook' to get participants involved in probation service programmes studied by Taylor *et al.* (1999: 31). Programme managers reported that the possibility of taking part in these activities attracted participants, and this was important as only when they were involved could the programme do other work with them. The attraction of the activities was important where participation was voluntary, but just as a means to gain engagement for the more significant part of the process. Activities with this capacity to attract participants was also a characteristic of successful programmes in the USA, noted by Witt and Crompton (1996). This use of sport accords with McGuire and Priestley's conclusion (1995: 3–34) that 'on balance the learning styles of most offenders require active, participatory methods'. However, they also note that 'programmes need to match the styles of workers and clients'. This suggests that sport will not be the best activity for all clients.

The negative role of sport

Little has been written on the negative role of sport, which reflects the influence of the positive value judgements discussed above. Sports participation is unequal between gender, age, class, ethnic group and those with different levels of education (Department for Culture, Media and Sport/Strategy Unit, 2002). All these factors inter-relate. Inequalities in sports participation can be seen as a dimension of social exclusion, although reducing them will not necessarily address the causes of such exclusion (DCMS, 2002). (The value of the notion of social exclusion itself is debatable as those using it generally fail to define when people are 'excluded' to an extent that public intervention is required to do something to reduce exclusion; what is the difference between this and differences between people that are acceptable reflections of attributes, ability or values; and who decides when social exclusion is a problem justifying public intervention.)

While gender inequalities are reducing (Sport England, 2001), especially among young people, a strong 'cult of femininity' as part of a more general patriarchal hegemony still militates against young girls' participation (Scraton and Flintoff, 2002). Sport is a more acceptable activity for males. As a disproportionate amount of crime is committed by young males (Audit Commission, 1996: 8), this supports the use of sport as an activity to gain their interest. However, this is limited by the high drop-out rates in sports participation after school age, and the greater participation by higher social classes. So, even though sport appears to be more attractive to young males, it is still not an activity they are strongly motivated to do. There will remain the problem that young women may be less attracted by sport, and may find it more difficult to progress through levels of participation and to sustain participation through parenthood.

Further, Jupp (1995) makes the point that the relation between sport and crime may be negative. Crime in sport includes the use of performance-enhancing drugs and violence on the field of play. Prominent sports people may provide role models of a competitiveness to win at all costs, including 'non-sportsmanlike' attitudes and behaviour (ball tampering in cricket, drug taking to enhance performance in athletes and cycling, violent conduct in football, etc.) The same point is made by Critcher (2000), extended to those leading sports activities. Jupp acknowledges that the extent of any negative impact of sport on participants in sports programmes to reduce crime is unknown, however, his, and Critcher's, observations provide a qualification of the view that sport is necessarily a 'good thing' and challenge the predominant value judgements.

The implications are that crime reduction programmes based on sport need to be aware of possible gender and class biases, and that the barriers for further participation may be the greatest for the most disadvantaged young people – those who are also at greatest risk of becoming involved in crime. Programmes also need to be aware of potential negative role models provided by prominent sports people, and may have to counter this with an emphasis on 'fair play'. Sport embodies no inherent pro-social values.

This initial romp through the traditional rationales for sport in crime reduction programmes shows how we need to be wary of the value-led general assertions for the role of sport, and need to understand in more depth the mechanisms by which programmes might reduce crime – how and why they might have this impact. The following chapter does this by synthesising contributions from criminology, youth work and adventure education.

3 A synthesis of theory from criminology, youth work and adventure education

This chapter outlines approaches from criminology and youth work that propose that crime reduction programmes should focus on development of cognitive skills. It also examines the risk/protection factor approach, which has also influenced criminology and youth work. These approaches are contrasted with a model of the process of personal growth in adventure education. A synthesis of these different approaches helps disentangle the role of sport in programmes and clarifies one of the major mechanisms by which programmes might reduce crime, incorporated into Chapter Six – personal development directed by pro-social values. This was the starting point for research into three of the case study programmes: Splash, Sportaction and Summit. This starting point – a combination of a theoretical description of the process and what is required to facilitate it – reflects the objective of helping managers design and implement programmes.

Criminological theory – the development of cognitive competencies

Ross and Fabiano (1985) reviewed fifty programmes designed to reduce offending behaviour and which had been the subject of, what they regarded as, rigorous evaluation studies. They concluded that 21 of the 25 programmes that had been successful in reducing reconviction rates were characterised by attempts to develop participants' cognitive skills. From this Ross and Fabiano developed an understanding of criminal behaviour as being predisposed by a set of cognitive deficiencies that were apparent in offenders. These included: an inability to solve interpersonal problems and deal with social relationships; a lack of self control; a lack of the ability to reason abstractly; low locus of control; and an inability to feel empathy with other people.

Ross applied this understanding of criminal behaviour to his own 'Reasoning and Rehabilitation' programme in Ottawa, and found it led to a significant decrease in offending (Farrington, 1994). The use of cognitive-behavioural programmes for offenders in the UK was appraised by Vanstone (2000) and by a Home Office review of research (Vennard *et al.*, 1997). Cognitive self-change programmes are now widely used in Britain's prisons (Rose, 2002; Hedderman and

Sugg, 1997). However, Pitts argues that, while Ross and Fabiano's programmes might appear to provide evidence to lead policy, the evidence can be challenged and appears to reflect a 'selective amnesia' (Pitts, 2003: 92) in relation to other research findings and alternative explanations. In particular, it is not surprising that successful programmes attempted to change the way offenders thought about crime, and their review of evidence ignored the 'findings of comprehensive meta-analyses of interventions with young offenders undertaken for the Department of Justice in the USA', which will be referred to later in this chapter.

Skills development in youth work

Very similarly to the cognitive skills development approach, in the UK, youth work has increasingly adopted a skills development approach. An influential contributor to policy formation has been John Huskins, a former Chief Inspector of Youth Work and more recently a consultant. His second manual, *From Disaffection to Social Inclusion* (1998) is labelled as a 'handbook for those working in youth programmes to address disaffection, including the Connexions Service ... and Youth Offending Teams'. Huskins (1996; 1998) emphasises that projects must first help people develop self-esteem and a positive life attitude. This is the initial requirement for encouraging participants to benefit from activities in which they increasingly take responsibility for themselves. Through these they can develop a range of social skills. Huskins defines these skills as: recognising and managing feelings; feeling empathy with others; problem solving; negotiation; values' development; action planning; and review skills. The development of these skills is progressive. 'Good quality' youthwork involves the progressive empowerment of the individual to take a more active and responsible part in their own development; to become more pro-active (Huskins, 1996).

The social skills' development, identified by Huskins (1996) as being important in youth work, corresponds to the 'cognitive competencies' identified by Ross and Fabiano (1985) as being developed by successful programmes aimed at reducing offending behaviour. Huskins's books prescribing the process of youth work have sold extensively, but this may be as much because they fill a theoretical vacuum, and because they appeal to a system led increasingly by targets, as because of their practicality for youth workers. They lead to a focus on the individual, in the same way that Smith has also identified in the Connexions and Transforming Youth Work agenda (Smith, 2003: 52). Both of these focus 'almost exclusively on the individual ... they both utilise what is essentially a deficit paradigm ... a public health model that identifies, isolates, and then treats the subject in order to restore him or her to good health ...'. Further, characteristic of contemporary youth work, Huskins offers a systematic use of performance indicators to ensure accountability. Smith (2003) and Pitts (2003) are both critical of this approach, firstly because of its obsessive collection of data to assure accountability, however unrefined or imprecise (Pitts, 2003: 41), but also because of its reductionist view of the development of young people.

Huskins shies away from specifying the values he wishes a programme to promote. This is common in youth work, reflecting the 'dominance of what is correct rather than what is right or good' (Smith, 2003: 49), although at the same time Huskins aims for young people to take more responsibility for their own development and for others. Huskins' work is not directly supported by research to show that if one pursues youth work in the way he proposes it will achieve the specific outcomes he predicts, although he has planned a practical evaluation (personal communication).

Criminological theory – the risk/protection factor model

The juxtaposition of risk and protection factors has a simplistic attraction (Farrington, 2000; Witt, 2000). Its starting point is the identification of factors that appear to have a causal relationship to crime because they have a strong statistical relationship to recorded offending.

The research on risk and protection factors is summarised by Catalano and Hawkins (1996). The risk factors that predispose an individual towards delinquency and drug abuse (which are not defined terms) include: 'community norms favourable to those behaviours, neighbourhood disorganisation, extreme economic deprivation, family history of drug abuse or crime, poor family management practices, family conflict, low family bonding, parental permissiveness, early and persistent problem behaviours, academic failure, peer rejection in elementary grades, association with drug-using or delinquent peers or adults, alienation and rebelliousness, attitudes favourable to drug use and crime, and early onset of criminal behaviour' (Catalano and Hawkins, 1996: 152).

One source of the identification of risk factors is Farrington's (1996) statistical analysis of a longitudinal study of 400 London males. Risk factors were deduced from their correlation with onset of offending. A limitation of this approach is that it does not help us understand the process by which these factors inter-relate and 'any theory of the development of offending is inevitably speculative in the present state of knowledge' (Farrington, 1996: 105). As Farrington states, as social problems inter-relate it is difficult to know what causes what. It is difficult to decide if any given risk factor is an indicator or a possible cause of anti-social behaviour. A methodological criticism is that Farrington's approach gives too much weight to the impact of circumstances and none to agency, the ability of the individual to react to these circumstances. As one of the few pieces of longitudinal research it is valuable; however, as Pitts notes (2003), it was specific to a particular population, place and time (white boys in 1960s London), which may limit its general applicability.

This approach has to explain why the risk factors have a differential impact, that is, not all people subject to them become involved in crime. This explanation is provided through the existence of protective factors, which include: 'individual characteristics, including resilient temperament, positive social orientation and intelligence; family cohesion and warmth or bonding during childhood; and external social supports that reinforce the individuals' competencies and commitments and provide a belief system by which to live' (Catalano and Hawkins, 1996: 153). Thus programmes such as Communities That Care (CTC) aim to provide these factors.

While these protective factors are intuitively plausible, the evidence supporting them is much more limited than that supporting the risk factors. A conclusion of an evaluation of the three UK pilot CTC programmes, conducted five years after they were set up, was that evaluation of outcomes needs to look at a larger sample of programmes, and over a longer period of time (Crow *et al.*, 2004). Catalano and Hawkins acknowledge (1996) that the understanding of the mechanisms by which the protective and risk factors interact is at present the subject of theory that needs to be substantiated by further research. They propose a 'social development' model that describes the process by which the individual is socialised into norms of behaviour. In general this involves four stages. The individual perceives opportunities for involvement and interaction in 'socialising units' of school, family, community institutions and peers. They then become involved in these and develop skills to do so. They receive reinforcement from the socialising unit in the role they take. This leads to a strong bond with the unit, and an identification with its norms and values, which then become internalised and act as a control over the individual's behaviour. This can explain socialisation into pro-social or anti-social norms. In essence this model emphasises the influence and constraints of social structure on the individual and gives little weight to personal agency – that is, the extent to which the individual freely chooses which 'social units' to interact and identify with. It does not consider how the balance between agency and structure will change at different times and circumstances. For example, although it states that perceived opportunities for involvement and interaction precede involvement in such units, the child has no choice of involvement in his or her family, which is a major source of norms and values. On the other hand, the adolescent has a very wide choice of 'social units' to affiliate to. However, their model is refined to emphasise the role of different socialising units at four stages in a young person's development. Implications for crime reduction interventions are that they have to operate to increase the influence of pro-social 'social units' at the various stages of development, although the examples given by Catalano and Hawkins (1996: 183) are just theoretical.

Similarly, Farrington, whose longitudinal research was influential in identifying risk factors, has proposed a model to understand involvement in anti-social activity. Farrington's model proposes three stages that lead to anti-social behaviour, which is a consequence of the interaction of energising, directing and inhibiting factors. Energising factors are: desires for material goods, status and excitement; boredom; anger; and alcohol and drugs. The directing stage is where the motivations in the energising phase are not able to be met by legal means. In the inhibiting phase, 'antisocial tendencies can be reduced (or increased) by internalised beliefs and attitudes that have been built up in a social learning process as a result of a history of rewards and punishments' (Farrington, 1996: 109). Farrington describes how these would include attitudes of parents and empathy between parents and children.

In common with Catalano and Hawkins (1996), this is a general theory of behaviour. Although Farrington acknowledges the interaction of the individual and the environment, his theory is not supported by qualitative research that attempts to describe how the individual perceives this interaction. In general, the explanation for offending is based on deductions from statistical relationships, so can be criticised as paying insufficient attention to subjective experience.

Farrington advocates a wide range of interventions to reduce anti-social behaviour. These include: adolescent pregnancy prevention; more home visits to pregnant women; pre-school programmes to help children with education; parent training; reducing socio-economic deprivation; reducing contact with delinquent peers; teaching children to resist delinquency; making school more acceptable to children; and changing the local community. These interventions are extremely broad ranging. Farrington's model of how people become involved in crime is not precise enough to decide which of these many interventions might be most useful in any particular circumstance.

Both Farrington and Catalano and Hawkins (1996) have put forward general models of how people become involved in crime, which are general models of how people adopt any particular behaviour. They have both seen the need to develop understandings of the processes by which people both become involved in crime and avoid becoming involved, and desist. However, these are not based on research and do not explore how individuals perceive their situation and how this perception changes. This reflects some criminological theories' emphasis on inferring causation from statistical regularities and an emphasis, until recently, on a single direction of causality from the environment to the individual, rather than understanding a dynamic interaction. Pitts (2003) has made a more sustained critique of the risk/protection factor approach, which he places in the context of the history of political strategies to address youth crime. These strategies have also led to the widespread adoption of cognitive skills development programmes, such as those of Ross and Fabiano (1985). As noted above, Pitts argues that the evidence for Ross and Fabiano's programmes ignores other research findings and alternative explanations.

The implications of the risk/protection factor model have been explicitly built into the 23 CTC projects in the UK (Communities That Care, 1998; Crow et al., 2004). This programme is an adaptation of one under the same name that has been implemented in the USA. The programmes aim to identify local risk factors and implement protection factors, through 'community mobilisation' of local people and professionals. The protective factors and processes include: strengthening bonds with family members, teachers and other socially responsible adults or friends; promoting clear and consistent rules and expectations about healthy and pro-social behaviour: giving young people opportunities for involvement and to feel valued; promoting social and learning skills; and giving young people recognition and praise. Three pilot programmes in the UK have been the subject of evaluation (Crow et al., 2004), though this has concluded that an evaluation of outcomes requires a longer-term perspective and a bigger sample of programmes.

Personal development theory from adventure education

In the same way that some theoretical contributions have started by focusing on sport, others have focused on outdoor adventurous activities as a medium. Again, the use of these activities reflects strong value judgements and assumptions. In a critique Brookes (2003) claimed that one of these is the common sense assumption that 'character traits' can be cultivated in one setting and transferred to another, contrary to evidence from social psychology. Further, the word 'adventure', the iconic symbolism of Kurt Hahn, and the disconnection from scholarly research in other fields, have all led to a less than critical approach. Nevertheless, the model below, of value-directed personal growth, is based on my own synthesis of the literature and focuses on the use of these activities as a catalyst and a medium, rather than an end in themselves.

Rather than taking as its starting point an identification of the factors that predispose an individual towards crime, this approach starts from a general understanding of the personal development of young people, drawing on the evidence of benefits of both crime reduction programmes and personal development programmes. It combines theoretical understandings of the process of adventure education with the evidence of case study participants from crime reduction programmes (Nichols, 2000a).

The focal point of this model is the participant's definition and redefinition of self-identity. Hendry *et al.* (1993: 31–57) identified this as the major task facing adolescents and for Giddens (1991) it is a major concern for everybody as a consequence of having to cope with greater uncertainty in our lives. (Giddens's case is contentious as he gives no evidence for an increase in uncertainty, and it can be argued that in many respects life in Western society offers fewer uncertainties and less risk than it did a hundred years ago.) Changed self-concept has also been identified as important in research by Graham and Bowling (1995) and Maruna (2001) into those that desist from offending. Graham and Bowling's research found that desistance from crime involved a reappraisal of personal value systems.

The focus on changed self-concept makes theoretical work in understanding the process of adventure education relevant because the focus of adventure education is the personal growth of the individual, especially young people (Hopkins and Putnam, 1993). It is mainly directed towards young people as it is believed they are at a particularly formative stage of development, but this does not preclude the approach being applied to adults. Although much of this theory has been developed with reference to programmes using outdoor activities with high levels of perceived risk, a more useful understanding of 'adventure' is as taking risks in self-concept. Drawing on theory reviewed in Chapter Two, the model proposes that self-development is facilitated by parallel increases in self-esteem, locus of control and cognitive skills, influenced or directed by values. Together these enable the individual to become more pro-active. In programmes that aim to reduce crime, an increase in pro-activity and pro-social values will be especially important in situations where individuals are subject to a high level of risk factors.

The most complete theoretical model of adventure education is provided by a synthesis of the ideas of Priest (1991: 157), Priest and Gass (1997:122), Mortlock (1984), Hopkins and Putnam (1993) and Csikszentmihalyi and Csikszentmihalyi (1992; 1991); summarised in Figure 3.1.

Figure 3.1 is an extension of Priest's (1991) model which showed the subjective perceptions of the juxtaposition of risk and competence experienced by a participant in an outdoor activity programme. The relation between the two is situation specific; for example, someone may feel competent canoeing on a gently moving river, but not on a rapid. Priest was merely concerned with helping an individual to obtain a more realistic perception of their own capabilities in terms of technical skills. In this, the task of the facilitator was to either show where the participant underestimated what they could achieve, or overestimated it. In contrast to Figure 3.1, Priest was concerned only to move an individual's perception of their risk/competence balance from an 'incorrect' to a 'correct' one.

The categories of experience (adventure, misadventure, etc.) are adaptations of those devised by Mortlock (1984) representing situations in which the individual feels progressively less in control. The category of 'peak adventure' is similar to Csikszentmihalyi and Csikszentmihalyi's notion of flow (1992). Flow is a state of mind in which there is a merging of action and awareness, and concentration is complete. The individual is completely engaged in the activity. For Csikszentmihalyi and Csikszentmihalyi, 'anything one does can become rewarding if the activity is structured right and if one's skills are matched with the challenges of the action' (1992: xiii). As in Priest's model, 'whether one is in

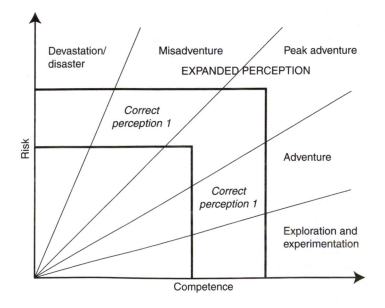

Figure 3.1 Personal growth through adventure

flow or not depends entirely on one's perception of what the challenges and skills are' (Csikszentmihalyi and Csikszentmihalyi, 1992: 50). Csikszentmihalyi and Csikszentmihalyi believed that flow, and learning to achieve it, was important because in an ever more complex life, flow experiences could give people a sense of control. It is important in describing leisure activities that are rewarding. They claimed that it is possible that through experiencing flow in leisure, individuals may learn to structure their everyday lives in a way that will create opportunities for flow.

The model above incorporates Hopkins and Putnams' (1993) objective of personal growth and the concept of flow, by showing how an individual could grow in ability to take on more difficult situations. This is represented by a move from the initial 'correct' subjective perception of the juxtaposition of risk and competence (Priest's original model), to the expanded perception. As Mortlock, and Hopkins and Putnam believed; this occurs through the facilitated progression through ever more demanding experiences. Consistent with their emphasis on growth of the whole person, risks include the social and the emotional as well as the physical. The most important aspect of growth is in the individual's view of themselves and the world. Learning about oneself is not just incremental but may involve a dramatic transformation (Putnam, 1985).

In common with Huskins's model, personal growth enables the individual to become more pro-active through increasing resourcefulness – 'the capacity of individuals to use their own and social resources to develop interests and pursue activities which yield personal and social satisfaction' (Rapoport, 1982, in Glyptis, 1989: 161).

The importance of values in the process of personal growth

Flow theory has been criticised as failing to distinguish between good and bad states of flow (Mason, 1999). For example, it would fail to distinguish between people involved in crime or sport. Further, its attainment is confined to the satisfaction of needs. 'There is nothing in flow theory which enables one to articulate the ethical ideal of attention to values which are separate from, or transcend, the satisfaction of needs' (Mason, 1999: 236). The criticism of sport as being just as likely to promote anti- as pro-social values could apply to any other activity used as part of a programme's content.

Thus, a crucial component of personal growth is the values that underpin it and give it direction (Nichols, 2000c). This emphasises the importance of the values of programme staff, as role models and mentors who are influential in directing personal growth. This was apparent in the author's evaluation of a sports counselling programme (Nichols and Taylor, 1996; Nichols, 1999a – case study below), in research into programmes run by UK Probation Services (Taylor *et al.* 1999: 42), and Collins and Kay's conclusion on an evaluation of Hampshire Sports Counselling: 'Its most important aspect for participants was the support of the sports counsellor, more important than the actual activities offered for three-quarters of them' (Collins and Kay, 2003: 186). In a survey of probation service programmes (Taylor *et al.*, 1999), managers consistently reported that high-quality staff were essential, and in assessing the quality of staff they put much more emphasis on the values they portrayed than technical skills.

Applications and examples of the personal growth directed by values model

As in the risk/protection factor model, and that of Huskins, this is a general model of personal development. It can encompass both programmes that aim to reduce crime through facilitating a changed self-concept in offenders and programmes that aim to contribute to the pro-social development of individuals who are subject to a high level of risk factors. It is more sophisticated than the risk/protection factor model because it can understand a dynamic process – the interaction between participant and programme. It shows how a sports leader or mentor can guide a participant through more challenging experiences. As the participant grows in self-esteem, locus of control and cognitive skills, they have the personal resources to take on more challenging experiences, and an increasingly pro-active approach to seeking them out. However, this growth has to be directed, and similarly to Catalano and Hawkins's (1996) model, this is achieved through the value systems of significant others – mentors, sports leaders, peers and 'social units'. The model matches Smith's aspirations for youth work 'having a vision of what might be possible, and looking to what is good rather than correct, allows youth workers to engage authentically as people with others' (Smith, 2003: 54).

This process of growth and change in self-definition directed by values is illustrated by examples in the case study programmes in this book, especially the West Yorkshire Sports Counselling Programme and Hafotty Wen, which were working with long-term offenders.

Understanding programme effectiveness in terms of helping participants to redefine themselves can be related to the concept of 'critical choice points' in an individual's 'career' (Craine and Coles, 1995). At these points careers are influenced by key authority figures. Maruna (2001), through interviews with long-term offenders who had desisted, came to the same conclusion – that desistance can be understood by a redefinition of self. However, in his study the criminal justice system usually reinforced the self-perception as an offender, in the same way as described by Pitts (2003). A likely catalyst for a change was trust shown by another person, such as a partner or probation officer. An especially significant reinforcer of this change was official recognition, for example when an ex-offender was supported in a court by the testimony of probation workers and others who testified to his or her changed character. This again emphasises the key role of a mentor as a significant other. The focus on understanding offending and desistence as a consequence of a changing sense of self is shared by Barry (2006), although for her the key conceptual tools are young people's need for social recognition, and the way this is linked, drawing on Bourdieu (1986), to the distribution of social, economic, cultural and symbolic capital.

The personal growth model, illustrated by the previous case studies, implies that a set of 'success factors' will benefit a programme. These include:

- A clear set of values associated with the activity leaders and the ethos of the programme – to provide a direction to personal development. These values are inconsistent with offending.
- The ability to adapt a programme to individual participants' needs – so needs and developing capabilities can be matched sensitively to new challenges, enabling 'growth' to occur, as represented in Figure 3.1.
- The ability to offer sustained work (18 months–2 years) to enable this process to occur, and viable exit routes where the participant can become involved in activity and further opportunities for development and taking responsibility independent of the original programme.
- The use of rewards of achievement, which will enhance self esteem in a way that is recognised by participants.
- A good relationship between participants and activity leaders; leaders taking a mentoring role.
- Sharing activity with pro-social peers – to reinforce positive values.

In addition the model clarifies the role of 'adventure activities' as a medium rather than as an end in itself.

This model goes beyond the simple countering of risk with protection factors, in the same way that Witt and Crompton (2003: 6), working with crime reduction programmes in the United States, have advocated that programmes should move from a simple 'deficit reduction approach' based on the risk/protection factor model. They feel this has been too limited and they now advocate 'positive youth development', achieved through a set of 'characteristics of environments that promote positive youth development' that are similar to the success factors outlined above. This seeks to 'increase the competency of all youth to meet the challenges of growing up' (Witt and Crompton, 2003: 5) and is very similar to the approach to youth work advocated by Smith (2003).

An implication of this model is that the redefinition of self-identity consistent with pro-social behaviour, or not offending, will be most difficult, and will involve most personal risk, for those most heavily involved in offending. Both of the case studies used as illustrations above were of long-term offenders. For work with low-risk participants, the main concern may be to reinforce a pro-social self-concept rather than to change an anti-social one.

A synthesis of theoretical perspectives to provide a model of personal growth directed by values

The theoretical perspectives above can be synthesised to provide a model of personal growth directed by values, which is proposed as one of the key mechanisms by which programmes might reduce youth crime. Although the risk/protective factor model, Huskins's model of youth work and the personal growth model from adventure education are developed from different starting points they have considerable points of convergence. The risk/protective factor model is based on the factors that predispose an individual to take part in crime, and the factors that appear to be able to nullify their impact. These protective factors need to be provided through the medium of a unit with which the participant identifies and which reinforces pro-social values. Huskins's model defines the social skills that need to be developed in parallel to self-esteem, and a willingness to take responsibility. The personal growth directed by values model is developed from evidence of benefits of participation in sport and outdoor activity programmes and theoretical understandings of this. It defines the outcomes of the process as increases in self-esteem, locus of control and social skills, directed by pro-social values. As a result of this the young person will become more proactive. It also describes the process through which this occurs. The two models offer a general explanation of the development of both anti- and pro-social behaviour and put a strong emphasis on the important influence of value systems of 'significant others', whether peers, programme leaders or 'social units'.

The personal growth model shows the mechanisms through which the protective factors and risk factors interact. This model is more detailed than the social development model of Catalano and Hawkins (1996) as it goes beyond this in its understanding of the process of personal growth. This involves the expansion of the individual's subjective perception of their capabilities and the challenges offered by their situation, leading to a more proactive approach to personal circumstances. In terms of social theory, this is a shift from an individual dominated by the influence of social structure to one who is more freely able to express themselves through social action. This is consistent with Barry's (2006) review of theories of the onset of offending and of desistance, in that the former tends to emphasise structural constraints, and the latter, free agency. As young people develop they will hopefully be able to become more proactive, drawing on an accumulation of personal resources to take charge of their own lives, and the role of crime reduction programmes is to help them to do this. An advantage of the personal growth model is that it helps understand how this has to be achieved through the individual being sensitively led through a progression of more challenging experiences, in a manner that accords with Huskins' (1996) model of good practice in youth work.

The personal growth model accords with the 'positive youth development' Smith advocates, in contrast to deficit-based models that focus solely on youth problems (2003: 51). It is not a coincidence that it draws on contributors from some very traditional institutions. Both Putnam and Mortlock spent many years delivering programmes in youth movements (Outward Bound and a local authority outdoor education centre respectively) that tried to achieve personal development through outdoor-based adventure. They, and the sports leaders in most of the programmes described below, would have regarded themselves as teachers following a calling rather than technocrats delivering a set of clearly measurable and accountable outcomes. Flair and integrity had an important role.

The personal growth model helps place programme activities in context as the medium for the process. It helps justify the use of some activities, for example those used as an initial attraction to help get people involved. It also helps put some in perspective; for example, the physical challenge of some outdoor pursuits activities might have been over-emphasised in the past compared to the key challenge of redefinition of self (Nichols, 2000a).

The model from adventure education comes to remarkably similar conclusions on the characteristics of successful programmes as did the meta-analyses of interventions with young offenders undertaken for the Department of Justice in the USA (Altschuler and Armstrong, 1984; Howell *et al.*, 1995). For them the characteristics of successful programmes included:

- They are holistic, dealing with many aspects of young people's lives as needed.
- They are informed by an underlying developmental rationale.
- They offer diverse opportunities for success and the development of positive self-image.
- They build on young people's strengths rather than focusing on their deficiencies.
- They are intensive, often involving weekly or even daily contact.
- They adopt a socially grounded rather than a treatment approach and emphasise reintegration.
- They involve young people in programme planning and decision making.
- They provide opportunities for the development of links between young people in trouble and pro-social adults and institutions.
- They give frequent, timely and accurate feedback for both positive and negative behaviour. (The existence of such feedback is a key characteristic of Csikszentmihalyi's flow model.)
- There are clear and consistent consequences for misconduct.
- They provide a forum in which young people are enabled to recognise and understand thought processes that rationalise negative behaviour.
- They offer opportunities to engage with the problems and deficits which got the young person into trouble in the first place.

However, there still remains a balance between structure and agency. In particular, an approach to reducing youth crime based on any of the approaches above still needs to take account of economic deprivation as a risk factor. While Farrington's longitudinal research identified economic deprivation as one of the factors that increased the propensity to take part in crime, the risk/protective factors model does not consider how this will be reduced. Neither does the Communities That Care project aim to increase local employment. The Commission on Social Justice (1994: 50) stated that: 'Unemployment does not turn a law-abiding citizen into a criminal. But whatever other factors are at work in rising crime, there now seems to be a clear association between unemployment and crime among young men between the ages of 17 and 25, who account for 70 per cent of all adults convicted or cautioned for a criminal offence.' Therefore a programme is more likely to help a young person stay out of crime if it helps them gain employment, either directly or through gaining employment skills. Employment might reduce the risk factor of economic deprivation, or it may give the individual a stake in society it is not worth losing (Roberts, 1992). Thus a further long-term success factor might be the ability of the programmes to contribute to employability.

For research, the model opens the 'black box' of the process. The understanding of the changing interaction between the programme and the participant as the participant develops is consistent with the notion of generative causality and the methodology of scientific realism (Pawson and Tilley, 1997), discussed in Chapter Four.

The synthesis of approaches provides a starting point from which to formulate questions. How important are the different components of the process? For example, it has been argued in the context of adventure education that the preoccupation with physical risk has obscured the understanding of psychological risk and personal development as a risk in self-concept (Ringer and Gillis, 1995; Ringer and Spanoghe, 1997; Nichols, 2000b). What can help a young person grow in proactivity? Which activities stimulate and which stultify the process for different people? How important is the role of a mentor? How much support does a mentor need to offer and when can this be withdrawn? The case studies in this book illustrate these points.

An initial conclusion on the role of sport

Chapter Two started with a review of the potential positive impacts of sport in crime reduction, but it was argued that this starting point itself reflected a preoccupation with the value of sport. Chapter Three reviewed the contribution of the cognitive development approach, and the risk/protection approach from criminology, before synthesising these with insights from outdoor adventure education.

This gives a much more precise understanding of one mechanism by which programmes might reduce crime: the contribution of long-term personal growth, directed by values. Within this, the activities – sport – are just a catalyst and a medium. Their effect will be specific to the programme and the participants, but one can still make generalisations. The role of sport is reviewed again after the accounts of the case study programmes in Chapters Seven to Fourteen. Before this we need to consider the nature of 'evidence' and the policy context.

Acknowledgement

The discussion of the process of personal development through adventure education previously appeared in: Nichols, G. (2004) 'A model of the process of personal development through the medium of outdoor adventure.' In Barnes, P. and Sharp, B. (eds) *The RHP Companion to Outdoor Education*. Lyme Regis: Russell House Publishing, pp. 26–33. www.russellhouse.co.uk.

4 What is 'evidence' and how do we get it?

In the same way that value judgements have informed the use of sport in crime reduction programmes, they also influence the interpretation of evidence derived by different methods. Policy makers and programme managers may favour particular research methods and this will influence the planning of evaluation and the extent to which policy is based on its results. Academic researchers may be influenced by similar value judgements, although in theory their debate about the most valid way to do research is carried to the level of epistemology and ontology – philosophical debates about how we generate knowledge about the world and the nature of reality. However, even this is not a rational debate but is a dispute based on different assumptions; and, one suspects, is also part of jostling for academic status and prestige.

The next chapter outlines four different approaches to research: the classic experimental design; qualitative methods; critical realism; and the 'theory of change' – in two different forms. This chapter is aimed more at the research student and the evaluator; however it is also relevant to programme managers planning their own evaluation, and policy makers deciding how to evaluate research evidence. It makes reference to the case study chapters where different approaches are illustrated. So the reader may also find it useful to return to this chapter after reading the case studies.

At this stage it is worth clarifying a distinction between research and evaluation. Weiss (1988: 4) defines evaluation as 'the systematic assessment of the operation and/or the outcomes of a programme or policy, compared to a set of explicit or implicit standards, as a means to contributing to the improvement of the programme or policy'. This implies the use of rigorous research methods (however this is defined – see the discussion below). Evaluation, as does research, may look at one or both of the process and the outcomes. For example, 'what has been the impact of the programme, and what elements of the process contributed to this?'. But a contrast with research is that evaluation makes judgements against expectations. It may ask 'has the programme reduced crime by as much as we expected it too, or as much as other alternative programmes?'. A second distinctive characteristic of evaluation is that it aims to contribute to an improvement of the programme or policy. This may be by helping policy makers choose between programmes when allocating resources, or it may be just by helping programme staff improve their programme to achieve their goals more effectively. It is easier to obtain full co-operation of programme staff if the evaluator stresses the ways in which an external evaluation can help them, rather than the role it may take in policy makers' decisions to continue to support the programme, though how easily this can be done will, of course, depend on who is funding the evaluator!

Philosophical positions

Before dealing with different approaches to research we need to grapple briefly with the philosophical assumptions on which they are based. Different assumptions justify different methods and, as noted above, can explain a divergence of views about what is valid research. Bryman (2001) gives a good introduction to the philosophy of research and the reader is advised to look at this, or one of the many alternative research methods text books for a more detailed account of methodological debates. For consistency I have used the same terms as Bryman to describe research: slightly different terms are used in other texts.

Epistemology is concerned with how we generate knowledge about the world, and thus what is (or should be) regarded as valid knowledge. Ontology is concerned with the nature of reality. The two 'ologies' are linked. Conflicting views on both of them help explain disputes over which research methods to use and the validity of results.

Positivism

Positivism, as an epistemological approach, maintains that we have to apply the same methods as are normally associated with the natural sciences to the social sciences, and only if we apply these will we generate 'valid' knowledge. Knowledge is confirmed by our senses (so it is not merely abstract concepts). Theory is used to generate hypotheses that can be tested, and this allows general explanations (laws) to be assessed. Thus we can deduce if a law is valid. However, by gathering facts we can provide the basis for laws; thus laws can be induced from these facts. There is an emphasis on the value free application of 'scientific' methods. Causality is thought of as a simple relation of cause and effect: I hit a pool ball and it goes in a certain direction; if I am any good, it will go in the pocket. This is termed 'deterministic' or 'successionist' causality.

Interpretivism

In contrast to positivism, the epistemological position of interpretivism maintains that understanding of social situations requires us to understand the subjective perception of social actors. To understand why a person does something I have to understand the conceptual map of the world that person has in their head – their own system of logic. I may not share that logic, but it helps me understand the way it has caused that person to act in a particular way. An example is religious belief.

A friend stood for a long time at a motorway junction trying to hitch a lift, and then decided to walk back to a station, and arrived just in time to catch her train. She told me she had responded to God's will, who had first directed her to wait at the junction, and then return to the station. I may not share this interpretation of divine intervention, but in order to understand my friend, I have to understand the way she sees the world.

Objectivism

The ontological position of objectivism is the belief that there is an external reality independent of the observer, and of social actors. Reality is 'out there' somewhere, and it will not be affected by our attempts to observe it. This fits well with the principles of positivistic method, as above. Therefore we do experiments that mimic the methods of the natural sciences to reveal this reality. In the example of researching a sports programme to reduce crime we might describe its structure and procedures: who manages and leads the programme; the content of the programme; how many people attend it; what they do; and for how long. We are describing a reality that is assumed to be external to the programme staff and participants. They experience the programme as an external reality to which they react – like the pool ball in an earlier example after it has been hit.

Constructionism

In contrast to objectivism, the ontological position of constructionism asserts that the social world is constructed by social interaction. We all have different world views and as a result of interaction we generate shared meanings. The implications for researching a sports programme to reduce crime would be that we need to understand it not as a reality external to the actors but as a result of shared and negotiated meanings; a socially constructed reality. The different programme leaders and participants might have different perceptions. A 'rule' might be regarded by objectivism as existing externally to the actor, but constructionism would emphasise the way understandings were the result of shared meanings and were continually being renegotiated.

This is one interpretation of constructivism, which implies the social scientist has to understand the conceptual frameworks through which individuals themselves understand their worlds. However, this can be extended to a second version of constructivism applied to the social scientist's own world view, in which case social scientists 'always present a specific view of social reality, rather than one that can be regarded as definitive' (Bryman, 2001:18). This second version implies that all knowledge is indeterminate, and is reflected in the position of postmodernism. This complete social relativism is not useful if one wants to use it to inform policy – as is the case in most programme evaluations – but it is a position from which research could be criticised.

The implications of philosophical positions for research design

Implications of positivism and objectivism

Arising from positivism and objectivism is what Pawson and Tilley (1997: 5) describe as the classic experimental design (see Figure 4.1).

Figure 4.1 illustrates that 'classic experimental research' starts with two identical groups. One group is given the treatment, and one group is not. Research is looking for measurable outcomes of a programme in the experimental group, and comparing them to the control group who have not experienced the same programme. If the group that had the treatment changes and the control group does not, it is deduced that the treatment caused the change. If numbers in the two groups are large enough, it can be ascertained whether the evidence of a causal relationship is statistically significant. Causation between the programme and intermediate effects, or the final outcome, is inferred from the repeated succession of similar effects after similar programmes. This model implies 'deterministic' or 'successionist' causation – the experience of the programme on the participant causes a change. This change can be objectively measured.

For the results of such research to be regarded as valid, in their own terms, they must meet several exacting criteria: the control and experimental groups must be identical; the only difference in their experience must be the programme itself; statistically validated tools must be used for measuring change (for example, a test instrument to measure changes in self-esteem or locus of control needs to be subject to rigorous evaluation itself before it is considered valid); and sample sizes must be large enough to produce statistically significant differences. Those involved in programme delivery will immediately suspect that this is a tall order in practice. How practical is it to set up a programme in which participation is voluntary and at the same time produce a group of volunteers who do not attend the programme to act as a control? How practical is it to use sophisticated measuring tools while at the same time trying to grab the enthusiasm of participants who probably have an aversion to questionnaire completion and a limited reading ability? Nevertheless, several reviews of 'evidence' of programme effectiveness, made from a positivist/objectivist stance, have systematically criticised evaluation results for not meeting these criteria.

	Pre-test	Treatment	Post-test
Experimental group	O1	X	O2
Control group	O1		O2

Figure 4.1 The classic experimental design

Source: Pawson and Tilley, 1997: 5

For example, Gibson (1979) reviewed 21 evaluations of the therapeutic impact of 'wilderness' programmes and listed their limitations, which included:

- bias in sample selection
- small sample size
- lack of adequate control group
- questionable validity of assessment instrument (for example, a questionnaire may not have been validated as measuring a phenomena; its construction may have been *ad hoc*)
- insufficient description of outcome criteria (poor definition of outcomes)
- inadequate statistical analysis of data (to show a significant relationship)
- lack of follow-up investigation (monitoring outcomes over a longer period than just after the programme).

Of the 21 evaluations he reviewed, all but three had more than one of these limitations.

Similarly, Coalter (1996: 15), in a review for the then Scottish Sports Council, concluded that there 'is a lack of systematic evaluation of the claims made for the preventative and rehabilitative properties of sport with regard to anti-social behaviour', although this criticism may have referred as much to the lack of a precise definition of the terms 'anti-social' and 'sport' as to the methods used in evaluation.

A criticism of the classic experimental research design is that the complexity of programmes leads to a degree of process complexity that it is beyond the capability of the research design to deal with. Once the objectives of research broaden to consider why a programme has an effect, rather than just if it has an effect, then a more sophisticated model of the process is required (see Figure 4.2).

Figure 4.2 illustrates that research is trying to show a causal relationship between the elements of boxes 1–5. It is not as simple as showing that participants on any one programme appear to experience a particular outcome while non-participants do not. The process of the programme is far more complex and

1	2	3	4	5
Type of participant	Process of getting involved	Programme content and process	Intermediate effects	Main objective – reduced propensity to take part in crime

Figure 4.2 The elements of the process of a crime reduction programme in sequence

Source: author

involves many different variables. As in the classic experimental design, research is starting from, and attempting to test, theory. It has already assumed that the type of participant, the process of becoming involved in the programme, and the programme content and process, will all determine intermediate effects. Within this there will be specific hypotheses – for example that particular qualities of the programme staff will have an influence on the outcome, or that particular activities will be more successful with boys than with girls. Further, there is an assumed relationship between particular intermediate effects and the final outcome, defined as a reduced propensity to take part in crime. If we are not able to measure the final outcome, possibly because it is beyond the time period of the research, we may still measure intermediate outcomes, but measuring these is justified by the theory that links them to the final outcome. For example, we may measure increased self-esteem in box 4, because we believe it is a contributory factor to reduced involvement in crime.

But it is very difficult to determine the effect of individual variables in a single process and to isolate them. For example, it would be difficult to ensure that all participants were black, middle class and female – thus removing the determining factors of ethnicity, class and gender. Even if this were accomplished, all the other potentially relevant variables, such as facilitator skills, would need to be held constant as well.

As noted above, the variable of the way in which participants become involved (box 2) is particularly difficult to eliminate. Where programme participation is voluntary there is always the problem that participants are more likely to gain benefits from it not because of the programme itself but because of their initial favourable attitude. The effect of voluntary involvement is very difficult to isolate if one is attempting to use a control group. (Illustrated in the example of the West Yorkshire Sports Counselling Programme, below.)

So, one set of criticisms of the classic experimental design is that it is just not practical to live up to the standards of methodical rigour demanded by the positivist approach. Pawson and Tilley (1997) make a more detailed critique, pointing out that, while it is not possible to hold all variables but one constant, the method itself is based on an assumption that we cannot observe the causal forces in a programme; all we can do, and all we need to know, is if it has achieved the final outcome – reduced participation in crime. So we are left no wiser about why an intervention has worked or not, and this does not help us understand how to improve it. This is a particularly important limitation to evaluation research, which aims to help programme staff improve their programme.

One limitation of the experimental design, which is common in evaluation of crime reduction programmes, is the inability of small sample sizes to produce statistically significant results. This is illustrated by the use of reconviction data in the case study of the Haffotty Wen programme. Within the positivist approach, one way of overcoming the statistical limitations of small samples is to generate a larger one by using a meta-analysis through pulling together independent empirical research results to produce big enough samples to provide statistically significant results, overall, and for specific variables. But within this, it is still extremely difficult to isolate the individual causal variables. This is illustrated by Hattie *et al.*'s (1997) aggregated results from 96 studies of outward bound courses. One criticism of this analysis is that it was attempting to 'add up' results from dissimilar programmes (Glass *et al.*, 1981). They ranged from a one-day abseiling course for adults to a 42-day course for 'low achievers' run by Outward Bound Australia. Another questionable assumption is that all the programmes had the same objectives. Hattie *et al.*'s (1997: 78) meta-analysis of evaluations still concluded that research had revealed little about the process of adventure education; as we have seen, this is a further limitation of the positivist research paradigm.

Implications of interpretivism and constructionism

Interpretivism and constructionism can lead to research that explores differences in perception. An example was Greenaway's research of participants (1995) on a management training course at an outdoor management development centre, who had a different perception of the course to those held by the course staff. This helped understand participants' reactions to the course.

While positivism typically leads to a quantitative approach where a large number of observations are collected to induce laws from statistically significant regularities, interpretivism is typically associated with a qualitative approach – often a small number of qualitative interviews, or participant observation. This can still lead to generalisations. Qualitative research has often been favoured by feminist researchers because they believe that it is important in gaining an understanding of how social constraints are perceived by women, especially those constraints arising from a set of social norms that favour men but which are subjectively assimilated by both men and women. An example is research proposed by Brown and Humberstone, using interpretive methodology, to explore how the Department for Education and Skills (DfES) Summer Activity Initiative in 2001 made a difference to young people with low motivation and/or skills. The initiative aimed to encourage young people aged 16 and over, who were undecided about their future, to re-engage with education and training. Qualitative methods were proposed, and the authors suggest that the rejection of their proposal by the Economic and Social Research Council might be attributable to 'resistance to forms of qualitative research' (Brown and Humberstone, 2003: 270). Whether this is the case or reflects the authors' sense of discrimination, it also illustrates a tension in the academic world between different methodological positions.

Although the combination of positivism and objectivism may appear to have clearer 'rules of engagement' as in the criteria for designing the classical experiment, there are equally rigorous procedures for conducting 'valid' qualitative research. (See, for example, Cassell and Synon's (2004) guide to qualitative research in organisations, which is written partly as a response to the dominance of the positivist paradigm in management research. Or Flick's (2002) introduction to qualitative research – Flick's major research area being public health.)

The debate between the two methodologies is not whether one is more objective than the other – it is equally easy to design leading questions in a questionnaire as it is to ask leading questions in an interview: the debate is between views of what is valid knowledge.

This is well illustrated by the acrimonious exchange in the journal *Evaluation* between Farrington, and Pawson and Tilley, over proposed methods to evaluate the Communities That Care (CTC) programme. Farrington came from the positivist/objectivist tradition. One of his major research projects was noted in Chapter Three, the *Cambridge Study* of 400 South London boys between 1961 and 1985. Farrington's (1997a) statistical analysis deduced 'risk factors' from their correlation with onset of offending. Although in the debate on methods to evaluate CTC, Pawson and Tilley were advocating a scientific realist approach – to be described later – rather than interpretivism/constructionism, this included the use of qualitative methods as one of a set of tools. Farrington (1997b, 1998) strongly advocated an experimental design. He was critical of Pawson and Tilley's suggestion (1998a: 87) that, within a scientific realist approach, 'research would be primarily ethnographic with the researcher following though the decision making process leading to the construction of the CTC programme in each community'. This would inevitably involve qualitative interviews to understand how key individuals in the CTC programme thought it would reduce crime. Specifically, Farrington responded with a criticism that a valid view of causality could not be obtained in this way – 'Many psychologists are reluctant to ask people to give reasons for their behaviour, because of the widespread belief that people have little or no introspective access to their complex mental processes. Hence, it is not clear that reasons in particular, and verbal reports in general have any validity' (1998: 207). To which Pawson and Tilley responded: 'Suppose a woman locks a door and is asked why she is doing so. If she says that it is a precaution against intruders, there seems no reason to us not to take her reply seriously' (1998b: 211).

As Pawson and Tilley observed in their first paper in the exchange, 'what we have at one level is the classic social science dilemma of incommensurable epistemologies and ontologies' (1998a: 74). Of course, at another level, the debate is also about status in the criminological evaluation community, and possibly a prestigious contract to evaluate the CTC programme (which was awarded to neither of the protagonists). One can sense similar undertones in Brown and Humberstone's (op. cit.) comments on the rejection of their research proposal. The very use of the words 'scientific realism' to describe a particular approach to research could be seen as an attempt to seize the high ground of validity in the popular view, although they were not coined by Pawson and Tilley. At least the protagonists in the *Evaluation* debate could add a couple more papers in a prestigious journal to their CVs!

As we shall see shortly, scientific realism allows for use of both quantitative and qualitative methods. But, why not use both anyway? Might a combination of quantitative and qualitative methods give us a better grasp of reality: it might show us what people do and why they do it. This pragmatic approach has been advocated by Tashakkori and Teddlie (1998). However, one factor determining the choice of methods is the research audience: if you are working for a PhD or writing for a top academic journal a philosophical fudge is not acceptable – so you need to choose one approach or the other. In other circumstances you may be guided by pragmatism, what is most practical, and the preferences of research funders and policy makers. This point is picked up later in the discussion of the 'theory of change' approach.

Scientific realism

Pawson and Tilley (1997), mentioned above, are influential proponents of scientific realism as an approach to evaluation in criminology. Their epistemological position is that causation in a programme cannot be understood through deducing how a programme works just through statistical regularities (as in positivism and objectivism). One has to understand why actors involved in the programmes chose to change the way they act. This is called 'generative causality', in contrast to the 'successionist causality' of positivism. Causality has to be understood as a combination of human agency and its reaction to new opportunities and resources. For example, to understand the impact of a crime reduction programme one would need to understand not only the new range of opportunities offered by the programme, but also the resources and attitudes the participants brought with them, and how these changed as the programme developed. As involvement progresses, the participant may be able to take advantage of a greater range of opportunities offered by the programme, and may in fact see them as opportunities only after some period of involvement. This was illustrated in the West Yorkshire Sports Counselling programme, the case study in Chapter Seven. In this, participants progressed through a range of increasingly demanding opportunities offered by the programme. As they developed in confidence and ability they were able to take on new opportunities. The interaction between programme and participants could be understood as 'generative causality', in contrast to positivism, where causality is a one-way process.

This approach tells us why a programme has a particular impact, for example, why a programme increases self-esteem (if it does). However, we still need to know how often or how much a programme causes a particular effect, and in what circumstances. How much has the self-esteem of participants changed and for how many has this effect been observed? In what circumstances does this happen? Pawson and Tilley use the concepts of 'regularity' and 'context' to incorporate these questions.

The three elements of mechanism, context and regularity are drawn together in Figure 4.3.

The mechanism causes a regularity, but this is contingent on a particular context. Some programmes will work with some participants, in some contexts, but not in others. An example is from research into the place adventure activities took in the rehabilitation of long-term drug addicts (the case study of Haffotty Wen, below). It was found that a key to successful rehabilitation was the ability to

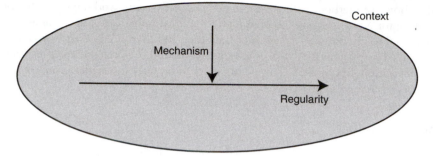

Figure 4.3 A context/mechanism/regularity configuration
Source: Pawson and Tilley, 1997

start a new life among new peers in a new geographical area. The area could be thought of as the context. If, having gone through rehabilitation (a process as long as 12 months), a former addict moved back to their former home area, then the pressures and opportunities to become trapped in a cycle of drug taking and crime were often too hard to resist. In this example, the rehabilitation programme and the role of adventure activities was the mechanism, the regularity (not measured in this research) was the rehabilitation rate, and the context was the area in which the participant found themselves after the rehabilitation process.

The general context/mechanism/regularity (CMR) model is the framework for hypothesis generation about context, mechanism and regularity configurations – as in the classic experimental design, research starts with theory. Hypotheses arising from this can be tested with a combination of quantitative and qualitative methods, the combination of which is justified by the epistemological position described above; that causation in a programme has to be understood both through statistical regularities and by understanding why actors involved in the programmes chose to change the way they act. This is in contrast to Tashakkori and Teddlie's (1998: 30) pragmatic avocation of mixed methodologies which 'eschews the use of metaphysical concepts (truth, reality) that have caused much endless (and often useless) discussion and debate' (brackets in original).

Pawson and Tilley (1997) want to explain the mechanism by which a programme 'works', but they still want to measure regularities (or outcomes). Thus, while we might interview participants to see how their perceptions changed while on the programme and how this can help us understand the programme mechanism (how it works), we still want to measure outcomes. For example; we might want to measure a quality such as self-esteem before and after a programme, or we might be interested in reconviction rates of participants against a control group.

The ontological position of scientific realism is that, as in positivism, 'there is an external reality to which scientists direct their attention' (Bryman, 2001: 13) but unlike positivism, 'scientist's conceptualisation is simply one way of knowing that reality'. Bryman quotes Bhaskar, the philosopher who founded this approach (1975: 250): 'Science then is the systematic attempt to express in thought the structures and ways of acting of things that exist and act independently of thought.' Scientific knowledge has a particular status because of the systematic way in which data is collected. But we still need to understand the different levels of social reality. Any mechanism has to be understood as embedded in its particular level of social reality. This provides a context on which it is contingent. This is common with interpretivism and constructionism: we need to understand the system of logic the actor uses to understand the world, so as we can understand their own rationality within this.

Pawson and Tilley's work is a response to the prevailing positivism in criminology. However, one might equally well make a criticism from the interpretivist tradition that Pawson and Tilley assume that there is some sort of reality that the researcher can get closer to than the actor. This is implied in their use of the word 'stratified' reality, in that the researcher is implied to understand a 'level of reality' superior to that of the actor, rather than just alternative to that of the actor. This may seem a reasonable view, given the researcher's superior knowledge of theory but, from the second constructionist view, one could argue that Pawson and Tilley's understanding of 'reality' may be no nearer to some ideal ultimate reality than the view of the actor: it is just an alternative. Other difficulties in scientific realism are that it is not clear what constitutes a regularity and how one defines a context. Further, while this approach starts from theory, which forms the basis of a CMR model from which hypotheses are derived, it is not clear how different from the hypothesised position a result has to be to challenge the original theory (Nichols, 2005).

The 'theory of change'

An approach that puts explicit emphasis on understanding the process of programmes, and on changing policy, and has been used in evaluation research, is the 'theory of change'. This sidesteps some of the epistemological and ontological questions above. The 'theory of change' approach starts by identifying 'a set of beliefs that underlie action' (Weiss, 1998: 55). This is 'A set of hypotheses upon which people build their program plans. It is an explanation of the causal links that tie program inputs to expected program outputs', and will include both the activities and the mechanisms of change. This would include the theoretical basis for the construction of a process map, such as that shown in Figure 4.2 (see page 33). This has been termed 'process evaluation' in that it seeks to understand the process by which inputs transform to outputs within a programme – the 'black box' that the classic experimental design can't unpack. The specific 'theory of change' is similar to Pawson and Tilleys' CMR configuration but does not arise from previous theory. In researching the impact of a programme, the hypotheses would be derived from interviewing programme staff and managers. They would describe the type of participants they worked with, the outcomes of the programme and how they thought their programme contributed to these. This focus on the process of the programme attempts to build consensus on the links between recruitment to the programme, what happens on the programme, intermediate outcomes, and long-term outcomes, as in Figure 4.2 (see page 33).

In contrast, scientific realism seeks to adjudicate between contrasting CMO configurations (Pawson and Tilley, 1998a: 84).

While the theory of change approach, as advocated by Weiss, examines the process of a programme, Connell and Kubish's (1998) approach also aims to change policy and practice. To do this it identifies key stakeholders in the policy community. These stakeholders are the most important judges of the validity of the research methods and results, though advice is still sought from academics. The key stakeholders are consulted, both to agree the initial hypothesis and also on how the research must be conducted to provide valid results. Connell, who introduced the theory of change to the UK, made the following points in discussion in 1998, with Rowan Astbury at the Charities Evaluation Services:

> The theory of change is a prediction about what leads to what; plausibility to relevant people is critical. They validate in advance; face validity is always important but especially where change (produced by the intervention) is likely to be small. Credibility of results is related to stakeholders having agreed not only ultimate outcomes, but also interim ones – i.e. if they agree at the start that activities abc, properly done, should lead to outcomes xyz – then if abc and xyz all occur as expected, they will have confidence that the outcomes are due to the interventions. Stakeholders agree in advance the standard of evidence which will convince them.

Thus the theory of change helps to circumvent the philosophical debates on methodology, especially in evaluation research, by recognising that the most important judges of validity are the stakeholders who are going to use the results. If these are policy makers rather than academics, preferences for particular research methods are less likely to be based on philosophical positions on the nature of the world and how to find out about it. This approach to evaluation was applied in a study of the Fairbridge organisation in the UK (a case study in Chapter Nine). So, there are two versions of the theory of change approach. For Weiss (1998) the focus is on constructing and systematically testing elements of the process. Connell's version takes this further – for him the 'theory of change' refers not only to the change in participants brought about by the programme, but also the change in policy brought about by the research.

An interim conclusion on practicalities and problems in research

So, where does this leave us? It partly depends where one starts. If one is planning research for a PhD, or is funded by an academic research council, or has to defend one's position in an academic journal, one has to be able to tell a logically consistent research story based on epistemological and ontological assumptions, so one can pick any approach that does this. Quantitative methods tend to tell us what has happened, but not how and why. For this, qualitative methods are more helpful. If one is a pragmatist, one may mix both – with no philosophical justification, except that such a blend might happen to impress significant stakeholders, so one's research is more likely to make an impact on the world. Further, a pragmatist may decide that, given the inherent difficulties in achieving the 'gold standard' of the classical experimental design, one will need to restrict oneself to small-scale case studies, juxtaposing quantitative and qualitative methods, asking 'how' and 'why' questions – but not 'how many' (Yin, 2003). This might be sensible for a student research project or one with limited resources and a case study approach is an academically valid way of adding to theory.

Scientific realism appears to offer the possibility of doing a set of small case studies, each their own CMR configuration, and adding them up cumulatively (Pawson and Tilley, 1997: 115). This is not the same as the meta-analysis used by positivist approach. But difficulties remain in defining a CMR configuration, and deciding when one is disproved.

Connell's version of the theory of change approach has the advantage that inherent difficulties in the research can be overcome by persuading the relevant stakeholders that this is really the best one can do in a specific situation. It does, however, require the establishment and maintenance of a stakeholder group. It also has the considerable advantage that the methods are developed to test the internally generated hypotheses and, as a consequence, the research process is recognised and valued by key stakeholders, including programme staff. This contributes to the ability to generate the research data. Evaluations that impose methods based on an externally generated hypothesis (as in the positivist approach) have often produced poor results; for example, an extensive survey of the impact of physically demanding programmes on probationers (Taylor *et al.*, 1999) had very poor response rates to pre- and post-programme questionnaires. One reason for this was that the programme workers felt no commitment to administering the questionnaires and that completing them interfered with the important initial contact with young participants (Nichols *et al.*, 2000). And of course, the major advantage of Connell's approach – assuming that one wants one's work to change the world – is that research is more likely to influence policy, as key policy stakeholders have already signed up to the validity of the methods.

My own view is that the generative causality of scientific realism makes more sense than the secessionist causality of positivism because it accounts for the dynamic interaction of agency and structure. To understand how and why programmes work, I need to understand how the staff and participants experience them, and what they mean to them. However, I still want to measure outcomes, and if these are only intermediate ones, as in box 4 of Figure 4.2 (see page 33), the link between the intermediate and final outcomes must be justified by theory. Research must start from theory – even research in the interpretive/constructionist paradigm does not start from a clean slate; there are already some theories underlying its instigation and design. It is very valuable to engage programme staff in making explicit the theoretical links in their programme because it may help them improve their work, but also it will gain commitment to the research process. But, this should be combined with links to what we know so far – such as the theory described in Chapters Two and Three. Pawson and Tilley suggest how this may be done through a scientific realist approach to interviewing that seeks to generate a shared understanding between interviewer and interviewee (1997: 165). Without going into details (this is discussed further in Chapter 15), this seems to be a far more realistic representation of my experience of interviewing than those that ignore the interviewer/interviewee relationship. Quantitative and qualitative methods both have a part to play: neither can be dismissed as invalid per se, but both must be pursued with the maximum methodical rigour.

The criticisms of different methods above do not imply that all the results derived from them are invalid – just that we need to be aware of their limitations. The theoretical frameworks in Chapters Two and Three are based on results from all different approaches.

Any research is a compromise between what one might ideally like to do and both the practicalities of the research situation and the resources available. The choice of methods, and the conclusions from them, must make clear these limitations. But on the other hand, one can still stick to the principles above to do the best job one can.

The points in this chapter are illustrated by the case study programmes that follow. Hopefully they will help researchers and programme managers plan evaluations, and policy makers judge the validity of the results.

Acknowledgement

Part of this chapter was adapted from Nichols, G. (2004) 'Research methods in outdoor education.' In Barnes, P. And Sharp, B. (eds) *The RHP Companion to Outdoor Education*. Lyme Regis: Russell House Publishing, pp. 34–42. www.russell house.co.uk.

5   The policy context

As we have seen in Chapter Four, the notion of valid 'evidence' is contentious and is affected by value judgements. The political context also determines how evidence is collected and interpreted. It affects the type of programme that is supported, the amount of support given, and the general approach to policy on youth and crime. This is, in turn, affected by the ways in which the media report specific cases and mould public opinion.

Policy as a reflection of ideology or of political pragmatism

Bateman and Pitts (2005: 248) have made the case that, while youth justice policy and practice are informed by evidence, 'the evidence is not the starting point of the policy making process'. They argue that the starting point is policy goals and that evidence is selected (or rejected) on the basis of its fit with these. These goals themselves are selected to appeal to the small proportion of the electorate who are liable to change political allegiance, and who also reside in the small number of marginal constituencies. Thus these few critical swing voters have a disproportionate influence on national government policy, and disenfranchise everybody else. This process has become more significant as politics has moved away from a link with ideological positions and towards a managerialist approach. In other words, political parties now claim that their party can do a more effective job in achieving a particular set of objectives, rather than trying to attract voters because their policies reflect a particular ideological position.

This interpretation is debatable. It is difficult to prove the claim that national policy is led by the views of a few key voters – and this is likely to be true only to the extent that political parties have made the effort to pinpoint the views of these voters (as 'New' Labour has). However, a historical perspective suggests a shift towards this position. A much more comprehensive overview of the development of national government policy on youth crime since the 1960s is given in Pitts (2003). Key points are summarised below.

The Children and Young Persons Act of 1969 can be seen as a high-water mark of a commitment to the idea that the welfare of young people needs to be of primary concern. This was influenced by the social scientists who contributed to the development of policy of the 1964 Labour government. Ideology probably had a greater influence here than the unknown views of marginal voters. In 1979 the Conservative Thatcher government was elected with an ideological commitment to reduce government spending and the role of the state. This was reflected in a youth justice policy of 'progressive minimalism', which drew on research showing that punitive programmes were often counter-productive. This policy aimed to reduce the amount spent on putting juveniles into custody, and reduced the interventions that had characterised the previous welfare-oriented policies. Instead Intermediate Treatment focused resources on reducing the offending of adjudicated offenders. This approach was enshrined in the Criminal Justice Act of 1991, which abolished custody for children under 15.

However, youth riots in the early 1990s, the highly publicised murder of a very young child by two ten-year-olds in 1993 (the Bulger case), followed by more media portrayals of young people involved in multiple offending, led quickly to the promise to create 200 places for persistent offenders in secure training centres. In this case the political imperative to act appeared to be the determining factor in policy formulation, and Bateman and Pitts' (2005) claim that youth justice experts were not involved in determining policy – just in advising on the means by which policy goals might be achieved. New Labour's 1998 Crime and Disorder Act led to all juveniles above the age of criminal responsibility (age ten in England and Wales) being treated as if they were physically and mentally capable of committing an offence, had an awareness that what they were doing was seriously wrong, and were therefore responsible for their actions. Prior to the 1998 Act this assumption of capability and intent had to be proved by a prosecutor in a court in respect of children aged between ten and thirteen. One could interpret this change as reflecting an ideological commitment to the notion of active and responsible citizenship, now applied to those aged ten to thirteen, but also as a reflection of the need to seize the law and order agenda from the Conservatives, as reflected in Blair's 'tough on crime and tough on the causes of crime' soundbite, made as Shadow Home Secretary.

So, there is a case that national government policy has moved towards being led at least as much by political pragmatism – in response to public opinion, the media, and a bid to seize the political advantage on the 'law and order' agenda – as it is by ideology and by evidence. A clear example of this was when a young person who had been attending an extensive residential programme was involved in further offending. The programme involved the young person working intensively one-to-one with a member of staff to plan an expedition to an African safari park. Media headlines following the young person's further offending were along the lines of 'safari boy commits more crime'. As a consequence, probation staff nationally were told not to support any programmes that involved young people travelling abroad. This posed some difficulty for the Probation Service's use of the Sail Training Association, which ran trips across the Channel in large sail boats. In this case probation staff turned a 'Nelson's eye'!

At the level of local government it is also likely that policies will be affected by both ideology and political reaction to local media coverage. However 'law and order' is not such an important issue in local politics in the UK and legislation is made at national level.

Policy as a determinant of the selection of evidence

We have seen in Chapter Four how the values of policy makers have influenced the type of evidence that is regarded as valid. Bateman and Pitts (2005; Pitts, 2003) take this further by arguing that evidence is selected and interpreted in a particular way because it fits the prevailing policy agenda. In the mid-1970s the view that offenders could be 'treated' in some way – a view that had emerged in the latter part of the nineteenth century and was associated with the welfarist approach to young people – was in decline. While Crow (2001: 35) identifies that this view was 'challenged theoretically, ethically and empirically, leading to the simplistic conclusion that "nothing works"', he, as does Pitts, notes that this change of policy has to be understood within the political climate of economic and social difficulties. These, and the 'treatment model' were characterised as consequences of a broad liberal ideology. An influential research report at this time was Martinson's (1974) review of 231 studies of a wide range of rehabilitative programmes. The main conclusion of this was that these programmes did not work, in the sense of reducing offending. Both Pitts and Crow point out that Martinson's conclusion could be criticised in many ways, not least that made by Pawson and Tilley (1997: 9) that it constructed: ' ... an impossibly stringent criterion for success. To count as a body of treatment that works, such programmes have to provide positive changes in the favour of the experimental group in all trials in all contexts. He is thus able to discount successful experiments by dint of them being isolated ...'. (See Pawson and Tilley's criticism of the classic experimental design in Chapter Four, page 34.) Interestingly, Pawson and Tilley (1997: 9) quote Martinson's original paper in which he said 'this is not to say that we have found no instances of success or partial success', and Martinson never actually said 'nothing works'. However, the interpretation of Martinson's review, and the weight given to the 'nothing works' conclusion, can be seen to have reflected the dominant political view at the time. In effect, Martinson's 'evidence' was given prominence, and interpreted in a particular way, because it fitted in with the contemporary political view that government intervention should be minimalised.

Bateman and Pitts (2005: 249) argue that the 'nothing works' orthodoxy was replaced, not because of new evidence but because 'by the late 1980s, a rising crime rate and growing concern about violent youth crime were placing mounting pressure on the Conservative government, the Home Office, and via them, academic criminology, to come up with something that did work'. Again this is difficult to prove. Crow (2001) reviews a body of research between 1979 and 1997 which supported the view that some programmes worked for some people in some circumstances – which was an alternative interpretation of Martinson's (1974) original review. It is interesting that a second paper by Martinson, published in 1979, and which reviewed new evidence to come to exactly the conclusion that some programmes did work, 'attracted little attention compared to the original article, and in any case by then the fate of the treatment module in its original form was sealed so Martinson's later article had little policy impact' (Crow, 2001: 61). So Crow is suggesting a relationship between the policy climate and the acceptability of Martinson's reviewed conclusions.

Approaches that came to prominence in the 1990s were cognitive behaviour programmes, based on the work of Ross and Fabiano (1985) and the risk/protection factor approach of Catalano and Hawkins (1996), both reviewed in Chapter Three. The evidence supporting both of these approaches can be criticised – see Chapter Three – but it could be argued that their general acceptance was due to a favourable policy climate in which there was a desperate search for something that 'worked'.

For Pitts the:

> ... rise to pre-eminence of Reasoning and Rehabilitation [Ross and Fabiano's programmes] as a mode of intervention is accounted for as much, if not more, by its ideological, economic and administrative fit with the new forms of penalty emerging in the US and UK justice systems in the late 1980s and 1990s and effective entrepreneurism on the part of its proponents, as its explanatory power of rehabilitative impact.
>
> (Pitts, 2003: 93)

A similar example of selective interpretation of evidence is the 1999 Policy Action Team 10 report to the government Social Exclusion Unit on how arts and sport can be used to reduce social exclusion, included in which was the reduction of crime (Department for Culture, Media and Sport, 1999). The policy priority was to reduce social exclusion; however, the evidence cited was extremely shallow and might all have been rejected as inconclusive under another political regime.

So, there is a case that the political context – the need to be seen to react to prominent cases and to sustain a particular public impression of dealing with law and order issues – determines policy, just as much as evidence. Further, that the prominent policy affects the way evidence is selected and interpreted. However, it is one determinant, and it would be too cynical to say it is the only one. As we have seen in Chapter Four, much evidence in this area can be interpreted through an optimistic or pessimistic perspective (beer glass half-full or half-empty) and virtually all of it can be methodologically challenged.

The selection of evidence facilitating accountability and control

Another reason why some evidence is preferred might be that it fits into an agenda of increased programme accountability and control. It might be argued that greater control over programme implementation is required because failure can be attributed to poor implementation. Of course, this assumes that one can prescribe a successful programme anyway. However, Bateman and Pitts (2005: 253) have argued that evidence leading to a particular approach is favoured if it can contribute more to the 'micro-management of the youth justice system, than its likely impact on re-offending'. Thus reasoning and rehabilitation programmes, based on Ross and Fabiano's cognitive deficit model, can be administered by relatively junior staff who can record in a 'tick box' format what they have done.

A similar criticism might be made of the ASSET form used by Youth Offending Team (YOT) officers to record in an interview with clients the 'risk factors' relevant to their lives (the validity of this tool being rejected as a method of evaluation in the case study of the Summit programme described in Chapter Twelve). Similarly Huskins's (1998) approach to youth work, in a section entitled 'project management', includes recommendations for process and control indicators. These include monitoring the progress of young people through the seven stages of his curriculum development module (1998: 104). On the one hand Huskins's tools for recording work (discussed further in Chapter Twelve) could be seen as a systematic way of ensuring that it is conducted and recorded in an appropriate way and someone is therefore accountable for what has been done. On the other hand Huskins's approach can be seen as a deskilling of youth work – a sort of 'youth work by numbers' that ignores a more holistic approach to young people. Similarly to the Reasoning and Rehabilitation programmes and the risk/protection factor programmes, it focuses 'almost exclusively on the individual ... they both utilise what is essentially a deficit paradigm ... a public health model that identifies, isolates, and then treats the subject in order to restore him or her to good health ...' (Smith, 2003: 52), and thus ignores the possibility that the problem might lie at the level of society. The recommended collection of monitoring data might contribute to the 'explosion in paperwork' feared by Smith (2003: 50). This concern is shared by Pitts, who comments that, 'on the face of it, it is a very good idea that YOT's should collect and collate data with which to inform the development of the youth offending service and professional practice within it. However, at present the evaluative tail appears to [be] wagging the rehabilitative dog ... This problem flows directly from the attempt of the Youth Justice Board to hijack data collection as a means of exerting greater managerial control over the YOTs' (2003: 41).

Thus, a case can be made that one factor in the selection of evidence is the degree to which it supports a political agenda of accountability and control. Perhaps, as in the risk/protection model, it also has the attraction of transforming a complex problem into a simple solution. In either case it undermines the ability of those working with young people to use their individual flair, imagination and creativity to match the needs of young people with opportunities for holistic development, as the personal growth model in Chapter Three suggests is required. It can devalue the qualities and skills of programme staff, which Chapter Seventeen emphasises are important.

Conclusion

Thus, the political context is one determinant of how evidence is selected, interpreted and used. Exactly to what extent can't be proven, and depends on how cynical one's standpoint is.

More specifically, with respect to evaluation studies, as Pawson and Tilley (1997) have noted, evaluation is generally concerned to inform the solution to 'social problems', so evaluation funding will be directed by the political definition of what is a problem and the priority given to it. Further, the results of evaluation, in terms of recommendations, will also be within politically determined parameters. Thus an evaluation is not likely to conclude that the causes of youth crime can be traced to excessive material inequalities, engendered by an over-reliance on free-market mechanisms to distribute wealth, in conjunction with the replacement of traditional moral values with individual avarice, which itself is doomed to failure because of the relative social construction of wealth and because of finite natural resources – unless, of course, one's evaluation has been commissioned by a party of socialist/Methodist/greens (I'm not discounting the validity of this standpoint). Rather, conclusions will be limited to less radical proposals, consistent with the prevailing social/political system. Of course, independent funders of evaluation, such as the Rowntree Foundation, have more licence to step outside the current political parameters, and may see it as an objective to do so.

6 A typology of programmes, with implications for evaluation

This chapter presents a typology of programmes that can guide their design and evaluation (Nichols and Crow, 2004). This combines a categorisation by the 'risk' level of participants, and a categorisation by the mechanism by which the programme operates to give a 3 × 3 typology in which programmes can be situated. Case study programmes in subsequent chapters are introduced here to show how they fit into the typology, and the implications for evaluation methods are discussed. The typology does not claim to be definitive – further research could develop it – but it does offer a useful framework. The chapter also previews the problems of evaluating different types of programmes and some of the implications described in Chapter Sixteen.

Thus, this chapter provides a bridge between the discussion in the previous chapters of mechanisms and methods; and the detailed case studies of programmes that follow. In the description of the programmes and discussion of their approaches to evaluation, there is inevitably some overlap with the individual case studies; however the case studies give much more detail.

A categorisation of programmes by risk level of participant

A categorisation of programme by 'risk' level of client builds on Brantingham and Faust's (1976) categorisation of programmes in terms of three types of crime reduction potential: primary, secondary and tertiary. In this categorisation, primary reduction is directed at the modification of the criminological conditions that are likely to give rise to offending. Sports programmes of this type would operate at the level of attempting to improve the community and reduce neighbourhood disadvantage as a risk factor. Programmes directed towards secondary reduction focus on the early identification of, and intervention in, the lives of those in circumstances likely to lead to crime. Sports programmes that operate in this way would try to target 'at-risk' groups of young people. Tertiary programmes work with those who have already been identified as offenders and they seek to prevent recidivism. Therefore sports programmes that seek to do this are likely to take referrals from a criminal justice agency such as a Youth Offending Team (YOT). Of course, these are pure types, and some programmes may operate in more than one manner. It is not always easy to place a programme in one of the

Brantingham and Faust categories and they might more realistically be seen as points on a scale in terms of the risk level of participants.

A categorisation of programmes by mechanism of crime reduction

Chapter Three developed a model of personal growth, directed by values, that represents a long-term mechanism by which programmes might reduce crime. To this are added the more simple mechanisms of diversion and deterrence. This is not to rule out any other mechanisms, but these three are seen as the main ones.

A diversion mechanism involves diverting the person from a place or at a time when they might otherwise be involved in crime. It could also include a diversion from boredom, and thus a reduction in the likelihood that they would get involved in crime. Thus, in the summer Splash programmes, supported by Youth Justice (see Chapter Thirteen), the place and time the programme was run was important, but also the fact that it was run in the school holidays when young people would otherwise be bored.

The mechanism of deterrence works when the person thinks they are more likely to be caught if they commit an offence. For example, if a programme is run on school premises people are less likely to throw a brick through the window when programme staff are present. So this mechanism is place and time specific. The mechanism of pro-social development is described in Chapter Three. As noted, it combines the juxtaposition of risk and protection factors with a model of self-development, facilitated by parallel increases in self-esteem, locus of control, and cognitive skills, directed by pro-social values.

A typology combining risk level and mechanism

The three risk levels and mechanisms can be combined to produce a typology of crime reduction mechanisms (see Table 6.1), which may be exclusive, though one programme might have elements of all three in different proportions.

Examples of programmes, with implications for evaluation methods

Below are brief descriptions of programmes featured in Table 6.1, described by their combination of participant risk level and main mechanism, and with implications for evaluation. A conclusion, illustrated by the case studies to follow, is that it is easier to evaluate programmes working intensively with high-risk participants than programmes working with low-risk participants, where the main mechanism is diversion. This applies to the use of both qualitative and quantitative methods. High-risk participants are more likely to have been convicted, enabling use of conviction records. Work with them will generally be more intense and over a longer period of time, allowing more scope for the use of in-depth qualitative methods. In contrast, programmes with low-risk participants

Table 6.1 A typology of programmes and mechanisms

Risk level/ mechanism	Tertiary – high risk	Secondary – medium risk	Primary – low risk
Pro-social development	Positive Futures/ Sportaction WYSC Hafotty Wen 14 peaks	Fairbridge Clontarf	Splash (long term)
Deterrence			Northtown Parks for All scheme Splash on-school sites
Diversion		Summit	Splash Many local authority holiday schemes

may not even have accurate records of who has attended, and the experience for participants themselves will be a much less significant part of their lives. However, an important message of the whole book is that the difficulties of evaluating programmes with low-risk clients are not a good reason for policy makers to disregard them.

High-risk/pro-social development

West Yorkshire Sports Counselling (WYSC) operated from 1993 to 1996. It was provided by a voluntary sector charity, West Yorkshire Sports Counselling Association (WYSCA) and delivered by four sports leaders based in local authority sports development sections. Probation service clients were referred to the project by their probation officer, though participation was voluntary. The basic programme was 12 weeks of sports activities delivered on a one-to-one basis to each participant, involving one meeting between the sports leader and participant each week. However, in several cases sports leaders maintained informal contact with participants and this allowed them to act as a broker of further sporting opportunities as well as take a more mentoring role.

The Hafotty Wen 14 peaks programme was run by what was at the time Merseyside Probation Service's residential outdoor centre in North Wales. It involved probationers climbing all of the 14, 3,000 ft and over, peaks in North Wales over 24 hours – a fairly demanding feat. The 14 peaks attempt was preceded by two or three training events. Qualitative research focused on participants who were experiencing drug rehabilitation – although these were not the only participants.

Southtown Positive Futures was one of 24 Positive Futures programmes supported by Sport England (2002a; 2002b). It was run by Sportaction, a registered charity with four trustees, instigated by the Chief Constable of the county constabulary and a group of local businessmen. Participants were referred from the local YOT as those at highest risk of offending. The programme offered one-to-one sports counselling over periods that varied depending on the willingness of participants to take part. This could last as long as a year or more, since participants could take sports leadership awards and become involved in leading other groups run by the Sportaction project, initially on a voluntary basis but with the potential to lead to paid work. This programme was tertiary as it was directed towards YOT clients with a long history of offending.

High risk/pro-social development programmes of this type tend to be easier to evaluate in terms of outcome measures. As participants have an offending record, evaluation can focus on individual reconviction, though it is unlikely that a good comparison group will be easily available. In the WYSC and Hafotty Wen cases it was possible to use the Offender Group Reconviction Score (OGRS), which compares actual reconviction rates to those predicted by a model derived from an analysis of a large sample of probationers, who in effect provide a control group. Thus, this is an example of the classic experimental method. In WYSC it was also possible to set up a control group and compare reconviction rates with participants, an approach that again replicated the experimental design. In WYSC, in spite of a small sample size, statistically significant positive results were obtained showing that those participants who stayed with the programme for 8 or more weeks were less likely to be reconvicted than expected (Nichols and Taylor, 1996). However, in the Hafotty Wen case the apparently positive result had to be qualified by the sample size, which made results inconclusive (Nichols, 2001a). So, despite the considerable work required to conduct the reconviction rate analysis, sample sizes may limit the validity of the results.

In both these cases, to gain a better understanding of the programme mechanisms, interviews with individual participants and individual case studies were conducted. Thus qualitative and quantitative methods complemented each other. The qualitative interviews and case studies of participants were extremely valuable in understanding the process of the programme and implications for its development (Nichols, 1999b). These illustrate a constructionist-intepretivist approach to research: it was important to understand how the participants experienced the programme and its place in their drug rehabilitation. Although the WYSC evaluation was not conducted as a conscious application of the scientific realist approach, methods in this study were similar to a scientific realist design.

The study of the Positive Futures Sportaction programme had to be limited to a few detailed case studies of participants as numbers were too small for any reconviction rate analysis or other quantitative measurement of outcomes – few people participated in the programme for any significant length of time while it was being studied. This meant that the study had to remain at a case study level, just asking how and why the programme had an effect, rather than for how many people was this significant.

In this type of high-risk/pro-social development programme, it may still be difficult to apply 'before and after' measures of characteristics of participants, as such measures, especially if academically validated, are often viewed by programme staff as being onerous to administer and counter-productive to establishing a positive relationship with participants. These difficulties led to the failure of such methods in an extensive study of probation service programmes (Nichols *et al.*, 2000), and they had limited success in WYSC. In contrast, the theory of change approach, applied to designing evaluation tools acceptable to programme staff, proved successful in the evaluation of Fairbridge, discussed below.

Medium-risk/pro-social development

Fairbridge is a charity that works with disadvantaged and disaffected young people. All agencies dealing with young people aged 14–25, including the youth service and probation service, can make referrals to the programme, and some young people refer themselves. Fairbridge aims to develop young people's personal and social skills and build their confidence, helping them to change their lives. A basic week-long course includes centre-based preparation and up to 3 days at a residential location. From this, participants develop a personal action plan for the next 6 months. The activities the young person might choose to take part in after that include workshops to develop life skills, programmes to develop skills for the workplace, follow-on outdoor activity courses, courses run by partner organisations such as The Prince's Trust, and individual counselling sessions. Thus Fairbridge aims to work through the mechanism of long-term pro-social development by intervention in the lives of young people 'at risk' and, in some cases, those who have already offended. This example illustrates that the Brantingham and Faust (op. cit.) categories are an ideal type, with some programmes overlapping between categories.

The Fairbridge evaluation included: a self assessment by the young person of their personal and social skills at either end of an initial 1-week course; detailed records of participants; structured observation of the courses; face-to-face semi-structured interviews conducted with 58 randomly selected participants 3 months after the basic course, and a repeat of the self-assessment of skills; and follow-up interviews with 30 young people a year after the introductory course. Much of the interview data was converted to quantitative form to permit a statistical analysis of the factors in the process most associated with positive dimensions of change.

This evaluation used Connell's version of the theory of change approach. Programme staff were initially involved in describing hypotheses about who the programme worked with, what it achieved, and what contributed to this. Methods were then designed to test the hypotheses. These included devising a 'before and after' measure acceptable to programme staff and participants. Large sample sizes allowed an internal validation of this measure. Consistent with Connell's theory of change approach, key stakeholders in the policy community were involved in the selection of methods to test the hypotheses, to ensure that the validity of potential results was accepted by them at this stage of the research design.

The other programme placed in this category is Clontarf in Australia. The Contarf Foundation delivers Australian rules football (ARF) programmes through academies, each of which operates in partnership with (but independent of) a school or college. The academies offer Indigenous young people top-class coaching in ARF. Participation in the football training and games is conditional on attendance at school. The nature of the programme means that it is relatively easy to collect data on school retention rates, graduation and employment rates of participants. In all of these respects Indigenous young peoples' achievement levels are far below the Australian population as a whole. Thus the rates for the Australian population, and for Indigenous young people as a whole, offer simple comparisons with the Clontarf students. This is a replication of the logic of the classic experimental research design, which shows very positive results. The case study does not include further evaluation into how and why the programme is successful.

Medium-risk/diversion

Easttown Summit was run by Easttown Recreation Department and was sold to Easttown Youth Offending Team. It involved sporting activities on a one-to-one basis with a sports leader. From 1998 to 2000, clients were referred from the probation service. After this date clients came just from the YOT, which contracted to buy places in 2000/2001 on what was essentially the same programme. One full-time member of staff was responsible for the programme and worked entirely on it, supported by a small pool of casual staff. The programme is regarded as secondary intervention because, although all the participants had been referred by the YOT, they had not been convicted and the focus was on reducing the potential for this to happen.

In this programme it was possible to use in-depth interviews with the sports leader and a set of case studies of participants to show that the programme was seen as primarily a diversion from crime, although the YOT officers used it because they felt it had a significant impact on long-term development. Some 'before and after' measures were attempted, but with limited success. It was also not possible to gain access to YOT records to track the re-offending of participants. Thus, research was limited to asking how and why questions in a case study approach – it was not possible to measure outcomes, as in a scientific realist CMO configuration.

Low-risk/deterrent

Northtown Parks for All scheme was instigated by Northtown Recreation Department in response to local residents who were apprehensive about using the parks, especially after the removal of on-site park attendants. Residents complained about vandalism to the park and young people drinking there at night. A presence in the park during the day and evening was provided by letting an unused building in the park at a peppercorn rent to a martial arts dojo (centre for the instruction and practice of martial arts). Not only were the martial arts instructors, and their pupils, present in the park, but the contract with the dojos also required the instructors to patrol the park periodically. This acted as a deterrent for people who might otherwise have engaged in casual vandalism. Importantly, it was also of great reassurance to local residents, and thus, in turn, supported local politicians' decisions to support the programme. Evaluation used records of vandalism collected by the park rangers and police records of reported incidents, though neither of these provided conclusive evidence of success. However, an advantage of these was that the records were related to the specific geographical area – the park. Just as important for the continuation of the programme was the positive impact on local public opinion.

The collection of records of vandalism was a quasi-experimental approach as it was not possible to set up a control park where exactly the same circumstances prevailed, except for the introduction of the new dojos.

Low-risk/diversion

Westtown Splash is an open-access sports activity programme, aimed at 8–18-year-olds, targeted on the most socially and economically disadvantaged areas of Westtown. The sites used by Splash are playing fields, parks and fields or hard surface areas adjacent to leisure and community centres. Paid staff lead a range of sports and games. Participation is free. The programme has been run by a partnership of Westtown Police and Westtown Leisure Services for over 10 years and is typical of many local authority-run programmes (Nichols and Booth, 1999b), apart from its long-term continuity over the last 10 years. In some areas other activities are offered during the school holidays and after school in the summer term. There is the potential for regular participants to attend a sports-related youth group run by the sports development staff throughout the year, and also to become involved in voluntary sports leadership. In 2001 and 2002 the programme was expanded with funding from the Youth Justice Board (YJB), which funded several other similar programmes, all of which the Board also called Splash.

The main mechanism – diversion – could be extended to a direct deterrent by running programmes on some school sites. Vandalism to the schools had been reduced, at least while Splash was on. The long-term continuity of Westtown Splash (in contrast to programmes that may be short-term as they rely entirely on the YJB annual grants or other short-term funding) means it also has the potential to contribute to long-term pro-social development through older participants acting as volunteers to help the younger ones, and this leading to sports leadership awards.

An evaluation method for this type of programme, which the Youth Justice Board asked programmes they had supported in 2000 and 2001 to implement, is to compare police records of crime and incident data of the categories most associated with youth offending in an area where a scheme has been provided with the previous year when it was not – a classic experimental design. There are several difficulties with this method, reviewed further in Chapter Thirteen: the area in which crime data is recorded may not match the area where the programme is running; changes in crime figures may be so small as to be insignificant; and the effort required to analyse the data may be beyond the programme.

In Westtown Splash, a self-completion questionnaire was sent to parents and interviews were conducted with participants. These methods required skill to implement and took considerable resources, but they gave positive results and a better indication of how the programme worked. They reflect an approach in which methods are designed to test specific hypotheses about how the programme worked, as in scientific realism, or the theory of change.

Even if Splash programmes were targeted on those most likely to offend and it was possible to record who attended the programme, there are still major difficulties in comparing in any meaningful way those who attend and those who do not. These include setting up sample and control groups and the small numbers involved in sub-groups – reviewed in Chapter Thirteen (Nichols, 2001b).

A combination of the methods above might provide some indication of programme effectiveness in crime reduction, but the resources required are considerable and, even then, small sample sizes may make changes statistically insignificant. The questionnaires and interviews used in Westtown Splash gave an indication of how and why the programme might reduce crime, in a case study approach, but did not show by how much. Again, research was unable to measure outcomes, as in a context-mechanism-regularity (CMR) configuration.

Example of low-risk/pro-social development

Examining the long-term impact of the Westtown Splash programme, characteristics of the programme that make this difficult include open access for participants (they can drop in or out at any time), the open-ended involvement of participants (they may be involved for a few days or a few years), the variety of 'exit routes' for participants that can be regarded as successful outcomes, and the general targeting of young people 'at risk', the numbers of which may be relatively small even when accurate records of participants are available.

One can not use 'before' and 'after' measures of individual participants, such as measures of self-esteem, changing relationship with the sports leaders as mentors or changed attitudes towards crime. In a situation where participation is open-ended and records of participation are unreliable, it is difficult to identify the group of participants one would expect to have benefited, and one may have only a small proportion of participants who completed both 'before' and 'after' measures. Given the large number of participants in many of these open-access programmes, the physical environment in which the programme operates and the resources required, it is not efficient to conduct 'before' measures with a large sample, many of whom will not become regular participants over the 2 years, or cannot be identified as such. Much of the data collected at the start of the study would be wasted.

Even if one was able to do this, it would be impossible to set up retrospectively a control group matched by age, gender and history of offending to see if those attending the programme regularly had changed significantly in relation to those who had not. A further difficulty is finding an instrument to measure such changes that is suitable for this type of participant and situation.

Similarly to measuring changes in the personal attributes discussed above, one could examine recorded offending rates of participants and non-participants over a two-year period. This would require access to local YOT records. Programme success would be implied if regular attendees had lower increases in offending rates than a matched sample of non-participants. However, the same problems of setting up a retrospective control group remain. In theory this would be possible if one had access to all youth offending data in a specific geographical area. However, the effort involved in such an analysis would be beyond the resources devoted to research by a typical local authority. If one was able to conduct such an analysis one would still be reliant on large enough sample sizes to lead to statistically significant results. This would be difficult as once one had identified a core of regular participants one would be working with relatively small numbers. One option might be a meta-analysis of a number of such programmes, though a limitation, as with all records of offending, is that they record only a small proportion of offences.

A further difficulty is that initial contact with a programme may lead to an 'exit route' involving long-term participation in another organisation, which confers the same positive benefits as the original programme. For example, a summer sports taster session may lead to a long-term involvement in a local canoe club, but this will be unrecorded by the original programme unless extensive follow-up research into all participants is possible. The resources to do this are not available, and thus this successful programme outcome would remain concealed. In such a situation it may also be asked whether any impact should be attributed to the longer-term involvement, or to the 'taster' session for getting the person involved to start with, or the combination of the two. These difficulties reflect the criticisms Pawson and Tilley (1997: 5) have made of the classical experimental research design. It is not practical in such situations and, even if it was, it tells us insufficient information about the process.

Evidence of the positive impact of participation on a young person's pro-social development can come from individual case studies but the evidence here is of process; that is, how and why a programme has had an impact on participants, rather than of outcomes such as a reduction in crime participation by participants overall. Detailed records of participation are still needed to show how typical these case study participants were, and therefore how many similar participants attended regularly to the extent that one might expect them to benefit in the same ways. Qualitative interviews with long-term Splash participants is an expensive option, but the research context reduces the ability of such interviews to explore in depth the causal relationship between the programme and long-term impacts. The participants' attention span and willingness to take part in an interview for more than 15 minutes is limited, thus restricting the interviewer's ability to elicit details about the impact of the programme. For any one participant it is difficult to triangulate data from other sources, such as parents or sports leaders. Even with sufficient detail, results show the relevance of this mechanism of pro-social development in a few cases, showing that the programme has the potential to achieve this, and the most important programme characteristics leading to this, but not how many participants have benefited in this way.

Implications

An initial implication of the categorisation above is that it can inform the selection of research methods in a deductive approach, starting research from theory. In any one programme, research starts from a general theory about the mechanism involved and the outcomes one expects, similar to Pawson and Tilley (1997) starting research from a particular CMR configuration.

One problem is that if research starts by looking for just one mechanism, then there is a danger that this is the only one it will find, and other mechanisms will be ignored. Starting research from this basis can be self-fulfilling. Preliminary research might be conducted prior to evaluation in order to identify what type of evaluation is necessary. There also needs to be regular checking of material to ensure that subsidiary mechanisms are not being missed, and to verify whether the programme's mechanisms have altered. As shown by the example of the Westtown Splash programme, all three mechanisms might be involved.

The ability of programmes to provide the evidence needed to evaluate them will vary. This determines the evidence one can reasonably expect a programme to provide itself, and that which can be provided by an external researcher. Just because it is harder to produce evidence for the effectiveness of programmes working with low-risk participants, does this mean there is less justification for funding them? Alternatively, the position of a programme in this categorisation should influence policy makers' judgements of what is acceptable evidence of effectiveness.

Evidence from programmes is scant because they do not have the funds or skills to conduct their own evaluation, and a higher priority is to assure next year's funding to allow them to continue. It is possible for programmes to be intensively evaluated by experts with greater resources than are available to the programme management. (WYSC is a good example, although in this case the programme itself funded the evaluation, so it was buying expertise.) But in these cases, the generalisation of results will depend on how precisely programmes can be replicated. It is possible to say that certain ways of working are more likely to bring the desired results in particular circumstances, but the problem is to define the circumstances. This reflects a general methodological difficulty of the critical realist approach, noted above, which is how to define a CMR configuration.

Implications are returned to in Chapters Fifteen and Sixteen, but for the moment the risk/mechanism typology is useful in situating the case studies that follow.

7 West Yorkshire Sports Counselling

Summary

This programme worked with relatively high-risk participants, many of whom had been through several other programmes offered by the probation service. Where it was successful its main mechanism was pro-social development. The evaluation applied the classic experimental design in the use of reconviction data (details are given of this method), other quantitative methods, and also qualitative case studies of participants to understand how and why the programme had an impact. Thus mixed methods complemented each other. As one of the authors of the evaluation, I recognise that the research started with theoretical hypotheses about the mechanisms by which the programme might cause change and in what circumstances, even if these were not made explicit. Thus the case studies were starting from theory – academic theory, rather than theory generated from programme staff – in the way that a scientific realist approach would start with hypotheses about CMO configurations. So, although the evaluation study was not designed to use a scientific realist approach, in practice it was very similar. The evaluation identified key factors that led to the programme's success. These included the good-quality mentoring relationship developed between participants and sports leaders and the way this was used to guide participants through a succession of developmental opportunities.

Introduction to the programme

West Yorkshire Sports Counselling (WYSC) operated from 1993 to 1996. It was provided by a voluntary sector charity, West Yorkshire Sports Counselling Association (WYSCA). Trustees included local authority sports development managers in the area. Initially the programme was funded directly by the Home Office, but shortly into its operation funding was devolved to the West Yorkshire Probation Service. Probationers from this service were referred to the project by their probation officer. Thus WYSC was separate from the probation service and was seen as such by the participants. Referral was voluntary and took place only after the client, sports leader and probation officer had discussed the project and the client had agreed to attend. Attendance was not a condition of a client's order. The project was initially aimed at those aged 16–25 years – a specification of the Home Office funding – but this was widened, and over the evaluation period 30 per cent of referrals were over 25 years of age.

The project offered a 12-week programme of sports activities. This was delivered by four sports leaders on a one-to-one basis to each participant, involving one meeting between the sports leader and participant each week. All these meetings would involve active sports participation, shared by the sports leader and participant. The one-to-one counselling allowed the programme to be matched to participants' needs, allowing the pursuit of individual sporting preferences and aiming towards an 'exit route' involving continued independent sports participation. The sports leaders were based in local authority sports development units. During the 12-week programme, each participant was introduced to local authority leisure facilities, given an opportunity to take part in outdoor pursuits and obtained a local authority concessionary use card for leisure facilities, where appropriate. Although the formal length of the programme was 12 weeks, sports leaders maintained informal contact with participants and this allowed them to act as a broker of further sporting opportunities. For example, one participant had a particular interest in swimming and wanted to take life-saving qualifications to help gain employment in swimming pools. A suitable course did not arise until some months after the 12-week programme and the sports leader informed the former participant of this opportunity. Whilst on probation the probation service would pay for clients to take such courses, so the unofficial brokering of suitable opportunities to former participants enabled them to take full advantage of this. After the 12-week programme there was the opportunity for participants to join 'drop-in' sessions in some areas.

In the context of WYSC, 'counselling' was used to describe the programme of meetings and activities between the sports leaders and participants, and the selection of exit routes. It did not formally include giving advice on other aspects of participants' lives, such as benefit claims, employment training or housing arrangements. However, the relationship of trust built up between the sports leaders and participants meant that sports leaders found that participants would turn to them for advice on these issues and other personal problems.

Evaluation and results

An external evaluation of the project was conducted by the Leisure Management Unit at Sheffield University (Nichols and Taylor, 1996). Within a case study approach, methods included:

- use of internal programme records
- reconviction rate analysis
- participant questionnaires to measure changes in self-esteem and perceived fitness
- interviews with sports leaders, participants, probation officers and programme managers
- case studies of individual participants.

Use of internal programme records

Over the period of study 329 probationers were referred and 212 withdrew early, but for 62 per cent of these withdrawals the reason was that they had been referred to the programme but had not been able to start it. This was because contact had been lost with them, clients had lost interest, clients had been given custodial sentences between referral and starting, and some clients reached the end of their supervision orders before starting. All these problems are typical of this type of programme working with this type of client. They were exacerbated in this case by the popularity of the programme with some probation officers, which meant that referrals were made at a faster rate than they could be given places. The longer the time period between referral and actually starting the programme, the more likely it was that there would be drop-outs, for the reasons above.

Referral was not even throughout the probation service; some officers were especially enthusiastic about the programme. This meant that not all probationers had an equal chance to attend. Six per cent of participants were female, and 8 per cent from ethnic minorities, in contrast to 9 per cent and 10 per cent respectively in the West Yorkshire Probation Service.

A total of 194 clients actually started the programme. During the study period 113 completed the 12 weeks, a considerable achievement with this client group. Of these, 29 obtained sports qualifications.

Reconviction rate analysis – comparative methods
with a control group

This section gives details of the reconviction rate analysis. The results of the analysis indicated that WYSC had an impact on reducing the reconviction rate of participants, but this needs to be interpreted with care and qualified.

The comparative reconviction rate study included participants who had been on the programme before December 1993, during the first year of operation. These were divided into those who had completed 8 weeks or more of sports counselling (25 participants) and those who had completed 7 weeks or less (13 participants) as a test of the importance of duration of attendance on the effectiveness of sports counselling. Each participant was matched to a probation service client who had not attended sports counselling. Participants and non-participants were matched as closely as possible by a set of characteristics that would have an impact on the likelihood that they would be reconvicted. These included: age; gender; date the current order started; length of current order; type of most recent conviction; seriousness of most recent offence; if the most recent offence was the first; previous experience of custody or orders; the probation division; and ethnic origin.

Thus for the purpose of analysis four groups were created. Group 1 had attended 8 weeks or more of sports counselling. Group 2 was a matched control group to Group 1 and had not attended sports counselling. Group 3 had attended 7 weeks or less of sports counselling. Group 4 was a matched control group to

Group 3 and had also not attended sports counselling. Differences in reconviction rates between Groups 1 and 2, and between Groups 3 and 4 would indicate if this had been affected by participation on WYSC. The participants and non-participants were compared according to whether or not they had been reconvicted in the period December 1993 to December 1995, and by the number of offences they had been reconvicted of during this period.

Over the 2-year period participants in Group 1 were significantly less likely to have been reconvicted than members of their control group, Group 2. Over the same period participants in Group 3 were not significantly less likely to have been reconvicted than their control group, Group 4. Details of this analysis are shown in Table 7.1, which used McNemar's test, a statistical test used to compare paired data.

Table 7.2 presents the data from Groups 1 and 2 in a manner that allows the application of the test. It shows that of the 14 members of Group 1 that were reconvicted, two of the corresponding matched pairs in Group 2 were not reconvicted and 12 were reconvicted. This indicates that there is a 2 per cent probability that there is not a difference between Groups 1 and 2 in their reconviction rates. It can therefore be concluded that there is a significant difference between reconvictions in Groups 1 and 2 – in other words, participants who had attended WYSC for 8 weeks or more were less likely to be reconvicted than probationers who had not attended at all.

Similarly, Table 7.3 indicates that of the 11 members of Group 3 who were reconvicted, four of their matched pairs in Group 4 were not reconvicted and seven of them were. Applying the same statistical test to the reconvictions of Groups 3 and 4 concludes that there is a 69 per cent probability that there is not a difference between their reconviction rates. Thus there is not a significant difference in reconviction rates between Groups 3 and 4 – participants who

Table 7.1 A comparison of reconvictions of Groups 1, 2, 3 and 4

	Reconvicted	*Not reconvicted*
Group 1	14	11
Group 2	23	2
Group 3	11	2
Group 4	9	4

Source: WYPS criminal records

Table 7.2 Participants who had attended 8 weeks or more of WYSC, and control group

	Group 2 not reconvicted	*Group 2 reconvicted*
Group 1 reconvicted	2	12
Group 1 not reconvicted	0	11

Source: WYPS criminal records

Table 7.3 Participants who had attended 7 weeks or less of WYSC, and control group

	Group 4 not reconvicted	Group 4 reconvicted
Group 3 reconvicted	4	7
Group 3 not reconvicted	0	2

Source: WYPS criminal records

attended for 7 weeks or less were no less likely to be reconvicted than the control group. The two tests above suggest that length of counselling makes a difference to its impact on reconvictions.

There was also some evidence to suggest that members of Group 1 were reconvicted of fewer offences over the period than their control group. Figures are given in Table 7.4.

The Wilcoxon matched-pairs signed-ranks test was applied to this data. (This test was used to compare the number of offences between Groups 1 and 2 and Groups 3 and 4. For each matched pair the difference in number of offences is calculated. The positive differences in the number of offences for each pair are then ranked, and compared against what would have been expected if the null hypothesis, no differences, were true.) The test indicated that those that had attended 8 weeks or more of sports counselling had significantly fewer offences than those that had not. This did not apply to those who had attended only 7 weeks or less.

These results indicated that WYSC had a positive impact in reducing the likelihood that participants will be reconvicted and in reducing the number of offences. A critical influence on this impact was the duration of attendance on the scheme.

The analysis above is applying the logic of the classic experimental design – the participants and control group are considered to be identical, apart from the experience of the programme. However, as noted in Chapter Four, a difficulty encountered by this type of study is that an apparently positive result may be attributable to the characteristics of participants that volunteer for a programme and sustain participation in it, rather than to the impact of the programme itself. It is virtually impossible to disentangle these two effects. Thus the results above could be interpreted as indicating that probation service clients who were more

Table 7.4 Offences reconvicted, December 1993 – December 1995, Groups 1, 2, 3 and 4

	Median number of offences	Mean number of offences	Minimum number of offences	Maximum number of offences
Group 1	1.0	2.4	0	9
Group 2	3.0	6.7	0	25
Group 3	1.0	1.6	0	5
Group 4	2.0	5.8	0	35

Source: WYPS criminal records
Base: 25 members in Group 1 and 2; 13 members in Groups 3 and 4

likely to volunteer to take part in sports counselling were also less likely to be reconvicted, and were more likely to remain committed to the programme for its full duration.

Bias in comparing WYSC participants to probationers in general could have occurred at three points: the point of referral; the time between referral and starting the programme; and the time between starting and completing the programme.

It is unlikely that bias occurred at the point of referral of clients to WYSC as not all probationers were offered sports counselling. The use of sports counselling was not evenly spread across probation officers and this would have been especially so when the project was establishing itself. This was the period prior to December 1993, when members of Groups 1 and 3 attended the project. There is also no reason to believe that probation officers in general offered sports counselling to clients whom they consider less likely to re-offend. Therefore, at the point of referral it is unlikely that those referred were untypical of probation service clients.

Not all referred clients actually started the programme. It is possible that those who started were those who were less likely to be reconvicted, firstly because they were better motivated and secondly because they had not been reconvicted and given a custodial sentence between referral and starting. Analysis of reasons for not starting the project for 80 cases where information was available, showed that only 17 did not start because they had lost interest. This indicates a proportionately small difference in motivation between those that started the project and those that did not after referral.

Once a client started the programme it is possible that those that completed 8 weeks or more were those who were less likely to be reconvicted because they were more stable and better motivated. It is at this point that it is most difficult to differentiate between the positive impact of participation in sports counselling and the impact of the personal characteristics of participants on their propensity to be reconvicted. However, it is also at this point that the results from the case studies and interviews, discussed later, indicated that participation did have a positive impact. Thus the different research methods support each other to suggest that the lower reconviction rates for participants on the project for 8 weeks or more can at least partly be attributed to the impact of the programme. Where the personal characteristics of participants may also have been significant, there has been an interaction between these and the impact of the programme – the generative causality of scientific realism. Thus, if a probation client comes to sports counselling with a positive approach and a willingness to take up all the opportunities offered, they are more likely to gain further benefits from it. Overall, the difficulty of distinguishing between the initial characteristics of participants and the impact of the programme on outcomes is common to all programmes where participation is voluntary.

The use of the reconviction prediction score

This research method used a formula devised by the Home Office research group (Lloyd *et al.*, 1994) for calculating the likelihood of an offender being reconvicted within 2 years of their last conviction. The formula takes into account variables of gender, age, number of previous youth custody sentences, previous court appearances where found guilty and the last principal offence. All of these factors have been found to predict reconviction in the probation population as a whole. This method was used by Raynor in an evaluation of the Mid-Glamorgan STOP programme (Raynor and Vanstone, 1994). It was replaced by the Offender Group Reconviction Score (OGRS), which was used in the study of Hafotty Wen, described in Chapter 8, which replaces the formula with a computer programme. This makes it easier to use. In his analysis of the STOP programme, Raynor adapted the formula to allow the examination of reconviction rates over a 1-year period. This was done by using a chart of reconviction prediction scores devised by Copas, Ditchfield and Marshall to be used by the Parole Board in assessing the suitability of prisoners for early release (Copas *et al.*, 1994). In the evaluation of WYSC the same method was used to scale down the probability of reconviction over a 2-year period to 18 months. This allowed the reconviction prediction score to be applied to a larger number of ex-participants of WYSC, that is, those who had completed WYSC 18 months before the study, rather than in the 2 years before.

The 2-year reconviction prediction score was calculated for 49 participants of WYSC who had completed 8 weeks or more of the programme and met conditions that enabled them to be included in the analysis. The results of this analysis showed that for these participants the actual reconviction rate was less than the predicted rate. The average reconviction prediction score for each of these 49 participants was 63.8 per cent. This meant that one would have expected 63.8 per cent of these participants to have been reconvicted over a 2-year period; 49 per cent of these participants had actually been reconvicted over this period. Therefore, as the actual reconviction rate was less than the predicted reconviction rate, this result supported the conclusion of the comparative reconviction rate analysis, that WYSC had an impact in reducing reconviction rates.

Scaling down the reconviction prediction score to cover an 18-month period made it possible to increase the number of participants in the analysis to 63. The result of this analysis was that the expected percentage of participants to be reconvicted in the 18-month period was 56.86 per cent but the actual rate of reconviction was 44.44 per cent. The results of the two sets of analyses are shown in Table 7.5. The differences between predicted and actual reconviction rates are statistically very significant.

Table 7.5 A comparison of predicted and actual reconviction rates

	Predicted reconviction rate %	Actual reconviction rate %	Sample size
Over 2 years	63.80	49.00	49
Over 18 months	56.86	44.44	63

So again this supported the view that participants who had attended 8 weeks or more of the programme had benefited from it, and this was reflected in lower rates of reconviction. This is again an example of the classic experimental design, only the control group is provided by all probationers (an analysis of the factors predicting reconviction being the basis for the reconviction prediction formula) so there is no need to match the participants individually to a control group. The method is not strictly a substitute for use of a control group as the formula is based on national averages and there may be local differences. And these results are subject to exactly the same qualifications as those from the comparative reconviction rate analysis, including the extent to which change can be attributed to the programme or to the characteristics of the participants.

Other quantitative methods

Changes in self-esteem were measured using a scale used by Warr and Jackson (1983) in a study of transitions between employment status of young workers – a similar study group. The scale had been adapted from one statistically validated. Eight questions each had a 5-point scale, which aggregated to a 40 point self-esteem score. Questionnaires were administered at the start of the programme, at the end, and at a 12-week follow-up meeting. Over the period between the completion of questionnaire 1 and questionnaire 2 (i.e. the length of the programme), 77 per cent of respondents increased their self-esteem score. The average increase was 3.2 points – see Table 7.6.

Although 39 per cent of participants continued to increase their self-esteem score between the end of the programme and the follow-up questionnaire, the mean score over this period fell by 0.5 points. However, for the 20 participants for whom it was possible to compare self-esteem both at the start of sports counselling and 12 weeks after the programme, 80 per cent increased self-esteem, with an average increase of 4.4 points. The figures indicated that while there was a general increase in self-esteem over the period of sports counselling there was a slight drop in the 12 weeks after the programme's completion. However, overall the programme had a positive impact on self-esteem when scores at the start, and 12 weeks after concluding the programme, were compared.

Table 7.6 Changes in self-esteem

Period	Mean change in self-esteem score	% of respondents with increased score	Base
Q1 – Q2	+3.2	77%	43
Q2 – Q3	−0.5	39%	18
Q1 - Q3	+4.4	80%	20

Key: Q1 = questionnaire survey at the start of the programme
      Q2 = questionnaire survey at the end of the programme
      Q3 = questionnaire survey 12 weeks after the end of the programme

Table 7.6 illustrates a practical difficulty with this method, which was obtaining a reasonable sample size for the questionnaires. Further, it could be argued that those for whom it was possible to arrange a 12-week follow-up interview with were not typical, and neither were those who completed the questionnaire at the end of the programme, as this did not include those who left the programme with no further contact.

A similar method was used to measure participants' self evaluation of fitness at the start and end of the programme, using a 5-point scale. This appeared to show a considerable increase in self-perception of fitness. However, the validity of this result as a generalisation across the programme is limited as only 52 of the 114 participants who started the programme provided this information at the start and the end. On the other hand, one could argue that for those who did complete the programme, and the end of programme questionnaire, there was a significant increase in self-perception of fitness.

Case studies of individual participants

The methods above indicated outcomes of the process – lower reconviction rates were the final outcome (as in Figure 4.2, box 5, page 33) and self-esteem and fitness were intermediate outcomes (box 4). But this still did not tell us how and why the programme had a positive impact. To do this, case studies were made of eight participants using a combination of methods. These involved: interviews with the participants, their probation officers and their sports leaders; records of participation in the programme; and the questionnaire data. It was not possible to link the case studies to the conviction data used in the statistical analysis of reconviction rates for reasons of confidentiality.

All these sources were synthesised into case studies, which were used to illustrate the benefits gained by participants from attending the programme and to develop an understanding of why they benefited – what was it about the programme that contributed to this impact? The case studies used pseudonyms. Participants agreed to be used in this way for the study and the final version was checked with them. An example case study is reproduced below.

> Debbie is a single parent with three children, all of school age, though one is disabled. She was unemployed throughout and after the period of sports counselling. She has a long history of offences. For 5 years she was addicted to heroin but has not used this for the last 2 years.
>
> Debbie felt that a major reason for her probation officer's strong encouragement for her to do sports counselling was that it would be an outlet for her aggression. On her questionnaire at the start of the programme Debbie had said that she wished to do weight training, boxing and kick boxing. Her probation officer reported that she thought that sports counselling would get Debbie out and involved in an activity separate from the domestic sphere. She felt that Debbie had an interest in sport in that she was interested in building herself up and that it would also build up her self-esteem. Prior to

her participation on the programme, Debbie had not been taking part in sport although she had done netball and swimming in the past. She did not have a leisure concession card.

Debbie was not particularly looking forward to the programme, apart from the weights, but thought she might as well try it. She was not concerned by the group sessions being male dominated and her confidence was reflected in her high initial score on the self-esteem test in the questionnaire administered at the start of counselling. She took part in the programme between September and December 1994. On it she did football, weight training and swimming. She also tried pot-holing, mountain biking and running.

Although she had never played football before, she became involved in the group sessions run in Calderdale and attended these regularly. These are attended by probation service clients who are waiting to start the sports counselling programme and others that have completed it. Debbie was the only woman at first, and quite a bit older than the other people at the group session, but she was not deterred by that. Debbie started playing in goal and then in other positions when another woman joined. Debbie began to play for a team in a local league, set up to make links between different groups in the community. Following the sports counselling programme, the sports leader linked Debbie to a volunteer from the probation service who took her on a 2-day course for helping disabled people to participate in sport. Debbie also took a Football Association Leaders Award over 2 days. The probation service paid for these courses. Debbie also continued to take part in regular weight training.

Debbie also attended a local women's group, where she was asked to organise a football team to play in a local cup, but she did not want to take this on. She would have been prepared just to have done the coaching. She has recently been approached by another club to act as coach.

Debbie thought the scheme had calmed her down a lot. She felt she had more self-control and this had helped her avoid violent behaviour that could have led to another offence. Her probation officer agreed that it had helped her to cope with confrontational situations and that the sport had been a controlled outlet for her feelings. Debbie felt it had helped her relations with her children and made her fitter. This was reflected in her increased score on her own assessment of her fitness between the start and end of sports counselling. Her probation officer confirmed that she was proud of her personal fitness and that she felt better in herself. Debbie also felt that involvement in sport and sports counselling had helped her to keep off heroin as she felt more able to cope with personal problems. This had helped her to keep out of related crime such as shoplifting.

A few months after completing sports counselling she was convicted of driving while banned, which led to a 3-week prison sentence and a further period of probation. Debbie reported that the driving offence was as a result of trying to get her children to school on time for the first day at a new school. In prison she was able to start a Community Sports Leader's Award, but her sentence was not long enough to finish it.

On the questionnaire Debbie completed at the end of counselling she commented that sports counselling had relieved boredom and got her out of the house. In the follow-up questionnaire completed 12 weeks later she again commented that sports counselling had kept her busy, given her a new focus and raised her self-confidence and self-esteem. Debbie continues to attend the regular group sessions.

When Debbie started counselling, her children were on the child protection register, which meant that social services could take them into care at any time. They have now been removed from this, through the support of her social worker, partly as a consequence of the change in her behaviour since being on the scheme. Her children are still on a care order, meaning that anybody looking after them has to be subject to a police check. Debbie hopes that they will be off this soon.

Her probation officer felt that Debbie had got more out of the project because she was a woman who had become involved in a typically male sport – football. She always put everything into it and this had helped her gain the respect of the other participants. This had helped her self-esteem as people looked up to her. There was a slight increase in her self-esteem score from before to after sports counselling, although this was from an already high level. Her probation officer had been able to use Debbie's experience of sports counselling as something very positive to refer to. The achievement of the certificate of completion and the two training courses have been major positive outcomes. Debbie felt she had a much better relationship with her sports leader than that with her probation officer. She felt that she could discuss personal problems with the sports leader and be supported; for example, he was supportive on the anniversary of her brother's death. The value of this new relationship was confirmed by Debbie citing the sports leader as one of the people she would turn to for personal help on the second questionnaire, completed after sports counselling. The sports leader will contact Debbie if he becomes aware of a good opportunity for her, such as a first aid course. The probation officer felt that the way the sports leader worked with clients was excellent, in that he appeared relaxed but was able to build up a very good relationship of mutual respect. He was seen as a role model and this allowed him to reproach clients for things in a way that they 'would not take off anybody else'.

The future difficulties Debbie could foresee in continuing sport were the cost of courses and of child care to allow her to participate. At present both of these are paid for by the probation service. She is now on probation for 2 more years following the driving offence, but once the order ends there would no longer be financial support with participation.

Debbie's case illustrates the value of the relationship with the sports leader, increased fitness and a positive direction offered to her life, which appears to have helped her cope with a mass of personal problems and to avoid serious crime. It illustrates exit routes of voluntary involvement and coaching schemes.

The case study participants were selected by the sports leaders, so one could argue that they were unrepresentative, not only because they were participants with whom the sports leaders had retained contact for some period after the initial course (so it was possible to interview them) but also because they were selected to demonstrate success. Even so, one of the case study participants, while successful on the programme, had subsequently died from a drug-related incident. However, even if one accepts that the case study participants were not typical, their success is precisely a justification for selecting them for study if one wants to understand how and why the programme had this impact, and if 'the investigator's goal is to expand and generalize theories (analytic generalisation) ...' (Yin, 1994: 10). In this respect the case studies were extremely valuable.

Conclusion on the programme and evaluation methods

The reconviction rate analysis suggested that the programme had reduced crime, and this could be equated with a specific number of offences. The measures of self-esteem and self-perception of fitness, combined with the case studies, suggested how and why the programme was successful.

Where the programme had been successful it was understood as helping participants change their behaviour through a new sense of self-identity. Aspects of the programme that contributed to this included: the voluntary involvement in the programme; increased fitness; increased self-esteem; new peers; the positive role model of the sports leaders – combined with a strong mentoring relationship; and the new opportunities provided by the programme, including employment.

Voluntary involvement in the programme was very important in ensuring that participants had a positive approach and were therefore most likely to benefit. This was in contrast to attendance at the probation service, which was a condition of probationers' orders. Of those that completed the programme, 98 per cent reported that they would recommend it to a friend, confirming that it had been a positive experience for them.

Sports counselling allowed participants to meet new peers; 27 per cent of participants completing the questionnaire 12 weeks after the programme reported that they had taken part in sport in a local club during this period. The case studies provided examples of participants who had become involved in local sports teams and gained some success or who had become regular sports participants. These participants were generally those that had previously had an interest in sport and been re-introduced or re-motivated.

The role of the sports leaders as a positive role model and the relationship between the participants and sports leaders was an extremely important contribution to the programme's success. In the same way that new peers could offer a new set of values, the sports leaders were individuals with whom participants could develop a relationship of respect. This was facilitated by the one-to-one counselling and the shared sports participation. It was also reinforced by the unofficial follow-up work sports leaders did with participants. A continued relationship was also maintained by ex-participants themselves who were able to ask the sports leader for advice about other personal difficulties. The significance of this relationship was examined through a question asked both at the start and end of the programme: 'If you had a difficult problem to sort out and wanted to talk to someone about it, who would you talk to?'. In 28 per cent of cases the sports leader was mentioned at the end of the programme but not at the beginning. Naturally this relationship with the sports leaders appeared to be very important for the case study participants.

At the start of sports counselling 84 per cent of participants were unemployed. The case studies provided examples where participants had been able to take further sports leadership qualifications through sports counselling, which could lead to improved employment opportunities. These included Football Association coaching awards, Community Sports Leader awards and life saving awards.

These benefits from participation can be understood as being inter-related and contributing to changed behaviour of the participant through a changed self-image. Increased self-esteem allowed the participant to take advantage of the other opportunities offered through the programme, particularly meeting new peers and taking further training. New peers provided a new set of values and the whole programme was underpinned by the values promoted by the sports leaders. The sports leaders were respected as friends but also had a paid job, a respected position in society and were not involved in crime. The positive role model of the sports leader might be maintained through a period of contact after completion of the programme. The 'exit routes' of training opportunities might lead to employment, or further involvement in sport.

This process through which the programme had an impact was summarised by one of the case study participants. To paraphrase his words, he felt that the major effect of WYSC had been to motivate him to do things, to become more proactive in taking charge of his life. He saw crime as addictive:

> To get out of it you have to first get away from friends who are committing crimes and then move to a new area. When you have little money it is very tempting to commit crime when you see friends walking down the road with new clothes and things they have got as a result of crime the previous night. Once you have got into crime you realise how easy it is. So it is hard to break out of it.

This participant had attended four courses in sports leadership following the sports counselling programme. At first he did not feel confident enough to attend these without the support of the sports leader but these led to voluntary work in a youth club. From this he had taken basic training in youth work and was planning to take further training to become a qualified youth worker, with the support of the full-time worker at his club. This particular case study illustrates the effect of the combination of increased self-esteem, the positive role model of the sports leader, new peers and new opportunities. It illustrates the cumulative effect of these in that his self-confidence had to be built up gradually until he was able to take training opportunities and become involved in voluntary work by himself. He had become both motivated and empowered to take charge of his own development. New peers were important in changing the norms of behaviour and value judgements that became integral to his new sense of self-identity. Thus the programme had offered him more than just the opportunity to take part in sporting activity.

The importance of understanding the interaction between the participant and the programme over time – how the participant sees new opportunities and develops the skills and confidence to take them – demonstrates the relevance of the scientific realist understanding of causality and approach to evaluation (Chapter Four). While this evaluation was not designed from a scientific realist perspective, it demonstrates the value of complementing quantitative and qualitative analysis to show how much the programme reduced crime, and how and why it had this impact. However, both methods involved considerable resources. Although WYSCA commissioned the evaluation, it is unusual for a programme to allocate this proportion of its budget (£16,000 in 1995). Further, the small numbers in the statistical analysis of reconviction rates meant that the outcome of this analysis could easily have been negative if a few participants' reconviction rates had been different, for reasons completely beyond the control of the programme. The limitations of reconviction rate analysis is illustrated in the Hafotty Wen case study in the next chapter.

Potential improvements to the programme

The programme was constructed around the belief that independent sports participation would lead to crime reduction, and for this reason, however sensitive they were at dealing with participants, the sports leaders came from a sports development background. One could argue that, while a commitment to the use of sport was valuable, the personal skills were the key ones. Maybe a broader perspective on the programme as personal development though sport might have altered the emphasis. The sports leaders might have had links to other agencies so as they were better able to help participants with the permutation of personal problems that were related to their offending, such as housing, employment training and health. However, the decision is whether to have a sports development programme that aims to reduce crime, or a crime reduction programme that aims to use sport. Perhaps the only practical solution is to recognise that a balance of skills is needed in the leaders – but that the most important skills are empathy and commitment.

This is related to a second issue – when to stop working with a client and leave them to their own devices. The sports leaders' willingness and capability to keep in touch with clients after the initial 12-week programme contributed to its success. But there is a tension between this and meeting output targets in terms of the number of clients dealt with. This may have been concealed by the use of part-time sports leaders who may have delivered some of the extra service in their own time.

A further problem was that the popularity of the programme with certain officers meant that referrals might have to wait some time before actually getting on the programme – by which time they might have lost interest or their probation order had finished.

Partnership working and termination

As noted in the introduction to the programme, delivery involved a three-way partnership between WYSCA, five local authority sports development sections, and West Yorkshire Probation Service (WYPS). Most of the trustees of WYSCA were managers of sports development sections. The sports leaders were based in these sections, which gave them access to a wide range of equipment, access to local authority facilities and direct contact with many sports opportunities for the participants. This made it possible to provide an individual programme for each participant and to arrange suitable 'exit routes'. This partnership between WYSCA and the local authority sports development sections worked well – the objectives of crime reduction through this type of intervention were shared between the two partners.

The partnership between WYSCA and WYPS changed during the operation of the programme and eventually ended. When WYSCA had been set up in 1992, it was with a grant directly from the Home Office, and at this time one of the trustees was a deputy chief probation officer in West Yorkshire. The Home Office subsequently devolved funding to WYPS. However, WYSCA had a formal contract with only one of the probation divisions in which it operated. This was in Leeds, where the project had been established later than in the other four divisions.

In its 1994/95 Probation Service Annual Report, WYPS stated its intention to introduce formal competitive procedures for externally provided services in line with guidance from Her Majesty's Inspectorate of Probation (HMIP). When WYSCA became aware of the intention to competitively tender sports counselling, the project manager gave the probation service advice on the details that WYSCA thought should be in the contract specification. By this time the WYSCA trustee who was a deputy chief probation officer had stood down as a trustee so this informal line of communication was no longer present. A new post of contacts adviser was created in WYPS to deal with contracting externally provided services and she wrote the contract specification.

Following its response to an invitation to tender, WYSCA was sent the specification for sports counselling in late November 1995. This specification differed from the existing work in that the length of the programme was specified as a minimum of 4 weeks with a possibility of extension to a maximum of 8 weeks. In addition, 10 per cent of the total fee was related to the number of participants in excess of 100 completing the programme, to a maximum of 120 participants. Thus a proportion of the fee was performance related. This was unacceptable to the trustees, who believed that to reduce the length of sports counselling from 12 to 4 weeks would make it ineffective so they attempted to negotiate the contract, proposing that 25 per cent of participants would complete the programme in 4 weeks, but 25 per cent would complete in 10 weeks. The rest would fall between these periods.

It appeared that while WYSCA might have felt it could negotiate the contract WYPS felt that through the competitive contracting tendering process it should define and obtain the service it wanted at the lowest possible cost. The service WYSCA provided was relatively expensive and WYPS wanted something different and cheaper. Three other tenders were received for the contract and it was awarded to one of these that both matched the contract specifications and 'was willing to be creative and flexible in the subsequent management of the contracted service' (Thurston, 1997: 51). This suggests that, from the view of the WYPS team responsible for awarding the contract, the new contractor would not only be prepared to deliver the service it wanted, but would also be responsive to suggestions to change it. Thus the contract between WYSCA and WYPS was ended.

Clearly the WYSCA trustees and staff were disappointed by this. Perhaps if more informal lines of communication had been used earlier, a compromise between what WYSCA wanted to offer, and WYPS wanted to buy and pay for, might have been achieved. This may be outside of the strict interpretation of competitive contracting procedures, but was not unusual at the time in contracting for local authority services. When one considers what made WYSC successful, it would be very difficult to write a contract that specified the commitment, enthusiasm and personal qualities that enabled the sports leaders to develop a good mentoring role with participants.

The successful contractor failed financially within a year. It attempted to reach the throughput targets by re-recruiting participants who had completed an initial 4-week programme on to a second one, thus saving considerable time in the referral process. Thus it might appear that two participants had each completed one course, rather than one completing two. This again illustrates the difficulty of building performance indicators into a contract in a way that will ensure the desired job is done.

Competitive contracting altered the nature of the partnership and put a strain on the relationship with trustees, who were acting as volunteers and who gave their commitment because they believed in what they were doing – and might not continue to do so if asked to do something else. Within a partnership both parties might expect to negotiate and discuss their commitment and obligations. In a competitive contracting situation the client defines the service it wants through the specification and the contractor undertakes to provide that service. In this situation the buyer defines the terms of the contract.

So, general implications are: in contracting a service it is hard to define the qualities of a programme that determine its success; and the process of contracting competitively might put a considerable strain on relations between the public and voluntary sector. Awarding the contract to the cheapest operator risks losing expertise and commitment. For a balanced discussion of the contracting of WYSC see Nichols and Taylor (1997) and Thurston (1997).

8 Hafotty Wen – 14 Peaks Programme

Summary

This programme worked with relatively high-risk offenders, many of whom had a long history of drug-related offending. Where it was successful it had helped participants start a new life and redefine their own sense of identity. The particularly physically demanding programme offered a point of reference and a catalyst for change. It illustrates the particular impact of 'outdoor adventure' type programmes and their relationship to risk: the significant risk is not an apparent physical risk from the activity, but the risk to self-identity. The case study illustrated the particular sensitivity and the long-term support required when working with this client group and also the way a residential setting could be used for participants to try out new behaviour. The case study concludes by drawing extensively on the views of the centre warden, who understood the key factors contributing to the programme's success to be the relationship of respect between staff and participants, and the centre ethos.

An analysis of reconviction rate data failed to show a positive impact of the programme. A detailed description of the analysis shows how this was limited by the small sample sizes once invalid data had been removed. This also illustrates the very significant amount of work required by such an analysis. In contrast, qualitative interviews of participants, ex-participants, probation officers, bail hostel staff and the hostel warden helped understand why the programme had an impact, when it did. Thus, as in West Yorkshire Sports Counselling, the case contrasts the use of quantitative methods used in the classic experimental design with qualitative methods that help understand the experience from the perspective of the participants.

Introduction to the programme

Hafotty Wen was an outdoor activity centre in North Wales, funded by Merseyside Probation Service. When it was researched, in 1999, it had been running for 15 years. Activities used on the courses included orienteering, mountaineering, climbing, mountain walking, gorge scrambling, navigation skills and mountain biking. Most work was with people aged 17–25 years. It ran a combination of closed and open courses, the closed courses being when the whole centre was booked by one specific group. These included bail hostels, drug rehabilitation centres, hostels for homeless people and a range of other courses run by, or associated with, the probation service. Open courses could be attended by any probationers. These included a national navigation award, an annual fun run, mountain biking expeditions, and a walk covering the 14 peaks of 3,000 feet and over in North Wales in 24 hours. The 14 Peak course is the focus of this case study although it has to be understood in the context of the rest of the centre's work, as probationers might well attend a series of courses at Hafotty Wen and build up a strong relationship with the staff. The 14 Peak course itself had been run since 1985 and involved four training days to become familiar with different parts of the route. In 1995, 30 people attended each of the training days and 17 completed the final expedition. The previous year two expeditions had been run to accommodate the 25 participants. Clients came from residential settings, such as bail hostels or drug rehabilitation units, as well as other areas of probation service work.

Evaluation and results

Methods included:

- analysis of reconviction rates
- in-depth interviews with participants
- interviews with probation officers and bail hostel wardens
- interview with the centre manager.

Analysis of reconviction rates

As the centre had accurate records of who had attended the programme since 1986 it appeared that this would be an ideal programme to evaluate using the Offender Group Reconviction Scale (OGRS), which had replaced the formula used in the analysis of reconviction rates in the WYSC study.

The OGRS was designed as an assessment tool for pre-sentence report writers to help them when considering what sentence to propose (Copas and Marshall, 1998). However, it has also been used as an internal management tool to help assess the performance of the probation service in reducing re-offending by offenders under their supervision. In this case analysis is at the level of the group rather than the individual. As in the reconviction prediction formula, OGRS uses records of an individual's gender, seriousness of last offence, previous custodial sentences, previous court appearances at which convicted, age of first conviction and age at current conviction to give a percentage score that represents the likelihood of reconviction in a 2-year period from the last conviction. This last conviction is termed the 'index offence'. In making these calculations convictions are not included if they were for a non-standard list motoring offence (such as speeding or drunk driving), or if they were related to an earlier conviction, for example, non-payment of a fine or breach of probation.

The analysis used the 1997 version of the OGRS formula, supplied by the Home Office in a form that allowed the relevant offender characteristics to be entered directly on to a computer package. This then calculated the OGRS score. As in the use of the reconviction prediction formula in WYSC, a major advantage of using the OGRS in evaluation is that it removes the difficulties of setting up a control group. In effect it uses all other probationers as a control group to show if any one probationer has re-offended less than one would have expected over a 2-year period.

The practical application of the OGRS

Records of offences were obtained from the Offender Index (OI), held by the Home Office. Although 94 offenders had attended the 14 Peaks programme, it was possible to use the records of only the 62 who had attended between 1990 and 1995 inclusive. The records of those who had attended before 1990 could not be used as the centre had not kept a record of their dates of birth, which was required to match participants to records of convictions. The records of those who had completed the course after 1995 could not be used because at the time of analysis records of reconviction, obtained from the OI, were available only up to 1997. It was not possible to obtain data directly from Merseyside Probation Service, who would have had access to the Police National Computer (PNC) as it had no time to provide it. However, there is a case for using the OI data in preference as this is the data that was used to construct OGRS. The use of OI data meant that only for offenders completing the programme in 1995 could one see if they had offended in the 2-year period after the programme. Of these 62, 32 others were excluded from the analysis. For two offenders the date of birth on the records from the centre did not match that on the Home Office records, so one could not be sure they were the same person. For 14 clients there was no data on their convictions, though it was not clear why this was the case. Perhaps the centre's records had been incorrect or these may have been course members without a record of offending – the centre worked with clients who were 'at risk' as well as those on probation. Three offenders had their first recorded conviction after the date they had attended the course. Again, this may have been because not all course members were convicted offenders. Fifteen offenders could not be used in the analysis because their index offence had taken place more than 2 years before they attended the course, therefore it was pointless examining records of re-offending over the 2-year period after their last conviction as this could not have been affected by course attendance.

So, after considerable effort from promising beginnings, this left a usable sample of 28 out of 94 potential clients.

Results – reconviction rates

The following results compare average predicted and actual reconviction rates for the 28 usable offenders and some sub-groups. With each comparison, a p value shows the statistical significance, using a one-tailed test, of the differences in rates. In each case a one-sided test was conducted as it was expected that the scheme would result in a reduction in reconviction rates. However, had a two-sided test been used, the conclusions would have been broadly similar; the two statistically significant results would have remained significant, albeit with slightly higher p values, and the two non-significant results would, of course, remain non-significant.

1   Of the total sample of 28 offenders, 46.4 per cent were reconvicted after 2 years, and the average predicted reconviction rate from the OGRS was 68.4 per cent. The difference is statistically significant, with a p value of 0.013. This means that there is only a 1.3 per cent possibility that this result could have occurred by chance. So this result suggests that the programme was a success in reducing re-offending.

2   However, as indicated above, some clients were in a residential drug hostel when they attended the course. This would have reduced the possibility of them offending within the 2 years from their index conviction as they were locked into the hostel. It was not possible to tell if they were in a hostel from the OI records, but this information was on the centre records. They may have been in a residential rehabilitation hostel for up to 9 months, although it is not known at what stage of their hostel stay they attended the 14 Peaks course. Some had also received a custodial sentence at their index offence. This means that, though they were not in custody while attending the course, they must have been for some of the 2-year period after the index offence. Again this reduces their chance of re-offending within the 2-year period but, similarly to the drug rehabilitation clients, it is not possible to tell the time they were actually in custody. This difficulty arises because the index offence was not immediately followed by the intervention – the 14 Peak course. Ideally, for purposes of the OGRS analysis, the intervention being evaluated would start immediately after the index offence so the 2-year period over which reconvictions were measured would equate with the 2 years after the intervention. In practice this is often not the case.

    Once these 13 clients who had either been in drug rehabilitation or received a custodial sentence were removed from the analysis, a sub-sample of 15 was left. Of these, 66.6 per cent had been reconvicted within 2 years of the index offence and the average predicted reconviction rate was 69.1 per cent. The p value was 0.55, which is not statistically significant. So, once one had accounted for the fact that some course participants had less than 2 years to re-offend in, then the OGRS analysis was inconclusive on the impact of the course on re-offending. One would require a very big difference between predicted and actual re-offending for a significant result with so few clients.

3   The analysis in 2 above excluded both those who had been in residential drug rehabilitation at the time of the course and those who had been in custody for a period after their index conviction. As qualitative interviews (discussed below) suggested that the course might have a particularly strong

impact on drug offenders who were in rehabilitation, a separate analysis of these was conducted. Of the 11 offenders who were in a drug rehabilitation hostel at the time of the course, 36.4 per cent had been reconvicted two years after the index offence, compared to a predicted average reconviction rate of 74.3 per cent. This difference has a p value of 0.009, a 1 per cent possibility that this result could have occurred by chance. This makes it appear that the course may be effective for drug rehabilitation clients.

4   However, the analysis in 3 above can be modified to take account of the fact that the drug rehabilitation clients will have a reduced opportunity to re-offend while they are in residential treatment, as noted in 2 above. So a further calculation was made of those who had reconvicted within 3 years of the index offence and this was compared to predicted re-offending over the 2 years from the index offence. This would eliminate any reduction in re-offending attributable to the period spent in a residential hostel. Of the 11 offenders who were in a drug rehabilitation hostel at the time of the course, 63.6 per cent had been reconvicted 3 years after the index offence, compared to a predicted average reconviction rate of 74.3 per cent over a 2-year period. This difference has a p value of 0.31, a 31 per cent possibility that this result could have occurred by chance, which is not statistically significant. So this analysis does not support the hypothesis that the course reduced re-offending.

Comparison of the analysis in 3 and 4 above shows how results need to be interpreted with care. While 3 appears to give a statistically positive result, the differences between expected and actual re-offending become insignificant if one extends the time over which one measures offending by a year, as in 4. This length of extension gives a conservative estimate as the maximum period in residential drug rehabilitation was 9 months.

Comparison of the analysis in 3 and 4 above shows the major impact on the statistical significance of the results of a few cases in a small sample. In 3, four clients out of eleven had re-offended over the 2-year period. In 4, seven clients had re-offended. This illustrates that extreme caution is required while using this type of analysis and small samples. It is easy to think of a permutation of circumstances that may have resulted in one or two probation clients re-offending or not.

This consideration of drug rehabilitation clients also draws attention to another limitation of the OGRS analysis. Standard list offences included in the OGRS calculation include those for possession of drugs. It could be argued that in some cases this may be a relatively minor offence and that if an offender had managed to avoid becoming re-involved with heroin but had been convicted for possession of cannabis this represented success.

Other general limitations of the OGRS analysis

The main purpose of the detailed description of the analysis above is to show that, even with a promising initial sample size and a great deal of work (at least 4 days for the 28 cases and the analysis), obtaining a statistically significant result may depend on just a few individual cases in a small sample. So, how valid a measure is this of a programme's success? The comparable analysis in WYSC produced positive results – but these might have been negated by a few more reconvictions.

There are some further difficulties with the analysis. Use of the reconviction prediction score has to consider the effect of crimes committed before the 2-year period of measurement, but for which a conviction was made during those 2 years. These are regarded as 'false positives'. For example, an offender may have committed a crime 3 months before the 2-year period of measurement, but they might only be convicted in court 4 months later, during the measured period. It is not possible to take account of these using pre-2000 OI data as this does not tell one when offences were committed. They can be accounted for using data from the PNC, as this includes the date of offence. However, as noted above, it may be better to use OI data with OGRS as the measure was devised using this data source. A similar limitation is crimes committed during the 2-year period of measurement but for which conviction would not be made until after the two year period. These are 'false negatives'. Analysis does not usually take these into account. Again one would need post-2000 OI data, or PNC data, to be able to do this. Analysis can assume that the two false scores will cancel each other out and that offences are committed and detected at a steady rate as a client gets older. However, this may well not be the case.

A further limitation is that the OGRS formula was developed to cover all offenders. It will be less accurate if used just for those with serious drug problems, or if factors specific to Merseyside alter the propensity to re-offend. Ideally the ORGS method would be combined with the use of a local comparison group, as in WYSC, though there are difficulties setting this up for voluntary programmes.

It is possible that the analysis could have used more up-to-date records of re-offending if it had been conducted internally by Merseyside Probation Service, using its own records, but this would have required several days work to evaluate a relatively small programme.

A further practical limitation was that, even given the guidance notes provided by the Home Office, there was still difficulty interpreting records of offences to ensure the correct ones were included in the analysis, and interpreting different sentences to categorise these as custodial. This second problem applied especially to youth custody sentences, which included a changing range of options over the period covered by the data.

Even if the OGRS analysis had produced a significant result, a low reconviction rate for programme participants may be explained by characteristics of the participants themselves rather than the impact of the programme; that is, those who are least likely to re-offend are also those most likely to volunteer to take part in the programme. It is extremely difficult to remove this potential bias when evaluating any programme where participation is voluntary. Again, a comparison group might have been used, but in this case it would have been very hard to set one up retrospectively and it is always more difficult to do this for voluntary programmes.

Qualitative interviews

Interviews were conducted with four probation officers (two female and two male) who had extensive experience of sending a variety of clients on centre programmes. Interviews were also conducted with five ex-clients (all male) who had used the centre over the last 14 years, three recent clients (all male) who had taken part in programmes at the centre in recent months, and the centre manager. Four of the ex-clients had successfully completed long-term drug rehabilitation programmes and were now involved in work with current drug users. The fifth had also been involved in drug-related crime and now manages an organisation that also works with young offenders. Thus the ex-clients could comment on the role the outdoor programme took in their own rehabilitation and how they used it with others.

Some of the interviews were transcribed verbatim and some were summarised. Analysis was by identifying themes and comparing perspectives between different interviewees. If more time had been available the transcripts would have permitted a more systematic approach, such as conversation or discourse analysis (Bryman and Bell, 2003). However, the willingness of interviewees to express their experiences meant that large sections of interview transcript could be used to express the participants' understanding more eloquently than could a researcher's summary.

A particular focus of the analysis below was concerned with the nature of risk. As noted in Chapter Three, the notion of risk is confused, especially in considering the role of outdoor adventure programmes. The physical risk involved in legitimate activities has been considered as a substitute to the risk in illegitimate ones, both falling into Lyng's (1993) concept of 'edgework', where the outcome is unpredictable but one has to draw on all ones resources of willpower and determination to achieve it. Both Giddens (1991) and Beck (1992) argue that in a state of late modernity decisions are less rational and more risky because of the lack of knowledge about outcomes. It is not that there are necessarily more risks in modern society but, for Giddens, the risks taken are of a different type. They involve having to cope with a general sense of anxiety because they are difficult to calculate. As noted in Chapter Three, Giddens's (1991) major concern is the risk we must all take of continual self-definition.

So the analysis aimed to understand the way in which the programme participants perceived risk, the way in which programme managers and staff perceived it and used it, and the role it took in the process that led to success in the programme. A further question, again arising from the literature on outdoor adventure programmes, was the extent to which the experiences on the programme could offer a constructive metaphor for the problems participants faced in the rest of their lives (Bacon, 1983; Nichols, 1998).

Given the extremely low success rate of drug rehabilitation programmes, as in the West Yorkshire Sports Counselling Programme, one could argue that the interview sample was unrepresentative. However, one could similarly argue that they represented critical cases, in that they helped to understand why the programme was successful, when it was.

Interview results – how and why the programme worked

The physical challenge and the management of risk

The 14 Peaks expedition would be a significant physical challenge for the average fit mountaineer, so it was a major challenge for the Hafotty Wen participants. However, speaking about the general courses run at the centre, the manager thought that the physical challenge of the activities was not a very important component of the programmes, seeing its value as initially bringing groups together. For some prospective participants the physical challenge was also not a concern but this was usually because they did not realise its extent before being involved in the activities; it is hard to imagine climbing a 3,000 ft mountain until one has tried it. For those in residential drug rehabilitation units a visit to the centre was seen primarily as a welcome change from a very structured routine, so they might not consider the physical challenge until they were confronted by it.

For other prospective participants the physical element of the courses could be a source of apprehension. Young males whose physical condition had been affected by drug use might feel that their self-esteem would be challenged by being unable to live up to male stereotypes, and a bail hostel warden explained that this was one of the apprehensions she had to reassure participants about before they attended a programme. An insensitive activity leader could set unrealistic physical expectations, and one example was given of where this had happened in the past, but experienced probation staff were now able to liaise closely with the centre before they visited and to ensure that the appropriate level of challenge was presented to all participants. For example, a drug rehabilitation officer described how:

> ... the mountains are a long day, some people may not be able to achieve that and we are not wanting to set people up to fail, so we will phone Hafotty and say, one or two are not going on this particular walk, one of our staff will stay behind, but rather than saying, 'maybe I should have gone', they will cook the tea, so when the group come back and they are tired they're all part of it.

The perception of the courses offered by the centre as mainly physical was a reason why some probation officers did not recommend them to their clients. This had resulted in a split within the probation service between officers who supported and did not support the centre. Those that used the centre regularly showed how the physical challenges, and other risks, could be made appropriate for the participants.

The 14 Peaks expedition was the most physically challenging programme offered by the centre. Although it involved two or three training events, participants still felt unprepared for the degree of challenge:

> Now, I look back now and look at my certificate and I can remember every single step of that 14 peaks. I felt every step. I can remember getting out of the van as clear as I'm looking at you now ... and it was absolutely teeming with rain. Going up Snowdon, I'd only taken about twenty steps and I was

thinking, how have I got here, what am I doing? I really found it hard to motivate myself at that point because I just felt like turning back.

However, experienced probation staff showed an appreciation that there were many other aspects of risk than the physical. These needed to be carefully considered in designing the programme and preparing the participants for it. A bail hostel warden gave an example of how perceived risk could be managed and used constructively in the case of young men experiencing horse-riding on a course:

> Now that in itself was another huge experience for residents because most of them had never seen a horse close up. But then they had to trust themselves on the back of this huge animal, and it was a very frightening experience. As I say, you are talking about people who think nothing about [committing violent crimes against individuals] ... , but really, really having quite a hard time sat on the back of a horse. Actually it's about keeping your nerve, trusting the animal, trusting yourself, not doing anything rash. In a very real way of getting a grip of yourself and learning to control.

In this case the bail hostel warden purposely did not discuss the activity beforehand because:

> ... otherwise then the exercise becomes meaningless, you are just sat on a horse aren't you. But for them afterwards to talk about how they felt. They would say to you 'I was really scared, I really bottled it on that horse, you know'. That is interesting because it is not a macho thing to bottle it on anything, ... This is now quite a big step here for these guys because they are actually admitting to fear, it means that they can actually take a different way out of a situation other than going back ... It's no good challenging the horse to go outside and have a fight, is it.

In this example the hostel warden, who was very experienced in sending groups to the outdoor centre, skilfully managed the participants' apprehensions to achieve an experience through which they could come to terms with expressing their emotions and seek constructive ways out of difficulties rather than resorting to violence. In contrast, the same warden explained how there were many other apprehensions that she had to alleviate to give hostel residents sufficient reassurance to ensure they would attend the course. These included fears of being made to appear inadequate if they had to complete a written exercise due to low levels of literacy, fears of bed-wetting due to physical conditions, fears of how they would cope without access to drugs and concerns about their arrangements for social security payments. This illustrates the great sensitivity that is required in managing risk for clients with a range of needs and conditions and who may well be lacking in self-esteem. It shows the importance of a worker who has detailed knowledge of the clients being able to liaise with the centre staff to ensure that the level and type of challenge is appropriate and managed. This bail hostel warden had learned the importance of this through having to deal with situations where a large number of residents had expressed an interest in attending courses but few had turned up on the day. This large drop-out rate had been remedied by sensitive preparation, but this did not happen in all bail hostels. It depended on the experience and commit-ment of the hostel staff, especially the warden. Thus the quality of risk management by probation staff was variable.

However, even the experienced bail hostel warden quoted above was still sur-prised by some course outcomes. She gave an example of how the shared experience of a course by staff and a client had led to unpredicted emotional risk-taking by the client. A young female member of staff had been employed at the hostel (which was for males only) to try to help male residents experience and develop the capacity to have normal day-to-day relationships with people of the opposite sex. She was supported in this challenging role but one client had not managed to come to terms with this and continually verbally abused her. The hostel warden explained how this relationship changed on a course:

> Well she [the female member of staff] said it happened in the middle of a river and she was stuck, they were doing a river crossing. He turned back and helped her, she was not in physical danger, she was stuck ... He was in front of her and he turned round and he saw her and she said 'can you give me a hand' and he went back for her, it was like that. You could not have set it up. Something happened in that moment, ... she had a very fruitful and produc-tive relationship with him thereafter.

This illustrates how the experience on the course acted as a catalyst for this client to take the emotional risk of offering support to the female member of staff. A change in relationship had been achieved that had not been possible through other activities. The activities had been a catalyst for risk-taking and change, in the sense that the client had challenged the way he related to the opposite sex, but in an unpredictable way. Similarly, another experienced proba-tion officer reported:

> I expect the Home Office would want to see a set of objectives, and we cer-tainly need to justify what we are doing there, but I am one of the most experienced probation officers that have used Hafotty Wen. I have been going for 15 years. It is certainly the best facility the probation service has got, and that's from experience, but if I was taking somebody out there the real answer is I don't know what they are going to get out of it. I know they will get something, but depending on the individual, 'cos you sit there, and say 'so and so is going to do this', and when you get there you find he does not do that, you find he is an entirely different person, with skills or a differ-ent attitude; or someone who will talk to you in the office in a monosyllabic conversation will sit down and tell you their whole life history. I have been amazed at some of the changes I had not foreseen.

Overall the analysis above shows the different perceptions of the centre manager and different probation staff of the risks taken by participants. These perceptions have consequences for the management of risk on the programmes. Where the perceptions are inadequate they may result in negative outcomes, an example being poor preparation of participants resulting in them not attending at all. The permutations of disadvantage faced by participants required a particularly perceptive and sensitive appreciation of their apprehensions and management of the programmes, although even then some positive outcomes were unpredictable.

Benefits of participation on the course and participants' perceptions

While participants might have been apprehensive about the physical challenge, overcoming it was a source of satisfaction. In particular, the achievement of completing the arduous 14 Peaks expedition, recognised by a certificate, was of major significance to all participants.

> I was elated after we'd done. Once we'd got back to the centre it was just wanting to get into bed, obviously. The next day at the presentation it was, to be honest with you, it was like the biggest achievement of my life

A client on one of the standard courses reported:

> You go up Snowdon. I'd never really done mountain walks before. I'd done hill walks but not mountain walks and I thought I'd never get to the top. At the beginning I really dreaded it, I really wasn't looking forward to it. Just going there in the van I thought oh, this is going to be testing. I used to look how far ahead you've got to go and it used to kill me. The top was there in the distance many millions and millions of miles away from me. It did seem like quite a hurdle at that time, to get up a mountain. You come to realise that it's not so bad, it's quite good really. The feeling gets better as you get closer to the top, I've got to admit.

For some participants mountaineering had become a major life interest and, in this sense, had replaced drug use, and for some an interest in outdoor pursuits had led to employment opportunities.

> ... it's given me an alternative to drugs but it's something that I enjoy more than taking drugs. You can say that it's a replacement but it's not a negative replacement, it's a positive thing because I've actually found something that I like doing that isn't having a detrimental effect on my health.

This participant 'enjoyed the adrenalin' of rock climbing, but for another participant who also experienced satisfaction and excitement on the programme, this was not a crucial part of a substitute activity for drugs:

Everybody's different and different things appeal to different people. The hard thing sometimes is finding what's on offer that will fill the void, if not to the point that drugs did, quite close to it. That does give you a good feeling, does give you a purpose in life.

This was reflected in a quote from a participant who put the satisfactions of outdoor pursuits in perspective when relating it to taking heroin:

... actually taking drugs, you do get something out of it. It is a good feeling, the actual drug itself. ... I think if you asked people and say if heroin grew on trees, and in any way didn't affect your lives or relationships with your mother or your family or your girlfriend or your wife or whoever, and give you this good feeling, I think there would be a large part of the population on it. At the end of the day it doesn't give you all that and it causes a lot of grief in your life. Therefore, sometimes it's hard to grasp what could give you an adequate feeling after drugs because you do tend to relate everything to the good feeling. Actually achieving something, actually just sharing, just being with people and doing outdoor pursuits, feeling good about yourself, that's a natural good feeling.

When you get off drugs there's a big void there, for me there's a big void. I've lost the drugs to fill this empty space inside me that used to give me a good feeling and now the drugs have gone I haven't got that good feeling. I know it really does fill a gap inside me. In a way it is addictive but it is a positive one.

Gaining a new interest, possibly leading to employment opportunities, appeared to be more important than excitement and risk as a direct substitute for drugs. These were similar characteristics to those experienced by successful participants in the West Yorkshire Sports Counselling programme. Increased self-confidence, and support from probation staff, was required to help clients establish a new self-identity that might be in sharp contrast to that of their former associates. One participant, a former drug dealer, developed an interest in conservation work, which led to voluntary work and later full-time employment.

I could not tell my friends and associates, 'that is a robin redbreast there, and that does stay here in the winter, and that is a blackbird and that is a song thrush'. That just would not have happened, it would not have gone down well, me street cred would have gone, so it was all suppressed. So coming here, people asking me, and what would I like to do personally, and it was like conservation, and it was great, there was no one judging me and saying, I don't like that.

This redefinition of self-concept in this case is all the more challenging because it is in such contrast to the participant's previous self-identity and that of his former peers. Hence it needed greater support to sustain. Similarly, those leaving the rehabilitation hostel to live independently needed support to redefine their

lives. It is interesting that all those who had successfully completed drug rehabilitation had started a new life in a new location.

Physical achievements, especially the 14 Peaks expedition, did act as a
metaphor for participants who were undergoing drug rehabilitation or trying to
start a new life.

> ... the first mountain I walked up, I kept tripping because I was looking at
> the peak and I was looking at the scenery and [the leader] said to me, look
> at your feet and every now and again you stop and check ... and have a
> look back at the scenery. I thought that would be like coming off drugs
> that, if I look at where I'm going, I'll fall over and if I look at where I've
> been to I'll fall over so I need to look at my feet, you know, every day ... So
> I translated that one thing he said, that on the surface was about mountain
> climbing, into the bigger thing.
>
> At one time I thought I'd never be able to get off drugs, I'll never be able
> to sort this one out. I often compare it with the 14 peaks. I said that when I
> was just first walking up them first few steps, which really stopped me from
> going any further especially with drugs, it really stopped me from getting
> over that threshold. I honestly believe in my heart now that it can be done.

The achievement of completing the expedition, recognised in a certificate, was
very important to participants. The centre manager reported that:

> My feelings when I meet them later on is this sense of enormous achieve-
> ment, of doing the 14 Peaks. One person rung up here and said, can I have
> another certificate as I've just had a big row with my girlfriend and she tore
> my certificate up. Most of them get them framed, and this was more impor-
> tant to this lad, that she had destroyed his certificate ... It gives an
> illustration of how important it was.

A similar example was a participant in the annual fun run with a prize for the win-
ner. A competitor who was an ex-offender had been missed coming in and the prize
had already been awarded by the chief probation officer. The competitor went to
the judges' table and said, 'I'm a criminal, I've committed offences, I'm the first
one'. So the cup was retrieved from the other offender who had been given it and
the chief probation officer felt so sorry for him he got him something else.

This was similar to the importance WYSC participants gave to their completion certificate. Experiences could also act as a metaphor to help clients put their
relationship to nature and others in perspective:

> I found it quite humbling, a humbling experience. I realised in a positive way
> for the first time in my life, that I was actually deeply insignificant when put
> next to all this stuff. How that helped me was because for years I had a typi-
> cal junky attitude and that the universe revolves round me and I am the
> most important thing in it, which a lot of people need to drop before they

become drug free. I have known quite a few other people have that experience at Hafotty.

The achievements on the courses, especially the physically demanding ones, could act as a metaphor for other challenges, such as coming off drugs. But this needed long-term support because of the risk of relapse, which was not uncommon. A client who had relapsed reported:

> I had to go back into the same situation that I came out of, sort of old haunts really. It was 18 months where I didn't actually use drugs but was being offered them constantly. We get tested enough, ex-drug addicts, on a day-to-day basis just walking along the road. You're always being tested in one way or another. You try and minimise it as much as you can. I wouldn't go to a friend's house where I know he has his mates round all using heroin because I know that's just not a good idea, it's a simple as that. You try and minimise those times and keep it as rare as possible. If you can foresee a time where you can put yourself in a vulnerable situation you will try, or I will now, try and avoid them.

As illustrated above, the major risk facing those on drug rehabilitation is relapse. Ex-addicts were aware of the dangers of going back to live in the same place, but living somewhere else offered other challenges.

> The problem is, most people, in rehabilitation you're wrapped in cotton wool, if you like. You're in an enclosed community, you're not dealing with the outside world. They do learn you skills to cope with everyday normality, whatever normal is. When you get outside, you get a flat and then you go pay your bills and stuff like that. You're unemployed, you haven't got a job because you've been out of work for years because you took drugs and it's like starting your life over, it's like leaving home all over again. You know how difficult it is to get a job and most people look at it and think, I can't cope with this, I might as well go back to taking drugs. You've got no support, a lot of people feel isolated again because they took drugs for years, all they've ever known is other drug users and to suddenly come out of that sub-culture and come back into society, you tend to be isolated because society doesn't really want to know them because they're a drug user or former drug user, and you don't fit into the drug culture any more because you no longer want to use drugs. You're sort of caught in the middle and either go one way or the other. Most of them tend to go back to what they know, which is drug use, what they're comfortable with.

The courses provided the catalyst for relationships of trust to develop between probation officer and client that could provide the long-term support required for drug rehabilitation. These moved towards 'pure relationships' in the sense used by Giddens (1991: 89), which became independent from the social structure of the probation supervision context. Unprompted, all participants commented on the good relationship they had developed with the centre manager, which for many had become a long-term significant relationship as they visited the centre on repeated occasions.

> ... meeting [the manager], he was from where I live, he's from Liverpool. He was born on ... Road in Liverpool and I'm only 5 minutes away. Just being from the same place I felt I could relate to [him] a bit. I seem to have hit it off with [him] ever since. Every time we've had a good chin wag about when he used to live in Liverpool.

Both the centre manager and probation staff might become long-term 'significant others'. A former client explained how his probation officer, with whom he had shared the 14 Peaks expedition 14 years before, had remained a close friend since then. This development of a trust relationship with an authority figure who acts as a role model is similar to the relationship between sports leaders and participants on the West Yorkshire Sports Counselling programme. It may be of more importance to participants who have few other relationships of trust in their lives.

Risk is relative to perception

The analysis above contrasted probation service staff's perception of risk on the outdoor programme and that of drug rehabilitation clients. The risks on the programme have been placed in the context of the major risk faced by those on drug rehabilitation, that of relapse, and the difficulties of establishing a new life and sustaining a new self-identity. Probation staff have to be extremely sensitive not only to the risks as perceived by disadvantaged clients but also to how clients' perception of risk changed.

One participant who had taken up rock climbing as a result of being introduced to outdoor activities later gave it up when he realised how dangerous it could be. In contrast, while on drugs he:

> ... used to inject half grams of heroin, which is a bigger gamble than the lottery. Basically what that type of behaviour says about somebody is that they don't care whether they live or die. I didn't at the time but I do now.

This illustrates that perceived risk is relevant to one's knowledge and perception. This participant's concern with the risks of rock climbing was a function of his awareness of the consequences of making a mistake. For some people this awareness of risk in rock climbing could enhance the experience, as in the rock climbers studied by Csikszentmihalyi and Csikszentmihalyi (1992) in their understanding of the intrinsically satisfying state of 'flow' (see Chapter Three). Others may not choose to take these risks. A second point is that risk is relative to the value of potential loss and gain. The participant above took high risks with drugs when he did not value his life, but low risks with rock climbing when he did.

Another ex-addict described the risks he took to get crack:

> Desperate for more crack I began stealing from the dealers. Letting myself in
> at 3 one morning I was pounced on by a dealer I owed £500 for a few grams
> of cocaine. He stripped me naked ... and beat me with a claw-hammer for
> nearly 2 hours.

The risks were balanced against the benefits of getting the crack, as perceived at
the time. An appreciation of this changing perspective on risk is useful in considering the validity of the argument that offenders would be less likely to
commit crime if they had a stake in society to lose. The two examples above of
drug addicts taking risks were people who felt they had nothing to lose, except
their next fix. Drug addicts on rehabilitation realised the risks they faced through
association with former peers and easy access to drugs when they felt insecure.
Gaining employment, if they could, helped alleviate these, but they needed more
than this stake in society. They needed help to 'start life over', to become established as a new person.

A more general understanding of the important characteristics of a residential group experience – the centre manager's view

While the analysis above has focused on the 14 Peaks course, and has been constructed round the nature of risk, the case study also illustrated important general
characteristics of the residential group experience. These were largely explored
through the interview with the centre manager. The centre manager's views were
not checked systematically against those of the other interviewees, but are
reported at length below as they articulate those of other managers of similar
centres and reflect considerable experience.

The centre manager took great care in staff selection. He had to be sure of the
way staff could deal with aggressive behaviour:

> Under no circumstances should staff respond aggressively to aggression, as
> once you do you have lost it. Anything we do here has got to be a platform
> for dealing with their lifestyle, and their lifestyle is about behaviour and
> offending.

Staff had to be well-rounded and mature people. They might have mountain
leadership and first aid qualifications, but they had to have the other qualities
needed for working with these groups. Setting an atmosphere and expectations
of mutual respect was the most important thing:

> If we attempt to treat people with respect then maybe they might respect other
> people's property. [Staff must] clearly be able to demonstrate that they have
> respect for someone. It is easy to use the word, it is not so easy for someone in
> a position of authority to turn round and be humble, and also to clearly be able

to show to a group that I as a person don't have all the answers. It's about honesty and integrity. It's about being humble, respectful and understanding. For example, you might tie a knot wrong and say to the group, oh I got that one wrong. ... That's not easy because some people are intimidated by offenders.

The centre manager was an optimist, and very positive about the potential of his work:

A large percentage of offending starts initially by chance, so a lot of people end up by becoming hardened criminals, but deep down inside their intention is not to be criminals.

An important part of the centre environment, in contrast to their home in Liverpool, was 'quietness and space'. Also, because the centre was only a very small organisation, staff 'could feel they are part of that team'.

The centre manager stressed that the centre environment was the opportunity for participants to experience a new way of behaving and living together:

I make them as much aware that they are the future society; and how they function in that society, that's the society they are going to have. We could not function without their respect for us and our respect for them. That respect goes right across the whole spectrum of what we do. This is also about respecting the environment, not leaving litter around, and respecting the centre. The centre is their responsibility, there is no one cleaning up after them. The centre is their home; when they leave it they have to clean it all up so it is ready for the next people that get here. We are dealing about behaviour now, whatever we are doing. [The climate of responsibility] ... starts with respect: there is no other way for it.

The centre manager reported that the initial briefing at the start of the course set out expectations of respect and responsibility, what that means to participants and what they will be doing. They were made aware that their support, in terms of how they behave, is needed for the centre to continue. They were told about the importance of local public relations. Simple rules were explained, components of the programme and that they were expected to commit themselves to it. This meant setting standards that must be kept. Drugs and alcohol were not allowed on the establishment. In practice only seven individuals had been sent home for misbehaviour, out of about 8,000 people going through the centre.

While the centre environment was important, so also was the contrast with the participants' home environment:

... it can help them to clearly identify that there are other ways of proceeding in their life. Whatever that is there is an opportunity to possibly identify it here. We clearly notice that people's skills and abilities do very much come to the fore.

To allow participants to behave in a different way it was essential that they felt safe:

> What is really beneficial for doing things here is that they feel safe. They are not undermined ... If they make a mess of orienteering or make a real balls-up of tying a knot they will come up and say that, but in their own environment they would not dare admit that they could not drink more than ten pints. This is what I mean by being safe. They might feel brutalised and isolated in society; whilst they are here it is about a caring society.

Being part of a group was important so participants could appreciate their inter-dependence to each other, and the small group size, of 10–12, meant people could not opt out:

> Whilst they are here they must eventually recognise that we can't work and operate in society in isolation, we need support from each other. They quickly realise that each person can give each other support. Whatever we do we give opportunities and examples for that support to manifest itself and also clearly give people opportunities for leadership. For example, a mountain rescue exercise where they do the planning and take responsibility for the exercise, or a river crossing exercise. It's about all the interpersonal skills that go on, and we video all that, and debrief it. It gives them an opportunity to function in a way that they maybe have not had before.

The small group size and the activities meant that participants 'clearly have the opportunity to see the effects of their decision making':

> One of the great problems I see with offenders is that when they do something they do not see the trauma they cause to the other person. If they get something wrong here, they can clearly see the consequences. For example, if someone gets something wrong on a bike expedition they can clearly see their effects on the rest of the group. Or if someone misbehaves, that could be the termination of the activity for all the group.

The ideal length of a course was seen as 5 days. Ideally, prior to the course, a 1-day assimilation visit was arranged, as the environment was so different to Merseyside. However, often the centre did not know exactly who would be attending a course until they arrived. This reflected the chaotic lives of many of the participants, both in terms of factors beyond their control and their own ability to make commitments. After the course a form was sent back to probationers' supervising officers, indicating suitable follow-up activities, but it was up to the probation officers to direct clients towards these. Alternatively, it was always possible for clients to come back on any of the open courses, as illustrated by several of the 14 Peaks interviewees. The probation service would pay for these.

The centre manager's overall views were:

In the end I say to people, I can't stop you offending, those decisions have got to come from you. You can't force people not to do something. You can make them aware and guide them, but it's something about their stability, employability, and their perception of what they see as right and wrong, that stops them. And also a component that is very important, the phase in their lives. If they have a long-term steady relationship with someone this is just as much a powerful experience as other things. The centre is more about changing their behaviour than the activity.

Conclusion on the programme and evaluation methods

Approaches to evaluation

The reconviction analysis did not show that the programme had a positive impact. However the qualitative interviews were very valuable in showing how and why the programme worked, when it did, and also the considerable difficulties faced by this particular client group – those undergoing drug rehabilitation. Again, they required considerable resources to conduct and the involvement of an independent university researcher probably gave them greater academic rigour and credibility. (In contrast to the WYSC case study, this research was carried out with only a small budget for travel expenses.)

A general lesson is that even evaluating a small programme using these methods requires considerable resources, beyond the capacity of most probation service research units. The OGRS analysis and the use and analysis of interviews together accounted for about a month's work for one researcher. As Merrington and Hine (2001) note, this approach may not be practical when evaluating a single local programme. There is a trade-off between using resources for evaluating programmes and for delivering them, and often decisions have to be made quickly. In this particular case Merseyside Probation Service decided to close the centre just as the data was being collected for this research. A general question then is how practical is it to base policy on evidence, given the resources required to collect it, and at what stage does one accept that one has sufficient information on which to make a policy decision? A further topic for research might be how programmes are justified, or the decision made to close them, given the difficulty of making an 'objective' judgment from the evidence.

How and why the programme worked

Within Hafotty Wen's programmes, the 14 Peaks case study showed that the considerable physical challenge meant that the sense of achievement was also considerable, and that the recognition of this, through a certificate and award, was important to participants. This achievement, and the memory of the expedition itself, could provide a metaphor for other challenges, in particular coming off drugs. The shared experience of the expedition was a catalyst for developing a positive relationship with probation officers and centre staff, which then enabled them to take a longer-term role in helping the participant. This relationship was seen as crucial. Thus the personal qualities of staff were very important, as was the ethos of the centre, and the ability of staff to offer long-term support.

In relation to clarifying the nature of risk, which was a focus of this study, risk can be used constructively in outdoor adventure programmes for offenders but this requires particular care and skill to take account of the circumstances of the clients. The analysis above shows that this particular group of clients had very diverse needs that only someone in long-term contact with them could fully appreciate. For example, problems with bed-wetting, which could cause a lot of embarrassment. Sensitive and skilled centre staff needed to liaise closely with probation officers who knew the clients to ensure that risk was used constructively. Probation staff needed to prepare clients carefully for the risks they would take on the programme, but this had to be part of a long-term process of supervision. If this was done, physical, emotional and social risks could be managed to achieve positive outcomes such as improved self-esteem, improved relations of trust with probation staff, and possibly a new interest that could lead to employment opportunities. The skills of programme staff needed to be particularly high to take account of the nature of risks faced by these clients and their considerable need for support.

Because the clients were disadvantaged they will face greater risks and therefore need greater support for a longer time; for example, those leaving drug rehabilitation for independent living. While for young people who are advantaged it may be reasonable for an outdoor adventure course to inculcate an approach to risk-taking that is seen as a means of taking responsibility for personal growth, disadvantaged participants may find it more valuable to be supported in strategies to minimise or avoid risk; for example, avoiding former associates involved in drug use.

The case study gave little support to the idea that risk activities can offer intrinsic satisfactions that substitute for drug use. The role of the activities as a medium for development was more important, but they could also offer a constructive, legal, leisure interest, and for some this could lead to employment opportunities. However, it is still possible that for criminals with different motives, not related to drug use, risk activities could provide a closer substitute for offending behaviour. This illustrates the difficulty of generalising between effective programmes for different offenders. A limitation of this study was its concentration on those involved in drug-related crime and its all-male sample of clients. This is likely to be reflected in clients' perceptions of risk, though the probation officers interviewed had experience of working with male and female clients.

Where drug rehabilitation had been successful, changed lifestyle, self-concept and peers had led to changed behaviour, reduced drug use and reduced offending. The analysis above clarifies the role of 'risk' in outdoor adventure activities, which can easily be obscured by the apparent physical risk of the activities that has led to much ill-informed academic debate and misleading media headlines (Nichols, 2000b).

Other important characteristics of the centre and the programme were: the residential experience in a small group away from the home environment; the ethos of the centre; and the ability for participants to take follow-up activities.

Funding, politics and operational difficulties

Shortly after this study was conducted, Merseyside Probation Service cut funding for the centre as part of a round of budget cuts. One justification for this was that a relatively small number of probation staff used it. Some may not have used it because they were put off by the image of the activities as 'macho', 'physical' and having an army culture. Some probation staff may not have used it because of unwillingness to put in the considerable extra hours required to take groups to the centre. Attending the residential courses was very hard work for probation staff: as there was no separate accommodation for staff they had to share it with the participants, who often had very irregular sleep patterns, partly because of their drug dependency. Similarly, bail hostel staff had been asked to attend the courses without being paid as bail hostels were constrained by the need to employ replacement staff to cover for those who were away. Budget constraints in the bail service had also restricted their ability to run day visits prior to courses. A further difficulty was that the popularity of the centre meant that bookings for closed courses had to be made 6 months in advance.

So, budget restraints had already affected the centre's work indirectly before it was closed. The uneven use of the centre across the probation service led to a split between those who did not use Hafotty Wen, seeing it as irrelevant to their work, and those who did, and were enthusiastic. So, political support was weak, but so was evidence of programme effectiveness in reducing offending. (The case study work above was not available at the time.) Of course, this relates back to the consideration in Chapter Four of what is regarded as evidence. How adequate would the case study evidence above been in persuading the probation service that the centre was worthwhile? Even though the reconviction analysis failed to show a positive impact, could one have argued that providing a turning point in just a few lives would have been worthwhile? The closure was a severe blow to the drug rehabilitation centre that had used Hafotty Wen extensively.

The centre's own evaluation involved a simple questionnaire completed by clients at the end of the course, including a question asking how they thought the course would help them reduce offending. They also used a self-assessment form signed by the client and supervisor at the end of the course, recording skills learned. These were not systematically analysed and their purpose was as much to give the client and supervising officer a record that could be built on in the supervision plan. So, the absence of more precise evaluation left the centre more vulnerable as it also lacked political support.

While the probation officers and bail hostel staff who had used Hafotty Wen had developed expertise in using the centre to complement their work, there did not appear to be a mechanism for disseminating that experience through other staff.

As the excerpts from the interview with the centre manager above suggest, he had very strong ideas about how and why the centre worked, and therefore how it should be run. He had set it up, on his own initiative, in 1984, and his approach permeated its work. As noted, he felt that the qualities of staff were crucial, but this may have made it harder for him to delegate responsibility. He was someone who had committed several years of his life to something he believed in. His integrity and commitment were a strength in his dealing with participants, but these qualities may have made it harder for him to work with those from the probation service who did not share his ideals and views. This is purely speculation, but the personal qualities required to set up and run an organisation working with long-term offenders, and where the odds of success seem to be stacked against you (as the manager of WYSC and the director of the Clontarff project in a following chapter) may not sit easily with those required to manage 'political' situations and meet externally imposed performance indicators. This may present a difficulty, given the political dimension of evaluation and evidence.

9 Fairbridge

Summary

Fairbridge used sports and other leisure activities to work with disadvantaged and disaffected young people at medium risk, but the programme takes at least 6 months, so it aims at long-term behavioural change. The considerable resources available to the evaluation allowed for far more comprehensive research methods than are usually possible in evaluation studies. These methods included follow-up interviews with participants a year after they had started the programme. The study took a 'theory of change' approach, led both by programme managers' hypotheses about how the programme achieved its objectives and by the views of key policy stakeholders on the validity of the research methods used to establish programme efficacy.

The evaluation showed that personal and social skills (measured by an internally validated, self-completion measure) had increased over the initial 5-day part of the programme, for a sample of 318 young people. While the gains in these skills did not appear to be maintained a year later, they were good predictors of the long-term behavioural improvements, which included better performance in jobs and education, stable housing arrangements, and having a positive attitude towards self and others. These results suggested that the gains in personal skills preceded the longer-term impacts.

Discussion considers the difficulties of determining the extent to which an initial apparent increase in personal skills, or a positive predisposition to the programme, was the most important factor determining long-term impacts. It is argued that it is more realistic to understand the impact of the programme in terms of generative, rather than successive, causality – one has to understand the dynamic interaction between programme and participant. Overall, it appears that the programme achieved positive results and that the supportive relationships with programme staff were of key importance in the long term. Initially the nature of the sports activities was important in gaining involvement. The results are consistent with these activities acting as a catalyst for the development of mentor relationships with staff and as a medium for longer-term personal development.

Introduction to the programme

Fairbridge is a charity. It is a major provider of personal development programmes for disadvantaged and disaffected young people in the UK. It aims to develop young people's personal and social skills and build their confidence, thus helping them to change their lives. Its mission is to offer opportunities for long-term personal development, which could enable young people from inner cities to gain the skills needed to meet the opportunities and responsibilities of society today. At the time of this study it operated through 12 centres in the UK (expanded to 14 in 2005) and, in 2001, across all of the UK sites approximately 3,000 young people overall attended Fairbridge courses. All agencies dealing with young people aged 14–25 can make referrals to the programme. These include the youth service and the probation service, though some young people refer themselves. Participation is voluntary.

Fairbridge offers an initial basic 1-week course, which includes centre-based preparation and up to 3 days at a residential location. Much of the residential course employs challenging outdoor sports activities such as canoeing and climbing. The aim is to use these activities as a medium to help participants learn about themselves and to develop a personal action plan for the next 6 months. Thus, the only common part of a Fairbridge programme is the initial week. Support after this is tailored to the needs of individual participants and can continue for a year. The activities that a young person might choose to participate in after the initial course include: additional outdoor activity courses; courses run by partner organisations such as The Prince's Trust (an organisation with similar objectives to Fairbridge but which focuses on helping young people set up their own businesses and develop community projects); workshops to develop life skills; programmes to develop skills for the workplace; and individual counselling sessions. Thus, while outdoor sports activities are part of the initial course and are often part of an individual's follow-on programme, they are used as a means to an end, rather than to achieve an objective of long-term sports participation.

Evaluation

Within a 'theory of change' approach methods included:

- use of programme records
- interviews with programme staff and managers
- a questionnaire for participants measuring personal characteristics
- a questionnaire for participants measuring self-perception of personal skills, administered at three times
- interviews with participants 3 months and 1 year after the initial course.

The theory of change approach to evaluation

The evaluation used the theory of change (TOC) approach as described in Chapter Four. So, the first step was to identify the programme staff's theory of change – 'a set of hypotheses upon which people build their programme plans ... an explanation of the causal links that tie programme inputs to expected programme outputs' (Weiss, 1998: 55). Staff at four of the Fairbridge centres, and senior managers, were interviewed to find out their beliefs about what characterises the young people who come to Fairbridge; the processes Fairbridge uses to bring about changes in young people; and the benefits resulting from participating in the Fairbridge programme. These beliefs were formally stated as the 'Fairbridge hypothesis'. This hypothesis proposed that young people coming to Fairbridge faced a mixture of personal problems over which they felt relatively powerless and reluctant to confront. They lacked personal and social skills and often had behavioural problems. The programme used exciting and fun activities and set up physical, personal and social challenges tailored to the individual needs of the young people in order to increase their personal and social skills. It was designed to help participants realise their own potential, and gain the ability to confront the problems they faced and their own behaviour. To accomplish these outcomes, close and sensitive support was required. As a result of their experience with Fairbridge, young people developed personal and social skills, enabling them to take responsibility for addressing their own problems and behaviours.

Thus the TOC approach to evaluation generated hypotheses from practitioners involved in the programme that was being evaluated, rather than from academic theory.

The final evaluation report (Astbury and Knight, 2003) did not review theory concerning the factors that determined the effectiveness of this type of programme or relate the findings back to theory – this would have been typical of a more 'academic' approach to research, led by the objective of adding to theory. In contrast, the main purpose of this evaluation was to inform and influence practice. This approach also meant that it was important not only to find out what influence Fairbridge had on participants, but why it had that influence; understanding the process was as important as the outcomes. Thus, in this sense, the theory of change approach was designed to understand what changed and why in order to inform policy and practice; Fairbridge wanted to both influence sponsors of its work and understand how it could improve its work. An important feature of this approach was the explicit recognition of the programme staff as key stakeholders in the evaluation – their involvement in developing the theory of change gained their commitment to the research.

The next stage of the research was to design methods to test the Fairbridge hypothesis. At this stage a second group of stakeholders were consulted, both to seek confirmation that the Fairbridge hypothesis was a reasonable starting point for the research and, more importantly, to get their feedback on how the research was to be conducted to provide valid results. The stakeholders were invited to join an advisory group that met over the period of the evaluation study. Members were selected as representatives of key policy makers, including the Youth Service at the level of national government, Her Majesty's Inspectorate of Education in Scotland, national government's Social Exclusion Unit, the Joseph Rowntree Foundation (a major independent social research foundation in the

UK), a former chief probation officer, and an academic expert. Maintaining commitment from this group was important because the purpose of the evaluation was to influence policy, and the representatives of the advisory group had direct or indirect influence on policy.

As noted in Chapter Four, because an objective of this version of the theory of change approach is to change policy, it was crucially important at this stage that key policy makers shared the plausibility of the hypotheses and the validity of the methods to test them. In effect they were committing themselves to agreeing that if particular methods produced particular results they would accept that the programme did what it claimed to. A further implication of the focus on changing policy was that planning the dissemination of findings was an important part of the evaluation.

Methods

The generous funding of the research allowed the use of an extensive array of methods to test the hypothesis.

1   A 40-item questionnaire, designed to develop a detailed profile of who was participating in Fairbridge, was administered to 318 participants as they entered the programme. The sample was the entire intake of four centres between 2 April, 2001 and 15 October, 2001. The centres were selected to be representative of the 12 UK centres. Two centres were selected from England, one in Scotland, and one in Wales. Across all of the UK sites approximately 3000 young people overall attended Fairbridge courses each year. The sample was very similar to the Fairbridge population in age and gender, but not in race – only 3.5 per cent coming from black ethnic minority communities. This was an under-representation of this group, who accounted for 9 per cent of all Fairbridge users, but reflected the demographics of the centres chosen for participation in the evaluation.

2   A self-assessment by the young person of their personal and social skills was conducted using a 'who are you' quiz. The quiz comprised 14 statements (e.g. 'How good am I at letting other people know what I mean') and scored on a scale of 'very good/good/OK/could be better/need to work on this'. The statements are reproduced in Table 9.1 (see page 103) in the discussion of results and were designed to test various aspects of the Fairbridge hypothesis. This self-assessment was completed at the beginning and end of the initial 6-day course. It was designed in close consultation with Fairbridge staff to ensure it would be practical for participants and staff to use. A total of 288 (n=288) completed sets of before and after responses were collected.

3   Structured observations of the Fairbridge courses were conducted by the research staff using a standardised recording sheet to determine the extent to which course activities matched the process components of the hypothesis. For example, the course characteristic 'gives young people experiences of success' was rated as 'none', 'some', or 'many'.

4   Records of data obtained from each participant and an assessment of their likely future involvement in the project and, therefore, in the research, were collected.

5   Information generated from the previous four components was compiled to provide the basis for selection of a sub-set of interviewees.

6   Face-to-face semi-structured interviews were conducted with 58 randomly selected participants, 3 months after the basic course. These were selected from the initial 318, sampled in method 1. An open question asked for up to four personal changes (such as confidence or skills) after participation in the Fairbridge basic course, and for each change participants were asked to rate the magnitude of the change on a 5-point scale (very positive change to very negative change). Further questions asked for causes of these changes, which were rated on a 3-point scale (very big impact, some impact, little impact). Similarly, a set of closed questions asked about longer-term behavioural changes in the young persons' lives, such as 'trouble with the law', and the causes of each of the noted items. The construction of the interview facilitated a quantitative analysis of results.

7   Follow-up interviews were conducted with 30 young people a year after the introductory course. Of these, 27 were taken from the 58 participants interviewed in component 6, and a further three from the initial sample of 318. The main questions replicated those in component 6 and included repeating the quiz used in component 2. Considerable efforts were made to keep in touch with this sub-sample to avoid non-response bias (i.e. interviewing only young people who were easy to reach). For example, one young person was interviewed in prison. However, there is still a possibility the sample may be biased against those with the most disorganised life styles. An incentive of £15 was paid to participants.

The main purpose of the interviews was to assess personal changes and behavioural changes in the participants' lives, and why these changes occurred. As a check on the young people's perception of change, the member of Fairbridge staff and the interviewer also made independent assessments of these changes. (Interviewers were paired with the same young people during the phase 2 and 3 interviews.) The interviews provided information that could be quantitatively coded into previously organised categories (such as employed versus unemployed). In addition, the interviewers provided qualitative information (e.g. 'she is desperate to work but is having trouble finding a job'). After the interviews were completed, the research team jointly developed a framework to classify and code both the quantitative and qualitative information. Seven main themes ('domains') covering long-term behavioural change (such as career) were identified, along with 16 sub-themes ('elements'; such as training and qualifications).

Similarly, reasons for change were coded into five 'domains': staff, group experience, peer group, activities, and ethos. Within these domains there were 19 elements. For example, within the ethos domain were elements such as respect, treated like an adult, new ways of working, challenge, safety and fun/excitement/stimulation.

The results reported here concentrate on those derived from method components 1, 2, 6 and 7. For purposes of describing the research, developing the Fairbridge hypothesis was conducted in phase 1, method components 1–6, in phase 2, and method component 7 in phase 3.

Results

Who came to Fairbridge?

The young people attending Fairbridge matched the target group upon which the Fairbridge hypothesis was based. Seventy-five per cent were aged between 13 and 17 and 75 per cent were male. Only 3.5 per cent were not white. Eighty-one per cent of those of school age were 'in trouble' at school, either as a result of their attitudes or truanting. One-third had difficulties in reading, writing and arithmetic. Sixty per cent reported difficult relationships with their family. One-third had issues with drugs and 40 per cent had issues with alcohol. One in four was in trouble with the law and 20 per cent reported that their main income came from crime. Twenty per cent had debts.

Although these findings were based on self-reports of information to an unfamiliar adult, the data confirm that Fairbridge was attracting its target group. A composite scale of difficulties was produced (including those associated with drugs, alcohol, personal and family difficulties, health, employment, and trouble with the law). Approximately 59 per cent of participants experienced four or more of these adverse prior circumstances. Attracting this target group to participate voluntarily could itself be seen as an indicator of success. In-depth interviews with the sub-sample showed many interviewees shared feelings of despair about their situation and worry about their lack of prospects.

What changes in personal skills occurred during the initial 6-day course?

The 'who are you' quiz was designed to be acceptable to the Fairbridge staff and practical for the target group of young people to complete. Some research into similar programmes has not taken sufficient account of these criteria and, as a result, has achieved very poor response rates to overly-complex questionnaires (Nichols et al., 2000). The TOC approach emphasised the importance of making the research tools acceptable to key stakeholders. This meant that the new measures had not been validated by previous studies; however, the large sample size of 288 completed data sets allowed for internal tests of reliability, discussed below.

There was a 13 per cent improvement in the average scores for personal and social skills, with some variation by item. Several non-parametric statistical tests were conducted, each based on matched pairs and comparing before and after scores. All tests showed that the improvements in scores were statistically significant (Table 9.1). The column in the table headed 'Pairs analysis' shows this.

Table 9.1 Changes in self-reported personal and social skills

	Mean score before	Mean score after	% change	Pairs analysis	Spear-man's Rho
1. How good am I at letting other people know what I mean?	2.57	1.95	24	<0.05	0.35
2. How good am I at understanding what other people are saying to me?	2.30	1.97	14	<0.05	0.40
3. How good am I at getting on with people?	1.91	1.76	8	<0.05	0.30
4. How good am I at making and keeping friends?	2.03	1.89	7	<0.05	0.25
5. How good am I at keeping my feelings under control?	2.79	2.44	13	<0.05	0.37
6. How good am I at understanding why I like some people and not others?	2.38	2.12	11	<0.05	0.35
7. How good am I at understanding that different people have different ways of thinking?	2.21	2.03	8	<0.05	0.32
8. How good am I at sorting problems out?	2.56	2.27	11	<0.05	0.33
9. How good am I at understanding other people's point of view?	2.47	2.16	13	<0.05	0.26
10. How good am I at give and take/compromise?	2.30	2.06	13	<0.05	0.26
11. How good am I at thinking and planning ahead?	2.58	2.24	13	<0.05	0.21
12. How good am I at learning from my successes and mistakes?	2.41	2.06	15	<0.05	0.31
13. How good am I at accepting my share of the blame when things go wrong?	2.73	2.35	14	<0.05	0.38
14. How good am I at thinking through what will happen to me and other people before I do something?	2.74	2.33	15	<0.05	0.40

The pre- and post-test scores were also correlated using the Spearman's Rho (Spearman's Rank Order Correlation Co-efficient). Scores on this measure ranged from 0.21 to 0.40. These correlations are moderately high (on a scale that, in principle, ranges from −1, a perfect inverse correlation, to 1, a perfect positive correlation. A correlation of 0 would indicate no relationship.). This means that, in giving their responses, young people were fairly consistent across the pre- and post-test administrations of the scale; the increases in the scores on individual questions are relatively similar. The results suggest that the test is 'reliable' in the sense that it will tend to produce similar results each time it is given.

Improvements were unevenly distributed across the sample. Thirty per cent of the sample showed marked positive changes, while 40 per cent showed some improvement and 30 per cent showed no improvement or a decline in scores. Females were more likely to show improvement than males, though this difference was not statistically significant. Twenty-eight per cent of males showed a decline, compared to 15 per cent of females.

The interviews found that 51 of the 58 young people surveyed felt the Fairbridge course had brought them tangible benefits including: increased confidence; improved family relations; improved communications; new friends; better understanding of people; improved fitness; more motivated; drinking less; feeling calmer; a greater sense of the future; ability to think more; help finding a job; taking drugs less; offending less; and taking up constructive leisure activities.

The 'who are you' quiz used before and after the initial course was also repeated during these interviews. Results showed that an increase in social skills after participating in the programme were not maintained. (Average scores at the three times of measurement were approximately 2.5, 2.8 and 2.0.) This pattern was common for all the 14 questionnaire items.

What was the long-term impact of the programme?

One criticism of previous evaluations of this nature has been the lack of long-term follow-up. The considerable resources devoted to this project allowed for follow-up interviews to be conducted with 30 participants, a year after the initial course. Tracking this type of respondent over this time period was not easy: for example, one former participant had to be interviewed in prison.

The interview structure replicated the measures and topics covered during the first interviews. There were four domains in which a significant percentage of young people reported long-term improvement: confidence (92 per cent), positive attitude to self (78 per cent), career (62 per cent; including jobs, education, training) and personal non-career (33 per cent; including housing, relations with law, pregnancy).

Data from three sources were compared with regard to long-term impact: participant self-reports during the interviews; Fairbridge staff impressions; and impressions of interviewers who conducted pairs of interviews of the same participants a year after the initial course.

Positive changes in three domains (positive attitude to self, career and personal non-career) were confirmed by positive correlations with the independent ratings made by Fairbridge staff and the interviewers (Table 9.2).

The three independent data sources also show significant agreement. All other domains showed low or negative correlations, so the triangulation of data sources did not support a conclusion that change had taken place. This conclusion is also supported by the positive inter-correlations between these three domains of

Table 9.2 Comparison of scores on domains in the interview with the young person, with interviewers' and staff ratings of positive changes in young people

Domain	Interviewers' rating of change	Staff ratings of change
Career impact	0.56	0.73
Personal non-career	0.67	0.79
Relationships	0.05	−0.02
Ambitions	0.16	−0.11
Positive attitude to self	0.47	0.50
Disposition to act	0.06	−0.07
Activities	0.05	0.04
Skills score	−0.17	−0.04

change (figures in bold), indicating that positive change in one domain is associated with positive change in the other two (Table 9.3).

Three factors – career, personal non-career and positive attitude to self – are significantly inter-correlated, with coefficients in excess of 0.4. Other relationships are weak or negative.

Why did these changes take place?

For the evaluation it was important to explain any relationship between changes in personal skills and the three positive domain changes reported in the longer-term. Had a change in personal skills enabled improvements in career, non-career and positive attitude to self, or was the causal relation in the opposite direction? There were significant correlations between the initial changes in personal skills scores, as measured before and after the 6-day introductory course (component 2) and the changes in the three domains of career impact, personal non-career and

Table 9.3 Inter-correlations between different domains in interviews with young people

	Career	Personal non-career	Relationships	Ambition	Positive attitude	Dispo-sitions	Activities	Skills
Career	1.00							
Personal non-career	0.48	1.00						
Relationships	0.13	−0.04	1.00					
Ambitions	0.26	−0.15	−0.15	1.00				
Positive attitudes to self	0.44	0.48	0.23	0.26	1.00			
Dispositions	0.02	−0.05	−0.02	0.22	0.12	1.00		
Activities	−0.15	0.02	0.18	0.02	0.08	−0.14	1.00	
Skills	0.01	0.08	0.13	0.13	0.24	−0.05	−0.14	1.00

positive attitude to self as reported independently by Fairbridge staff (0.55), ratings from the interviewers (0.36), and the Fairbridge participants (0.22) in component 7. This showed that the more a participant had made an apparent increase in personal skills during the introductory course, the more they were likely to have made increases in career impact, personal non-career and positive attitude to self over the following year. In the evaluation report it was concluded that these results showed that short-term gains in personal skills, experienced during the initial 6-day course, preceded the improvements in important 'domains' of participants' lives, which occurred over the subsequent year. 'Changes in feelings about self and others translate into increased competence to deal with external challenges, such as jobs, education, and housing.' (Astbury and Knight, 2003: 21).

The research analysed what was important in determining change by first asking the young people in the phase 3 interviews. The young people believed that participation in the Fairbridge programme had led to the improvements they reported; staff and interviewers concurred. Further, as noted previously, young people's responses regarding the aspects of Fairbridge that were important were coded into five domains: staff, group experience, peer group, activities and ethos. A multiple regression analysis was conducted using these measures as independent variables and tested their power to predict the long-term outcomes, as measured by an overall impact score, derived from quantifying the positive impacts reported in phase 3. These five domains together predict 55.8 per cent (R^2) of the variance in outcome. Of these five, staff (comprising the elements support, role model and practical help) had the most significant predictive power, followed by activities (comprising the elements learning new skills and sense of accomplishment).

Further analysis showed that young women were significantly more likely to benefit from Fairbridge than young men. This finding held for outcome measures based on young people's self-reports, staff assessments or interviewer ratings.

Conclusion on the programme and evaluation methods

The Fairbridge programme appears to contribute to the positive development of young people. The initial apparent changes in personal skills, and the link between these and long-term positive outcomes, compares favourably with the risk/protective factor model; an increase in these personal skills (as reflected in the 'who are you' quiz scores) appears to have a casual relationship to long-term positive behavioural changes. However, the success of the programme has to be qualified by the findings related to fewer changes in personal skills scores for males and for those with high initial 'risk' scores, and the apparent decrease in personal skill scores a year after the introductory course.

Determining causality

As in the West Yorkshire Sports Counselling case study, there is some difficulty distinguishing between the impact of a programme and the importance of the characteristics and attitudes young people bring to it. This is the same as the criticism Pitts makes of the evaluation of Ross and Fabiano's Reasoning and Rehabilitation programme: (2003: 91) 'Whatever it was that motivated prisoners to volunteer for the programme, rather than the programme itself, may well have enabled them to avoid reconviction upon release.'

Again, a better way to view the relationship between the programme and the participant may be generative causality – rather than a programme having an impact on a participant it is necessary to understand the interaction between the programme and the participant. Understanding the interaction between programme and participant would explain why those young people who have a more positive initial disposition towards Fairbridge, and who are experiencing the least 'risk factors', may be expected to have the most positive outcomes; these individuals can build on their initial advantages. However, this is not to discount the overall positive results of the programme, which as component 1 showed, are achieved with the generally disadvantaged young people who come to Fairbridge.

But if increased personal skills are associated with positive behavioural change, why did the personal skills scores fall consistently between the initial course, their measurement in phase 3, and the follow-up interviews with 30 participants conducted a year after the introductory course? One possible explanation is that rather than actually measuring these particular social skills, the increase in scores over the period of the initial course reflected an underlying positive attitude towards Fairbridge and what it can offer, i.e. an initial receptiveness to the idea that Fairbridge would have a positive impact on skills development. The 'who are you' scores were statistically reliable, in the sense that the same person would tend to achieve similar scores at the same time, but may not be a valid representation of personal skills. It may be that it is the attitude the young person brings to Fairbridge, their willingness to 'buy into the Fairbridge experience', rather than the apparent increase in personal skills, that determines the long-term positive outcomes. The apparent fall in social skills after a year might reflect a greater maturity in self-evaluation and a greater willingness to acknowledge one's own limitations, and, in this respect, represents a positive outcome. It is debatable the extent to which one can both achieve and measure a change in personal skills in this type of participant over a week, although achieving this has been the aim of the UK Government Department for Education and Employment summer programmes for 16-year-olds, and its evaluation claims to have measured this outcome (Hutchinson *et al.*, 2001). (See Nichols, 2001b, for a critical review.) As gender was a determinant variable in positive long-term behavioural change, this favourable disposition towards Fairbridge could also explain why young women showed both a greater increase in personal skills, as measured in phase 2, and better long-term outcomes.

Why did Fairbridge have this impact? – the relationship to the model in Chapter Four

The staff and the activities were key factors. As in WYSC, the activities were a significant 'hook' to get participants involved and may have provided a catalyst for the development of strong mentor relationships with staff. As in WYSC and Hafotty Wen, staff were able to provide a mentor role – only, unlike in WYSC, the programme allowed for this to be maintained for at least 6 months. Sports activities have different roles at different phases of the programme. Initially their importance is to attract the young person to voluntarily participate in the programme. At the same time they may act as a catalyst for developing the crucial mentor relationship between young people and programme staff. However, in the context of the young person's personal action plan, which follows the initial 1-week course, sports activities provide a medium for skills' development and achievement. This is not to discount the possibility that the use of outdoor adventure activities may deter some participants who perceive them as too risky – either physically or to their fragile self-esteem, as in Hafotty Wen. In the long term, it is also possible that other activities, such as art, may prove to be just as effective a medium for personal development, and the wide choice of personal action plans allowed for this.

The 'theory of change' approach to evaluation

The theory of change approach allowed a focus on the process as well as the outcome.

Programme staff were committed to the evaluation both because they were involved in initially developing the Fairbridge hypothesis and also because they were involved in designing practical methods of research that would enhance their work. The approach aimed to change policy – although it is not known if it did this. It was not designed to add to theory – but, as the discussion above shows, the results could be used to do this.

10 The Clontarf Foundation's Football Academies

Summary

The Clontarf Foundation's Football Academies work with Australian Indigenous boys through providing coaching in Australian Rules Football (ARF), conditional on school attendance. The programme is not targeted at offenders, but at a group who are at a high level of risk from their circumstances. It helps participants develop skills and confidence to establish themselves in Australian society. This case illustrates how this sport provides a unique bridge between the very different cultures of the Australian Indigenous and white communities, including the development of respect between Indigenous youth and the football coaches. The case study is shorter than the previous ones because it relies entirely on evaluation data collected by the programme itself. It demonstrates how simple monitoring data collected by the programme can be compared to national statistics, and complemented by qualitative letters of support. These are incorporated into the Foundation's annual report.

Key success factors are the quality and commitment of the coaches and the leadership of the managing director (a former professional football coach of top level Australian Rules football teams), as well as the role of ARF in engaging Indigenous young people. The Foundation is in a strong political position because supporting the Indigenous population to integrate successfully into Australian society is a high political priority.

Introduction to the programme

History and description

The Clontarf Foundation's mission is to 'improve the discipline, life skills, and self-esteem of young Aboriginal men and by so doing equip them to participate meaningfully in society'. Its programmes are delivered through academies, each of which operates in partnership with (but independent of) a school or college. The academies offer Indigenous young people top-class coaching in ARF. Participation in the football training and games is conditional on attendance at school. In 2005 three academies were running (expanded to six in 2006). The Clontarf Football Academy was the first to be established in 2000, and is on the Clontarf Aboriginal

College Campus, in a suburb of Perth. Most of the students are residential. Since then two other academies have been established, in Kalgoorlie (Goldfields) and Geraldton (Mid West), both in Western Australia (WA).

The Clontarf school had been in existence in Perth, Australia, from 1901 to 1975 as a Christian boys' orphanage. From 1976 to 1983, it was run as a residential school for emotionally disturbed young men. It closed in 1983 due to lack of funding. In 1986 it was re-opened as an Aboriginal college, providing education for the Indigenous community. However, as in all of Australia, there was a very high turnover rate of students, very few of whom stayed to age 14. A good attendance on any one day might be 30 young people.

The Foundation was started by Gerard Neesham in 1999, and he remains the managing director. He had worked as a professional football coach of top-level ARF teams, including the Fremantle Dockers, for 12 years. He also had 3 years' experience as a teacher at the Clontarf School, working with pupils with severe behavioural problems. In 1999 he was working for the media as a commentator on football games.

The Indigenous population in Australia has severe social problems (Steering Committee for the Review of Commonwealth/State Service Provision, 2005). Although they are 2 per cent of the population, they represent 50 per cent of those in juvenile jail. Indigenous people are 11 times more likely than other Australians to be imprisoned. After adjusting for age differences between populations, both Indigenous women and men experienced more than double the victimisation rates of other women and men in 2002. For juveniles this figure was 20 times. Twenty per cent are unemployed, but a large proportion are on welfare-related employment schemes. The Indigenous population labour force participation rate is just over 75 per cent of that for non-indigenous people in 2002. The life expectancy of Indigenous people is estimated to be around 17 years lower than that for the total Australian population. Suicide rates are very high – between 12 and 36 per 100,000 people. Indigenous students are half as likely to continue education to year 12 as non-Indigenous.

While there have been improvements in some of these indicators between 1994 and 2002 – for example, in retention rates at school to year 12 – in general the Indigenous population suffer multiple and inter-related disadvantages.

The programme

The Clontarf Foundation provides high-quality coaching in ARF for Indigenous men aged 13–18. This includes physical conditioning and health education. This happens before and after the normal school day and at weekends. It also runs camps. In order to remain in the Academy, members must attend school regularly, apply themselves to the study of appropriate courses, and 'embrace the academy's requirements for behaviour and self-discipline'. The Academy runs a football team that competes locally. The first academy was set up next to the Clontarf School, to which it is linked. This has set the model of academies being linked to, but separate from, colleges.

ARF is very popular with the Indigenous population as 10 per cent of Australian Football League (AFL) players come from this group. It is also very popular with Australians as a whole. Thus it is probably the best activity to provide a bridge between cultures of the Indigenous population and other Australians, which otherwise have very little in common.

Indigenous boys are recruited to the programme. The pilot year had 25. Attendance was good, and all wanted to return for a second year. At the end of the first year an overnight induction camp was run for the following year and 91 boys attended. This demonstrates the popularity of the programme. Boys came from as far as 1,000 km away. This has to be placed in the context of the distribution of the Indigenous population. The vast majority of Australians live in the urban areas, but for Indigenous people the Review of Commonwealth/State Service Provision reported that 23 per cent lived in outer regional areas, 9 per cent in remote areas, and 18 per cent in very remote areas. So the Indigenous population is far more widely dispersed, and far more likely to live away from a town.

The Academy coaches aim to provide a non-judgemental, non-authoritative figure the boys can relate to. Many of the coaches are ex-AFL high-profile players, which again helps them gain the boys' respect. However, Gerard Neesham reported that it is most important to employ coaches for their motivation. They must want to 'make a difference – not a dollar'.

The aim is to use football as a medium to improve the health, employment potential, education and life skills of the participants. Boys are shown a new set of opportunities. Staying at school to the normal leaving age of 17 is very unusual in the Indigenous community, but doing so provides a great sense of achievement for the Clontarf boys.

The Clontarf Foundation is able to help boys find jobs because of its links with a wide range of employers. Australian employers have a target proportion of Indigenous employees, which they find very hard to fill as so few graduate from school. This makes it easy to find work for the Clontarf graduates. The Clontarf Academy staff continue to support boys if there are any difficulties at work, and employers can contact them directly. The Clontarf Foundation also provides reasonably priced residential accommodation in Perth – essential for an Indigenous boy who has come from the country and wants to work in the city. Originally there was only accommodation for 18, but this has been increased to 50. Thus the Clontarf Foundation might remain supporting a student up to age 23/24, while they establish themselves as an independent member of the community. Thus, by providing a supported path into employment it is hoped to break the generational cycle of poverty and disadvantage, and to help Indigenous people find a place in Western society, which is so alien to their culture.

Gerard Neesham is still based on the Clontarf site (in 2005). He knows, and takes a personal interest in, all the boys there. Clearly his leadership skills, experience of working with disadvantaged young people and motivation have had a positive impact on the success of the Foundation. However, the two academies set up in other locations have so far had similar success, judged on retention rates of students. So the formula for success is transferable to other sites.

The academy was initially privately funded. In 2005 its funding was a third each from state government, national government and private support. In 2004 the total operating costs over the three sites was Aus $1.17m, which equated to Aus $5,500 per participant.

Evaluation and results

In this programme all the evaluation reported below was carried out internally and used in its annual report. Methods included the use of internal records, a comparison with national statistics and letters of support.

Monitoring data

The nature of the programme means that it is relatively easy to collect data on school retention rates, graduation and employment rates of participants. In 2005 there were 81 students enrolled at the Clontarf Academy, 53 at Goldfields and 80 at Mid West.

Across the three academies the attendance rate for students is 80 per cent or above, with the exception of years 10 and 11 at Mid West, where it is 69 per cent and 73 per cent. The target is 80 per cent. All the academies achieve at least the state average for Indigenous male students but generally exceed the WA average by up to 17 per cent.

Retention rates between school years is calculated on all students who re-enrol, re-enrol at another school, or go on to further study or to the workplace. Table 10.1 shows the retention rates at Clontarf and Goldfields academies for different school years between 2003 and 2004. These can be compared to the national average. The differences between retention rates for the Indigenous and non-Indigenous populations (as reported in the Steering Committee for the Review of Commonwealth/State Service Provision Report, 2005) become progressively greater between years 9–10 and 11–12.

The comparisons with the national figures are generally favourable, although it is not known if the national data is calculated in the same way. For example, it is not known if the national figures are able to include students who go on to further study or to the workplace. If they do not, the Clontarf rates would be

Table 10.1 School retention rates

Retention rates (%)	Clontarf Academy	Goldfields Academy	National average (indigenous)	National average (non-indigenous)
Yr 9–Yr 10		87	84	98
Yr 10–Yr 11	90	52	60	90
Yr 11–Yr 12	88		40	77

expected to be higher. In addition, the academy figures are relatively small, and a few students will make a significant difference to the percentages.

Of the 20 school leavers in 2002 and 18 in 2003, 75 per cent and 83 per cent respectively gained employment – well above the average for the Indigenous population. The national labour force participation rate for Indigenous people aged 18–64, was 64 per cent in 2002, although it is not clear what proportion of this 'participation' was accounted for by those on welfare-related employment schemes. In 2003, in WA, only 224 Indigenous students graduated from year 12. In the same year, 12 graduated from Clontarf. Assuming that half of the graduates in WA were male, at least 10 per cent of the graduating boys in WA were accounted for by students at Clontarf.

Letters of support

The Foundation's annual report in 2005 also includes a sample of six letters of support received from parents, community development officers, police officers, education officers and principals of two schools. These give qualitative evidence of the Foundation's work, especially the behavioural outcomes which the monitoring data does not measure. They also act as testimonies from significant community figures. For example, the Acting Superintendent of the Goldfields – Esperance District of the Western Australian Police Service wrote:

> Since the inception of the Academy in 2002, not only has there been a significant reduction in crime within the Kalgoorlie Boulder area, but incidents of antisocial behaviour involving youth has declined. The partnerships between the Academy, police officers and football team members have been instrumental in building positive relationships and a good rapport with all involved. The positive effect the Academy has had on the youth participating is nothing short of outstanding and the families associated with these youth have also assisted and form a part of this wonderful programme.

How and why the programme worked

Given that the evaluation reported above was all internally conducted, the impressions on how and why the programme worked are derived from my own visit and interviews with staff.

Probably the most important factor contributing to the success of the programme is its ability to gain the engagement and continued participation of the Indigenous young males, and crucial to this is the role of ARF in their culture. The Australian Government report (Steering Committee for the Review of Commonwealth/State Service Provision, 2005: 7) recommended that 'a greater recognition of Indigenous culture can be an important element in giving students the skills and knowledge they need to "walk in two worlds"'. Football provides the unique common denominator between the 'two worlds', with 10 per cent of AFL players being from the Indigenous population. At the same time,

AFL is Australia's most popular spectator sport (Stewart *et al.*, 2004). In 2002–3, the AFL Grand Final was the second most watched sporting event on TV (the first was the Rugby Union World Cup Final, in which Australia was playing).

This means that Gerard Neesham, and the coaches at the academies, already have a high status among young people in the Indigenous communities because of their association with the game at a high level – so there is already a strong basis for a relationship of mutual respect. Although not a primary objective of the academies, the relative success of Indigenous players in the game means that good-quality coaching is seen as a great opportunity to make a professional career in football. Success playing in the game may lead to increased self-esteem, and this is a general objective of the programme in helping young Indigenous people gain the confidence to take a full part in Australian society.

The importance of the motivation of the coaches is recognised by Gerard Neesham in the importance of employing people who want to make a difference, rather than achieve high earnings. The mentor relationship between students and coaches is probably important, and in a visit to the school it was clear that Neesham had a strong relationship of mutual respect with individual students.

The ability to match students to employment opportunities and liaise between students and employers is probably very important in helping students become established in the workforce. The long-term support of coaches as mentors is combined with the practical support of providing accommodation.

As founder of the project, Gerard Neesham had a particular combination of educational and coaching skills, credibility from his role as coach of a top AFL team, and a personal determination to make it work. One could argue that this might give an advantage to the Clontarf Academy, where he is based, over the other two. It is too early to make any judgement on this but, even if this were the case, all the other success factors apply across all three academies.

Politically the Foundation is in a strong position. The problems of the Indigenous population are a continual item on the Australian political landscape, though priorities may vary between national and state governments. A programme that can show success will be highly regarded – Clontarf was recommended to the researcher by both officers of the West Australian State Office of Crime Prevention and staff from the Criminology Department at the University of Western Australia.

Conclusion on the programme and evaluation method

Unlike the previous programmes, where evaluation was by external organisations, all the evaluation data in this case was collected by the programme itself. Evaluation measures are practical and simple and are incorporated into an annual report. It is relatively easy to collect data on enrolment, attendance, graduation and retention rates, because this will be collected automatically by the schools associated with the academies. Data is compared to national averages, which act as a control group – in effect a reproduction of the classical experimental method. As in the use of reconviction rates in WYSC or Hafotty Wen, one could argue that it is possible that those members of the Indigenous community who volunteer to attend the academy are not typical, because the same motivations that prompted them to volunteer might also lead to their superior school performance. However, similar to WYSC, only a small proportion of Indigenous young people have the opportunity to attend the programme – and one can assume that many of those in other parts of Australia would have joined the programme had it been available.

It might also be possible to include records of specific academic achievements. Records of employment must depend on the ability to follow up students, though this is built into the programme. The letters of support are a valuable complement to the other data because they provide testimonies from respected community figures of the outcomes that are harder to measure.

The programme does not have a specific goal of reducing crime and, as its annual report notes, key areas, such as behaviour, cannot readily be measured. However, given the multiple indicators of disadvantage among the Indigenous population, and Clontarf's mission of equipping young Aboriginal men to participate meaningfully in society, it is reasonable to assume a causal relationship between improved educational performance, establishment in employment and a reduced propensity for criminal activity. The managing director explicitly recognised the need to break the generational cycle of poverty and disadvantage.

The participants are at a high level of risk, given the national statistics on their relative disadvantage, although a record of offending is not a criteria for entering the programme – merely a willingness and commitment to take part. The programme is concerned to achieve general pro-social development of the participants, but the more tangible outcomes are in educational achievement and employment.

Further information on the Clontarf academy is available on its website: http://www.clontarffootball.com.

11 Positive Futures/Sportaction

Summary

Positive Futures was the name of a national initiative in the UK, which usually represented a pot of funding grafted on to an existing programme. So, at a local level the programmes took different forms. This chapter first describes the national initiative, and then a detailed case study of one local programme, Sportaction (pseudonyms are used throughout this case study). In this study it was not possible to measure outcomes, as only a very small number of clients took part in the programme for any significant period – a finding in itself. So a case study approach was used to find out how and why the programme had any impact on these few clients – which were at the relatively high risk end of the spectrum, but, as they were referred from Youth Inclusion Programmes, were younger than clients in the previous case studies. The main conclusion was that where the programme had an impact it was through the process of long-term personal development, though there was no clear evidence of identification with pro-social values, and an increase in self-esteem was not necessarily helpful. The quality of the relationship between client and sports leader was crucial. Sport worked well as a medium for the clients with which the programme had success, though it may have put off others. Even with the clients the programme worked most with, it could not deal with the permutation of factors contributing to offending and, because all the clients were on a final warning before custody, maintaining prolonged contact was precarious.

Introduction to the programme at the national level

Positive Futures was a partnership between Sport England, the Football Foundation, the Home Office Drugs Unit and the Youth Justice Board, launched in 2000. It funded at least 24 programmes across England with the aim of using sport to reduce anti-social behaviour, crime and drug use among 10–16-year-olds within local neighbourhoods. These tended to be additions to the work of existing organisations, as was the case in Sportaction, the example examined in detail in this chapter. From 2006 to 2008, the management of Positive Futures has been outsourced through competitive tendering to Crime Concern, a national charity.

In practice the large majority of the programmes were extensions of existing ones, as in the Sportaction case study: an existing organisation or partnership had already been doing work that met the Positive Futures objectives, and was awarded additional funding through Positive Futures. From the point of view of Sportaction, Positive Futures was another pot of money to bid for. The key criterion for awarding funds appeared to be that the organisation would do a credible job.

National evaluation and results

In September 2001, Sport England commissioned Leisure Futures (a commercial consultancy) to carry out a review of impact and good practice on both its Active Communities and Positive Futures projects (Sport England, 2002a; 2002b). The time-scale and resources allocated to the research meant that it was limited to 12 site interviews and 12 projects researched by phone calls. It was aimed to telephone a lead officer from each project and three other people who were involved, including partner organisations. Thus 24 projects were covered in total. This included Sportaction, which was researched by telephone interview.

The research was commissioned to give a quick overview so necessarily lacked detail on any one project. For example, the Sportaction programme did not provide figures of those involved – and the evidence in Table 11.1 (see page 123) shows that they had little success recruiting participants. In the Leisure Futures report, where there was evidence of crime reduction this was derived from the respondents' own reports, but in most cases the data was also provided to the research team. In ten programmes this showed reductions in local crime rates (Sport England, 2002a: 12), by comparing periods before the projects with periods when they were running. All but one of the projects where data was provided showed a decrease in crime. The report does not indicate if in the other 14 projects, where data indicating changes in crime were not reported, there was no data available, or it was available and showed either an increase in crime or no change. Where the data is used it does not appear to have been collected sepcifically for the project – it records general youth crime levels in an area – so it is reasonable to assume that it was available, or could have been accessed, in the areas where it was not reported. Thus, it is possible that local crime data might have indicated a decrease associated with the time the project was running in the 10 cases where this was reported, and an increase in the other 14 where it was not. It is more likely that this data was just not collected by the programmes. Several projects commented on the difficulties of attributing changes in local crime data to specific projects because several projects might be working in the same area. For example, the Positive Futures programme may be part of a Youth Inclusion Project. The difficulties of using local area crime statistics to do this are reviewed in detail in the Splash case study in Chapter Thirteen.

The one project that examined individual offending rates (Salford) was able to do this for only the eight out of 48 participants who had an offending history, and of these three had not offended since starting the programme, three others had committed minor offences, and the other two remained 'persistent offenders'. The projects noted the problems of overcoming 'multiple risk factors', but on this evidence concluded that Positive Futures had a 'positive impact on around 75 per cent of offenders, but is less effective for those with more deep-seated problems' (Sport England, 2002a: 13).

The overall results were published by Sport England (2002c) in a publicity report released on 11 July 2002. Sport England stated that there was 'a reduction of up to as much as 77 per cent in recorded crime in every area where Positive Futures are happening'. It is difficult to see how this conclusion was reached because crime data was provided for only ten of the 24 areas, so only in those areas was it possible to make a statement about crime. In only one of these areas did an apparent reduction equate to 77 per cent.

The general conclusions of the report need to be read bearing in mind the interests of the stakeholders: Leisure Futures would probably not want to produce results too critical of Sport England who were paying for the report; Sport England would want to publish favourable results; and the 24 projects interviewed would all want to give a favourable impression of their work to ensure continued funding. For example, the general conclusion that 'there is strong evidence to show that Positive Futures is having a real impact in terms of increasing regular participation in sport amongst participants to the programme and that a number of these are developing their sports skills' (Sport England, 2002a: 22) gives a very favourable impression. However, the conclusions noted that the skills and enthusiasm of project leaders were crucial. Also that longer-term funding is required to attract and retain the right calibre of staff and give them time to build up relationships of trust with young people.

In relation to outcomes, the report states that

> ... given the number of other influences and interventions at play in any area, it should also be recognised that it would be both unrealistic and inappropriate to try and isolate the Positive Futures Project as the 'cause' of a social change relating to the Positive Futures project objectives.
>
> (Sport England, 2002a: 22)

It then goes on to state that the qualitative evidence is strong.

It is interesting that, despite the bold headline figures of the Sport England press release – 'Sport is getting youngsters away from crime and helping fight drug abuse, new findings reveal' – the report cautions against making claims for the effectiveness of Positive Futures in terms of increasing sports participation, reducing crime and reducing drug use. The main qualitative finding is the importance of the skills and enthusiasm of the project staff. Overall it is unreasonable to criticise the Sport England evaluation as superficial, as to achieve much else one would have needed to have devoted a considerable amount of resources to any one programme, and as the programmes were all different it would have been difficult to apply a common evaluation approach. However, its conclusions from the evidence are optimistic. This illustrates the interaction between a political agenda and the way 'evidence' is interpreted – discussed in an earlier chapter.

A local programme – Sportaction

Description of the programme

Sportaction was instigated by the Chief Constable of Southtownshire Constabulary and a group of local businessmen in 1993. (Psudonyms are used in this case study.) In October 1994 it became a registered charity with four trustees. The trust mission statement described Sportaction as 'working to create, within the communities of Southtownshire, sustainable sport and recreational initiatives that, develop citizenship, promote a healthy drug free lifestyle and provide diversion from crime; by giving young people a sporting chance'.

In 2000 the programme had four staff: two seconded from the police; another employed by the Trust (though underwritten by the constabulary); and the fourth was funded through a 'modern apprenticeship' (a government employment programme) and worked as a sports leader. As the most experienced sports leader, Jimmy took this role in the Positive Futures programme, which worked with Sportaction's most difficult clients. Other staff were funded by various grants and schemes. These included 'New Deal' and a Lottery grant. There was a pool of other sports leaders, some voluntary and some paid on a sessional basis. Most of the coaches involved had been trained through the project, so participants could progress to become voluntary or paid sports leaders.

The core funding and support to establish and run the project initially came from the police. Later, for three years from January 2000, the major funder was the National Lotteries Charities Board, under their Community Involvement Poverty and Disadvantage Programme. Other income came from user organisations and grants, which enabled Sportaction to diversify its work. For example, a golf training programme was funded by a local businessman.

This changing permutation of funding is typical of projects and has several limitations (discussed generally in Chapter Fifteen) – it is difficult to plan beyond the period of the immediate funding, a significant amount of time is spent applying for funding rather than delivering the service, and, as noted in the national evaluation of Positive Futures, it is hard to attract and retain good staff. Different funding sources mean that the project will be pulled in different directions depending on the priorities of the funders. There is less incentive to invest in long-term evaluation, and a priority is responding to the short-term performance indicators of this year's funder.

Sportaction ran a range of programmes that provided synergy with the Positive Futures scheme. Some were just directed at young people at risk, and some at young people who had been excluded from mainstream education. These included:

- Summer 'road shows' in priority areas, defined by high levels of crime and deprivation, which offered a taster of activities for three days.

- Football coaching schemes.
- Multi-sport schemes offered every Saturday in three locations.
- A scheme to provide golf training to young people.
- Work for special educational needs groups whose members had been excluded from mainstream education, through 'Step Forward', a charitable trust set up to offer alternative programmes for these young people. Sportaction contributed the sporting element of these programmes, providing about 2 hours of activities per week. Most work was with 15–16-year-olds, but some were younger.
- Work with young people referred directly from the local authority special education unit. From this they might go on to Step Forward, or directly back to mainstream schooling.
- Sports leadership training, including Football Association Junior Managerial Awards, Community Sports Leadership Awards and Basketball Awards.

Sport England was looking for credible partners for its Sporting Futures funds and Sportaction met this criterion. Sportaction started work with Positive Futures clients in October 2000. (From now on the Positive Futures work is referred to as Sportaction.) Clients were referred from a Youth Inclusion Programme (YIP) set up to work with the fifty highest-risk young offenders in the SRB5 area of Southtown. Over the period (October 2000 to July 2001), 21 clients were referred. The referral process from the YIP involved little contact with and knowledge of the client. In some cases the YIP did not know the client's correct address and in several the client did not want to participate in the programme once Sportaction had contacted them, so did not start. From the perspective of Sportaction it appeared that the YIP could meet its performance targets just by referring clients to another organisation.

Attendance was voluntary. The programme took the form of one-to-one sessions with the full-time sports leader, Jimmy, and was completely flexible, depending on the client and how Jimmy felt that client could progress. The sessions would ideally progress from establishing interest, commitment and rapport with the client to helping them progress through voluntary leadership and obtaining sports qualifications. The range of programmes offered by the main Sportaction programme meant that it was relatively easy to introduce Positive Futures clients into voluntary leadership, and potentially paid work as sports leaders.

Local evaluation

A case study approach at the levels of both the programme and individual participants used methods designed to test the hypotheses arising from the theoretical model in Chapter Three. These included:

- programme records
- interviews with staff
- interviews with participants.

Methods

The research used a case study approach to ask how and why the programme had an impact (Yin, 2002). It was designed to test specific hypotheses about how and why the programme 'worked', using the model of value-directed personal growth developed in Chapter Three. This was at the level of the programme and individual participants. So, in this sense it started from theory, in the same way that scientific realism (Chapter Four) would, and the hypotheses provided an articulation between the theory and the methods.

To be more specific, the hypotheses arising from the model in Chapter Three were:

- The programme contributes to the personal development of young people, guided by values. This contributes to a reduction in offending.
- This process involves a growth in self-esteem, locus of control, cognitive skills and the establishment of a personal value system that makes the individual less disposed towards crime. These will contribute to personal growth such that the individual will be able to take a more proactive role in their own further development.

Key contributory 'success' factors to this process are:

- An attractive activity to get participants initially involved.
- The ability to adapt a programme to individual participants' needs.
- The use of rewards of achievement, which will enhance self-esteem.
- Sensitivity of staff in matching a progression of activities to participants' needs and development.
- A good relationship between participants and activity leaders; leaders taking a mentoring role, such as they become 'significant others'.
- The ability to offer long-term follow-up and viable exit routes where the participant can become involved in activity and further opportunities for development independent of the original programme.
- Sharing activity with pro-social peers.
- A clear set of values associated with the activity leaders and the ethos of the programme. These values are inconsistent with offending.
- Sport is a catalyst to this process.

However, unlike in a scientific realist approach, it was not possible to measure outcomes to construct context-mechanism-outcome configurations.

The difficulties of gaining access to participant records of offending through the Youth Offending Team (YOT), and the small numbers involved, meant that it was not practical to try to conduct the type of reconviction analysis as in the WYSC and Hafotty Wen case studies to quantify the impact of the programme. It was also not possible to measure other quantifiable outcomes, such as changes in self-esteem, locus of control, cognitive skills and the establishment of a personal value system. However, detailed case studies of clients were able to give a qualitative impression of these outcomes – as will be illustrated below.

Methods included the use of programme records to identify the two participants with whom the programme had done the most work. These 'critical cases' were then studied through records of sessions kept by Jimmy and interviews with the participants and Jimmy. These were supplemented with interviews with other programme staff.

Jimmy was briefed to keep records of his sessions with individual clients, and discussions with the researcher about the nature of his work probably sensitised him to think more carefully about this and become more observant of clients' development of personal skills, their attitudes and willingness to take responsibility. In this way, to some extent, through influencing the data collection the researcher was influencing the process being researched. Jimmy provided 29 and 27 accounts of individual meetings with the two case study clients, respectively.

Detailed interviews were conducted with these two clients, Adam and Marvin, and in one the client's mother also contributed. Interviews with staff and clients took a 'realist' approach in that the researcher came to the interview with a particular theoretical framework, which was reflected in the questions (Pawson and Tilley, 1997: 166). In this the object of the interview was to explore and test the theoretical views of the interviewer through presenting them for scrutiny by the interviewee. This takes account of the interaction between interviewer and interviewee, and is more realistic than the assumption that the interviewer has no influence on what the interviewee says, and is a mere neutral recorder. However, this approach was more practical with the programme staff than with the case study participants, who were less confident of their own views, and were less willing to challenge those of the researcher.

Several interviews, concerned with research into the general Sportaction programme, were conducted with Sportaction staff. Only a part of these was specifically about the Positive Futures programme, but they contributed to general conclusions about the operation of the programme. The evaluation of this programme was part of an academic study and was not externally funded.

Results

Programme records

Table 11.1, compiled from programme records, shows the very variable success of the programme in making contact with clients and then maintaining it. It allowed the identification of cases 3 (Marvin) and 16 (Adam) for intensive study as the clients who had participated the most. The time spent with these two clients was far greater than that spent with all the other clients combined. If the programme was to have an impact on anybody, it would be on them. Conversely, if it had made little impact on them, it was not likely to have done so for any of the other clients.

Table 11.1 Records of Sportaction work with clients – October 2000 to July 2001

Case	Hours completed	Achievements of client	Comments
1	17	Attended youth games	Now mentored by Enthusiasm[a]
2	8		Moved out of area
3	85	Basketball level 1, CSLA[b], assisted with coaching	Marvin
4	3		*Reason for leaving not known*
5	6		Chose to leave programme
6	11	Canoeing	Moved out of area
7	8		Chose to leave/refer to Enthusiasm
8	7		Mother sees programme as a treat, so has not continued
9	42	CSLA, basketball level 1, volunteer coaching	Sent to detention centre
10	14		Now mentored by Enthusiasm
11	26		Now mentored by Enthusiasm
12	0		Moved out of area
13	2		*Reason for leaving not known*
14	0		*Reason for not starting not known*
15	0		*Reason for not starting not known*
16	121	CSLA, Junior Team Manager (JTM), Basketball level 1, voluntary coaching	Adam
17	0		No response to correspondence
18	0		*Reason for not starting not known*
19	0		Shows no interest
20	0		Shows no interest
21	0		Wrong address given

Source: Sportaction

a Enthusiasm were an alternative organisation clients could be referred to.
b CSLA, Community Sports Leader Award.

Case studies

Adam

Adam was 16 when he started working with Positive Futures in January 2001, and had not attended school since his expulsion in September 2000. He lived at home with his mother; and a younger sister who had also been referred to Positive Futures. His father had been in prison for some years. His mother was very supportive of his involvement with Positive Futures.

Between January and July Adam had attended 121 hours with Positive Futures, the most for any one client. After a few sessions it was clear he had natural sports leadership ability. He was confident, articulate and was able to build a quick rapport with groups he worked with. By March he was identified as a potential future mentor to work with Sportaction and from April he was helping coach regularly at its Saturday morning sports sessions. He was keen to take sports qualifications and registered for a Football Association (FA) Junior

Manager's Award and a level one basketball coaching award a month after he started with Positive Futures. He passed both of these easily, as well as a first aid certificate. He was identified as the best student on the basketball course. He also took a Community Sports Leader Award (CSLA), did not complete it at the first attempt but returned to finish it with Jimmy. In general his attendance record on Positive Futures was very good.

Adam had no educational qualifications, although he had boxed at a local gym since the age of 10. He had trophies from this and the only paper qualification he had was his licence to box. He had also taken part in football, basketball, tae kwon do and karate. Before taking part in Sportaction he had wanted to be a professional boxer. From the first session with Sportaction he expressed a desire to become a sports coach.

Throughout his involvement in Sportaction Jimmy noted that Adam had difficulty controlling his temper and could easily be 'wound up'. He had a record of violent offending since he was aged 13/14 and was arrested for assault in April 2001 while on the Sportaction programme. At the time he was interviewed, in August, he was waiting to appear in court for an assault on a police officer. This assault occurred when the officer came to Adam's house to arrest him for a crime which evidence suggests (in Jimmy's view) he is not likely to have committed. Subsequently Adam was sent to a detention centre for 6 months, but was due for discharge in December 2001 if his behaviour was satisfactory.

This illustrates one of the difficulties of the Sportaction programme. As clients are on their last warning, a lot of work may be invested in them but they only need to be convicted of one offence and they will be sent to detention. Sportaction was keen to resume work with Adam on his release. Although Adam showed great potential as a sports leader, and would have been offered some paid work with Sportaction over the summer of 2001, they were not able to employ him because of his arrest for assault on a police officer. This was a particularly difficult situation for Sportaction, which was managed by seconded police officers.

Analysis in relation to the research hypotheses

Adam's long-term interest in sport made the Sportaction programme immediately attractive to him. The one-to-one counselling and the other range of Sportaction sports sessions enabled the work with Adam to be adapted to fit his needs. His initial action plan was adapted as he progressed rapidly and as soon as his natural skills at sports leadership became apparent he was given leadership responsibility. This occurred as early as the fifth time he attended, and he was given responsibility for a warm-up session with younger children. The progression through coaching courses and leadership experience illustrates Jimmy's skills in matching the progression of activities to Adam's needs and the ability to do this through Sportaction.

Adam already had high self-esteem and illustrated Emler's (2001) point that this does not necessarily lead to reduced offending. He was very confident. By March Jimmy reported that, 'in the future I hope he ... will be able to attend as a mentor'. But, in Jimmy's view, his self-esteem combined with his temper had led him to car theft and violent assaults at the ages of 13 and 14. It appeared his reputation as a boxer had led him into situations where he was either expected to defend friends or might be goaded into fighting. Jimmy reported several occasions when he was concerned about Adam's temper and had to counsel him about it. So the combination of boxing skills, high self-esteem and volatile emotions had contributed to Adam's offending.

However, although Adam did not appear to gain significant self-esteem from his achievements on the programme, which were considerable in terms of gaining sporting qualifications, he had gained the recognition and respect of the Sportaction workers. This mattered to him, and especially the fact that it could lead to paid employment with Sportaction. Adam viewed Jimmy as a mentor: 'I've got a better relationship with Jimmy (than with my YOT Officer) because I know him better.'

The mentor relationship extended to Adam aspiring to do Jimmy's job: 'My goal is to do what Jimmy is doing in the future.' The mentor relationship had developed sufficiently by late March that Jimmy could talk to Adam about controlling his temper, and later about the implications of being arrested.

Sportaction was in an excellent position to offer Adam long-term follow-up through a progression of voluntary and then paid sports leadership opportunities. Adam also felt he could obtain similar work in other organisations.

Jimmy thought that negative peer influence had led to a lot of Adam's offending. Recognising this, Jimmy had attempted to refer one of Adam's peers to the programme but was unable to do so as he lived outside the relevant area. This is supported by Adam's own account of how the programme had prevented him offending:

> It did keep me out of trouble because I was enjoying it and all my time was on that. I wasn't on the streets with bad influences and messing about. ... When you are bored and you are just sitting about that can lead to trouble because you've got nothing to do and then when you are out on the streets and there is a group and you've got nothing to do, you might get yourself into mischief. But if you've got something to do then you are not really thinking about going out and messing about and doing this, that and the other, and you've got a goal. You want to be doing something, so you can't really be messing about.

Thus sharing activity with pro-social peers, or at least being away from anti-social ones, was an important part of diverting Adam from offending. However, although he attended at least 28 sessions over less than 6 months, some of these taking all day, there were still the opportunities to offend at other times.

Another positive influence of Sportaction might have been that it promoted pro-social values. There is evidence that Jimmy attempted to counsel Adam on controlling his temper. This shows that, although Jimmy was relatively young and not trained in dealing with offenders, the understanding he gained of Adam though the long-term contact and position of trust led him to a deeper understanding of the factors leading to Adam's offending. Adam began to identify with Jimmy to the extent that he aspired to do his type of work and he was prepared to ask Jimmy about sensitive issues, such as the impact of his offences. This might represent an identification with the pro-social values of Sportaction, or it might just represent a concern with the implications of how Sportaction viewed his offending for his employment prospects.

Adam was concerned that his offence in April might have led to him being dropped from the programme but this might just have been because he enjoyed doing it and it would have led to paid work.

> What I really need to do is start getting some income. I need some work and coaching was going to be my thing. I was going to start getting paid this 6 weeks' holiday, then everything mashed up and that isn't good at all. So now I'm sitting here watching my television all day.

Overall Adam was upset that it had turned out like this and regretted being in trouble. Again, talking with reference to not being able to obtain work, he reported:

> I'm not bad and I don't go out there looking for trouble. So I'm just a name and a number and, if I am in trouble, I am in trouble and that's the way they look at it. I don't even, like, want to be doing this, I'm not really a trouble kind of person, and it all mashed up. I don't know why it mashed up, but it did.

His mother supported this:

> I think that if he hadn't got in trouble this time by now he would have been settled and quite happy with what he had got before him, because he'd been offered two days' work a week.

As Jimmy reported:

> I think employing him would have done him the world of good. He would have got a bit of extra cash, recognition for what he had achieved, more recognition off other bodies, such as the city council, as his name would have gone into a database. And he would have been able to, if police checks had let him, be employed throughout.

Conclusions

Sportaction was immediately attractive to Adam because he had always been interested in sport, and he quickly saw it could lead to qualifications and possibly employment doing something he enjoyed. The intense one-to-one counselling and Jimmy's skills enabled a mentor relationship to be established, in the course of which Jimmy could understand better the problems that had led to Adam's offending and try to address them through the sports counselling (although Jimmy had no formal training in this). Sportaction provided Adam with a diversion from offending opportunities and anti-social peers.

It contributed to his personal development to the extent that he developed skills through the sports coaching courses he attended. However, there was no need to develop his self-esteem and the counselling could have only a limited effect on his self-control. Thus it could not keep him from his particular pattern of re-offending, involving impulsive losses of self-control. For Adam one of the major potential benefits of the programme might have been paid employment, doing something he enjoyed and using the skills he had. Jimmy regarded Adam as a natural sports leader and this was proven by his success in quickly leading sessions with children only slightly younger than himself. But, paradoxically, his assault on a policeman prevented Sportaction offering him this opportunity in the future. Sportaction might have had a stronger effect on reducing his offending if he had been involved in paid sports leadership earlier and understood that this position was conditional on not re-offending.

Marvin

Marvin was 15 when he started working with Sportaction in October 2000, as one of its first clients. Jimmy reported that Marvin had originally lived in another town but had been thrown out by his parents after being involved in a robbery. He had come to live with relatives in Southtown, but his relationship with them had been strained by his behaviour. He had left them and been living with friends. He had not attended school since living in Southtown. He was due to attend the Step Forward programme for young people excluded from school, but he did not. In late March he had moved into a flat provided by the National Association for the Care and Resettlement of Offenders (NACRO). This address allowed him to claim benefit from April, though most of the time he lived at a girlfriend's house nearby. The flat had nothing in it except minimal furniture, a cooker and a fridge. Since January 2001 he had been involved in a range of offences.

From October 2000 to July 2001 Marvin had attended 85 hours of activity with Sportaction. He passed a Community Sports Leader Award, a basketball level one coaching award and a Football Association Junior Manager Award. At the beginning of February he started on a Step Forward programme, which involved activities each weekday and attending Sportaction on Saturdays. However he attended only the Sportaction activities. From April he started helping as a voluntary leader at Saturday morning sessions run by Sportaction for younger children, with the intention of helping regularly. He did not maintain this and attended only two more sessions in this capacity up to the end of June. Marvin had been accepted on a full-time course in sports and leisure at the local college, due to start in September 2001. This 1-year course would require attendance for 14 hours per week. Marvin applied for this while with Sportaction.

Apart from his personal circumstances, the major difficulty identified by Sportaction staff was his aggressive, erratic and unpredictable behaviour in groups of peers. It meant that Marvin had to be introduced into different social situations with care, and also had to be warned about his behaviour on several occasions. His aggression toward Jimmy almost led to him being removed from the programme in June, and it meant that he needed careful supervision whenever he was in a coaching role. However, he appeared to enjoy coaching younger children and got on well with them. At the time of interview Marvin was due to attend court for a further offence. This was part of an incident in which several peers were involved.

Analysis in relation to the research hypotheses

Marvin had originally been interested in the programme because he had played basketball at school. The programme was adapted to meet his needs and progress through new experiences. Jimmy explained how he had to build up Marvin's skills and match them to the courses he attended.

Researcher: Was this progression planned?
Jimmy: It was planned to do courses as and when they came up, depending on how far he had got down the programme, on attitude and how he developed in himself, as obviously those courses take a lot of brain power and concentration. When I first met him he would not have been capable of doing a course like that. As they came about he was capable of doing them, so we paid for him and I took him, and off he went.
Researcher: Is it a concern that if he was not ready for it, it would not be the right thing for him to do?
Jimmy: That's right – have to be careful not to push him into something, or any of them. Put them on a course with lots of different people they have not met, especially someone like Marvin, they would have found it very difficult to communicate with those people on the same sporting level.
Researcher: Is that the more challenging part for Marvin, relating to the other people on the course?
Jimmy: That's right. No problems with his confidence in delivering what's on the course, but the people what run the course are very astute. The other people [on the course] can be very intimidating for someone like Marvin. [This was confirmed when Marvin was interviewed. He was shy and found it difficult to articulate his ideas.]
Researcher: So more a matter of checking he can cope with the social challenge rather than the intellectual?
Jimmy: Yes. He can tackle the intellectual bit; it's integrating with people that challenges him the most.

This shows that Jimmy had carefully matched the challenges he presented Marvin with to Marvin's developing ability. He felt the Community Sports Leader Award had built Marvin's communication skills before he had to coach specific sports at the Saturday sessions. By October 2001 Marvin had built up the confidence to challenge the Positive Futures staff at basketball. The sports leader reported: 'He wants to play us, not we want him to play, but I don't think he would have been like that it we had not given him so much support'.

Marvin also had to be guided carefully in the voluntary work. After the CSLA course he had to complete a certain number of voluntary hours, so these were scheduled to be completed at the Saturday morning sessions, also run by Sportaction. Jimmy described how, while other coaches were running the sessions:

> I just stood and supervised him solely. Did not take part in much coaching, just watched him and looked at his progression. Then spoke to him after, listened to his views, and the problems he found with it, such as difficult questions the children asked him and different coaching techniques he may not be aware of. So he did ask questions and I was there to answer him, whereas other people may not have had time.

However, Marvin's erratic behaviour made it difficult to give him greater responsibility for sessions.

Marvin's self-esteem was not at as high as Adam's and this was confirmed by his approach to the personal interview; however, it was boosted by his achievements on the programme. He was also far less articulate than Adam, with less developed communication skills. Marvin felt satisfaction from his achievements in passing the coaching awards, which he had been apprehensive about. He was proud of his score in the football manager course in June: 'I got 28 [out of 40] so it was all right.' He also appeared to gain from the relationship with the children he coached. Jimmy described how 'he assists with the coaching of young people there, does a good job, the kids love him'.

Through taking part in sports coaching awards other skills had been developed. Jimmy reported that:

> CSLA built up his communication and involved team building exercises, so he learnt to communicate effectively before he had to coach anything specific. CSLA builds confidence and ... organisation skills.

As with Adam, Jimmy had developed a mentoring role with Marvin. Marvin said Jimmy was one of the few people he could phone up about problems and Jimmy confirmed he had done this: 'Yes, he talks to me about personal things. Mostly it's just a bit of advice, how to deal with a situation.' Jimmy felt his relationship with Marvin was not as a role model, but more as a 'mentor, friendship type thing, someone he can go to for support'. This was in contrast to: 'A lot of the other agencies working with him, the people are sort of corporate-minded. It's all about statistics, and you need to be telling him what to do.'

This led to Jimmy taking a much broader role in supporting Marvin. The records of contact show that his major needs were recognised as housing, the ability to claim benefit, the need to eat, and the need to comply with the demands of the justice system. Records show how Jimmy had attended and arranged meetings to deal with all these aspects of Marvin's life. He had taken him to his Step Forward interview, his new accommodation in March, social services, the housing office and his solicitor. Jimmy confirmed specifically that Marvin would not have obtained the NACRO flat unless he had helped him do so. In comparing Adam and Marvin, Jimmy confirmed the work was completely different: 'With Marvin it was supporting his housing, college and money situation; with Adam it was his sports, which is what it was meant to do.'

This illustrates the difficult balance between establishing a mentor relationship and as a result of this recognising and helping deal with a lot of the client's basic needs; and the sports leader using sport to contribute to personal development. In addition, there is always the possibility that the client may just take advantage of the sports leader's willingness to act as a mentor, a 'taxi driver', and the sports leader's genuine concern for the client's welfare.

With Jimmy the mentor role extended to advising Marvin on his personal behaviour, which became challenging to the extent that Marvin hit Jimmy twice during a session in June. While there is evidence that guidance to Marvin on his personal behaviour might have had an immediate effect, for example in the way he reacted to other clients or the sports leader, there is no evidence of long-term impact. Even when interviewed 4 months later Jimmy reported that, 'he still gives me the odd dead leg now and again and gets a bit feisty, but that's something you will always have to watch with Marvin'. There is no evidence that a mentor role developed such that Jimmy was perceived as a role model by Marvin, in terms of his values.

As with Adam, Sportaction offered long-term viable exit routes of sports coaching, although this was not viable in Marvin's case until he learned to control his aggression. However, it had led to enrolment on a college course. The research was concluded before this started, so it is not known if Marvin actually attended.

Conclusions

Sportaction was attractive to Marvin because of his interest in sport. The one-to-one counselling enabled a mentoring relationship to be established and developed. As a result of this, the sports leader became more aware of Marvin's needs and that unless these were met the effect of the sports counselling would be insignificant and they would prevent his full participation. Thus Jimmy's work became diverted from providing sports opportunities, which he felt was his proper role, to one he was unqualified for but felt obliged to fill. However, this did make a difference: in particular, it led to stable accommodation and the ability of Marvin to claim benefits. It appears that Marvin gained in confidence and social skills as he progressed through the coaching awards: it is not so clear if it made him any less likely to be involved in crime. The most direct evidence came from Adam, who commented: 'I'm proud of Marvin because he was bad, bad, but now, like, he loves his coaching and he's doing something with his life, you see, and it's all right now.' Unlike Adam, Marvin was not explicit about the impact of the programme on himself, although he said that for people in general it might reduce crime because it 'reduces boredom – something to do, keeps them off the streets and things'. In the long run, if it leads to a college course and subsequent employment, it will contribute to financial security. The development of confidence and social skills may have helped in this, but we can't be sure they were decisive.

How and why the programme worked

The case study clients both acknowledged the simple mechanism of crime reduction through diversion from boredom. Both had nothing else to do as they were neither at school nor employed. However, the research was constructed around an examination of the hypotheses that the programme would contribute to long-term pro-social development involving a growth in self-esteem, locus of control, cognitive skills and the establishment of a personal value system, and would be facilitated by the success factors identified in Chapter Three. So, did it do this?

Adam already had self-esteem and relatively high social skills, such as good communication, and these increased through the sports coaching courses. He did not have control over his temper or a job. A close peer had led him into offending. The programme did not modify Adam's temperament. There is no evidence that Adam changed his value system as a result of participation in Sportaction. It did keep him away from his anti-social peer while he was on it. It would have led to part-time employment over the summer of 2001 had he not offended in the way he did; assaulting a police officer made it too difficult for Sportaction, run by the police, to be seen to offer him employment. In contrast, his earlier offence of assault in April had not led to him being removed from the programme.

Adam illustrates 'generative causality' in that the 'generative mechanism' that the programme released, 'by way of providing reasons and resources to change behaviour' (Pawson and Tilley, 1997: 79), was the new resources of the coaching qualifications and contacts with Sportaction, combined with the desire to obtain paid work as a sports coach. In this sense he illustrates a changed locus of control as he gained the ability to obtain paid employment doing what he enjoyed. But this was frustrated by his most recent offence.

Marvin had a more complex set of related problems that sports participation could not solve, and which themselves would prevent participation in the programme if they were not addressed. Housing and the ability to claim benefit were more important. Nevertheless, he did gain in self-confidence during the programme. There is evidence that Jimmy attempted to address values related to offending, or at least behaviour (emotional volatility and aggression) with Marvin, but there is limited evidence that this had an effect. Adam reported that Marvin was less 'bad' than he used to be.

For both Adam and Marvin, the experience of sports coaching introduced them to something they had an aptitude for and could get immediate feedback for doing well. Thus, to a degree, the programme contributed to personal growth directed by values in both case study clients. And this in turn could have led to the opening of further opportunities such as employment and college attendance. The programmes provided coaching qualifications and experience; associated skills; opportunities to progress in this area; and the resource of the sports leader as a mentor. For Adam it provided a goal, in that the sports leader became a role model in terms of employment ('my goal is to do what Jimmy is doing in the future') and being paid for what he enjoyed doing. With Marvin, the causality was not so clear; although it is very likely that the experience of Sportaction affected his motivation to apply for the college course and provided him with valuable coaching experience.

But Adam and Marvin continued to offend, illustrating the limited potential of the programme to divert high-risk participants from offending totally, although it probably reduced it.

What factors helped the programme succeed?

Both participants were attracted by sport. Both benefited from the great flexibility of the programme and the skills and ability of the sports leader to match their needs with a progression of activities. However, while this was in respect of the demands made by the particular courses and leadership opportunities, the progression was not so clear in terms of taking personal responsibility, for example, for their own behaviour or for attending sessions. As another Sportaction worker commented when asked what had been important in getting the clients to continue attending, 'I think the fact that Jimmy knocks on the door and puts them in the car has a lot to do with it'. But perhaps this willingness to give clients responsibility for a 15-minute warm-up sports session, but not for making their own way to it, shows the sports leader's skills in matching expectations with capabilities.

In this programme the links with all the rest of Sportaction's work was a major practical advantage in ensuring the availability of a structured route into sports leadership roles and long-term exit routes. The one-to-one counselling was important in adapting the programme for participants and also in developing the mentoring relationship, which was good. The coaching courses offered the satisfaction of achievement, which in the case of Marvin had contributed to self-esteem. In Adam's case self-esteem was already high and was a contributory factor in offending.

For Adam keeping away from anti-social peers was important. It is hard to see a clear set of values associated with the activity leaders and the ethos of the programme, which are inconsistent with offending, as a major factor. There is evidence of Jimmy confronting particular behaviour, but not of participants affiliating with the pro-social values of the programme or leaders in the way that Catalano and Hawkins (1996) understand a programme providing a 'protection factor'. Rather, Adam's affiliation was pragmatic rather than affective: he wanted a paid job out of it.

The role of sport

Sport was an effective medium in terms of providing an attractive activity for Marvin and Adam, who were willing to become involved in the programme. However, as the YIP had no knowledge of most of the people it referred, not having been able to meet them itself, a lack of sporting interest may account for some of the low take-up level. Of six people referred by the YIP on one particular day, three did not start, one could not be contacted as Sportaction was given the wrong address, and two were detained by the police before they could be contacted. Sport attracted Adam and Marvin because they were already interested in it, and they, luckily, had not been detained at the time.

Sport provided a medium for developing a mentor relationship (Jimmy described how he had gone three boxing rounds with Adam!). It provided the medium for a structured progression through nationally recognised coaching awards, which themselves involved the development of the package of social skills associated with programmes to reduce offending. It offered practical exit routes.

Farrall's (2002) research into the impact of probation indicates the importance of Sportaction's ability to offer employment or lead to it. For Farrall, legitimate employment 'will in turn help to foster the sorts of ties and social contacts which allow for the development of social capital' (Farrall, 2002: 226). For Adam, the possibility of employment was potentially a major impact of Sportaction. For Marvin, his projected college course could enhance his employment prospects.

General limitations of the programme

The extremely poor referral mechanism from the YIP (noted above) was a significant problem, leading to considerable time being spent just contacting prospective participants only to find that many were not interested.

The programme was not designed to deal with the multiple problems experienced by the clients, such as housing and employment, but the sports leader found himself being drawn into these as they had to be dealt with if the participants were to be able to continue on the programme. While it was valuable for the sports leader to act as a broker to help young people find their way around other agencies, this role was not clear at the outset of the project. The sports leader was relatively young (aged 21) and had not been formally trained to deal with this particularly difficult client group. A difficulty is knowing where to make allowances for clients' problems and where to urge them to comply with the requirements of the programme. The programme was good at adapting to the needs of the individual clients but, on the other hand, it had no structure and no defined end. It was not clear when work would end with these clients, and one could argue that they sucked up an enormous proportion of its resources.

The case study clients were critical examples, in the sense that they were those who had experienced Sportaction the most. If it did not have a positive impact on them, it would probably not have on others who experienced it less. It did have a positive impact on them, not to the extent that it prevented them re-offending, but clearly it probably had less impact on the six out of 21 clients who attended for fewer than 10 sessions (see Table 11.1, page 123) and none on the eight who attended none at all. If one was going to comment on the overall performance of the programme this indicates failure. However, given the conservative estimate of the average economic and financial cost of a youth crime in 1994 as £2,800 (Coopers and Lybrand, 1994), it is still possible that the work with Adam and Marvin could justify the whole project.

Conclusion on the programme and evaluation methods

Evaluation

The small number of participants in this programme would have made any analysis of offending data meaningless, even if the YOT had been prepared to provide it. One could criticise the conclusions from the data provided by the Salford project, reported in the national evaluation (Sport England, 2002a: 13) on this basis. Further, the understanding of these client's lives provided by the interviews showed that very many offences would have been unrecorded anyway, thus invalidating the analysis. Thus the evaluation could not have adopted a scientific realist approach (Chapter Four) as it was not possible to measure any regularity in a context/mechanism/regularity configuration (see Figure 4.3, page 38) – either in terms of reduced offending or intermediate outcomes. It had to restrict itself to a case study approach, asking questions about how and why the programme worked, when it did, starting from a theoretical model on which to base hypotheses. Of course, one could also have asked how and why it did not work – this would have required a considerable effort in tracking down and interviewing the participants whom the programme had worked with only briefly and had lost contact with, or never even managed to contact in the first place! Indications of reasons for failure were provided in the interviews with staff.

However, as in scientific realism, research started from theory – the model of value directed personal growth (Chapter Three). This focused the research methods and was similar to the Fairbridge evaluation starting from a 'theory of change'; apart from that the theory in this case came from the researcher's own synthesis of theory, rather than from that of programme staff. The national evaluation (Sport England, 2002a) shows that evaluation is determined by the resources available (Chapter Sixteen), and that the interpretation of the evidence you have – as in the 'nothing works'/'something works' debate, is also influenced by political factors (Chapter Five).

The programme

At this end of the risk spectrum the programme was working with clients with chaotic lives, multiple problems and for whom just one more offence could lead to custody. So one could argue that to work with 2 out of 21 participants for the prolonged period that they did constituted success. The route to this success approximates to the model of personal growth facilitated by success factors outlined in Chapter Three. However, the contrast between the two case study clients shows that it may be as valuable to constrain self-esteem as to boost it (Emler, 2001). And a route to legitimate employment may be as valuable as any other part of the programme. As in WYSC, Sportaction shows the value of linking the crime reduction project to an organisation offering a broader range of sports development activities, which in this case made it easy to feed the clients into opportunities for voluntary leadership and gaining sports leadership qualifications, and potentially some paid work. However, it also illustrates the choice between using a well-motivated leader with sports skills and the ability to develop a rapport with these difficult clients; and using a worker who may have a better knowledge of the support services that clients experiencing multiple 'risk factors' may need. I'd conclude that motivation and rapport are essential as, if one can't build a relationship with the client, no other work is possible. Again, as in WYSC, and to a point in Fairbridge, there is the difficulty of deciding when work with any one client will end, and thus allocating resources between existing clients.

12 Summit

Summary

The Summit programme worked with medium-risk clients, referred from the local Youth Offending Team (YOT). It was based in a local authority and sports development officers worked on a one-to-one basis with clients, offering them a range of sports opportunities. An aim was to move towards independent sports participation, on the assumption that this would act as a diversion from offending. Unlike WYSC or Sportaction, the programme had a defined end, which was necessary to manage the contract with the YOT. Evaluation took a case-study approach, using a triangulation of methods at both the programme level and that of individual clients. It shows how several methods of data collection could be built into the programme's own monitoring, but how it was still difficult to measure intermediate outcomes, and not possible to measure reduced offending, and relate this to a control group. The case studies of clients were very valuable in showing how and why the programme worked, but they were also labour intensive, and beyond the scope of an internal programme evaluation. The programme illustrates the value of synergy between different objectives within local authority work – in this case crime reduction, sports development and the reduction of social exclusion. Rather than representing a weakness due to a lack of programme integrity, this synergy is a strength to be built on.

Introduction to the programme

The Summit programme was delivered by the sports development section of Easttown local authority's (pseudonyms are used in this case study) recreation department. The project started in 1998 and the case study work reported here was conducted between 2000 and 2002. As in West Yorkshire Sports Counselling, it involved sporting activities taken part in on a one-to-one basis, with a sports leader.

From April 1998 to April 2000 clients were referred from the probation service. After April 2000 all clients were referred from the YOT, which contracted to buy 100 places in 2000/2001 on what was essentially the same programme. The YOT clients were aged 14–17, younger than those from probation.

The initial referral meeting involved the YOT client, the YOT officer and the sports leader, to ensure that all three were clear about what the programme would involve, and that expectations were realistic. Rather than a set number of sessions, the programme involved specified hours of contact time. This meant that, depending on the client's needs, time might be allocated in different blocks. For example, a 3-hour session might be appropriate for one particular activity and 1-hour for another. The initial plan, agreed at referral, meant that at any time in the programme the probation officer knew what the involvement of the client should be. After each meeting between client and counsellor, details were sent back to the probation officer. This meant that it was theoretically easier for the YOT officer to use the sports counselling experience as part of their overall supervision plan although this was not so relevant for YOT clients, who might not be in regular contact with their YOT officer. It also meant that if there were any problems, such as the client not turning up, the officer was immediately aware of this. Summit was not intended as a substitute for probation or YOT supervision, but was one option YOT officers could offer clients. Participation was voluntary and the officer might not see clients after they had been referred, though officers interviewed in the Easttown YOT followed up clients with some home visits.

A principle underlying YOT work is that most young people who commit crime are not serious offenders. Early intervention is intended to prevent a downward spiral of court appearances, criminalisation and further offending, with consequences both for the young person and the criminal justice system. A large proportion of the young people dealt with by YOTs are on a 'final warning'. They will be sent to court if they are apprehended for another offence but technically they have not been convicted of an offence. Thus the YOT clients on this programme could be regarded as medium risk, on a secondary programme, in terms of the typology in Table 6.1 (see page 51).

Summit was broken down into bronze, silver and gold level awards – the aim being to give the client a structured set of rewards for completing the different levels. A bronze award required completing 5 hours' worth of the programme satisfactorily and the silver award required 10 hours. These would normally take 10 weeks. After this the client had the option of completing the gold award level. To do this the sports leader and client would agree a further programme of activity, a characteristic of which was that the client must show commitment to sports participation and take greater responsibility. Typically this might involve the client arranging some of the activities themselves, making their own way to the venue and back, and possibly taking a course of instruction. The gold award was designed to encourage independent sports participation and involved a further 10 hours of activity.

One full-time member of staff was responsible for administering the programme and worked as sports counsellor on it. He was supported by a pool of casual staff. Clients were allocated to one staff member.

From February 2002, Summit negotiated a new contract with the Easttown Intensive Supervision and Surveillance Programme (ISSP). This was part of Easttown YOT and dealt with young people aged 10–17 who had been sentenced for a criminal offence on four or more occasions, had served a term of custody and/or had a court order a community sentence. The Summit programme was part of the ISSP work with these clients, but attendance of these clients on Summit was compulsory. The work under this new contract was outside the study period of the research reported here, but it illustrates the way programmes adapt in response to changed funding opportunities. The work with ISSP clients might be expected to be different from that with YOT clients, as ISSP clients were at a higher level of risk, as in Table 6.1 (see page 51), and compulsory attendance might have altered the relationship between client and sports leader.

Evaluation

Methods

As in the Sportaction programme, research took a case study approach, both at the level of the programme and, within that, individual clients. It focused on how and why the programme had an impact, and used a triangulation of methods. These included:

- records of participation kept by the programme
- a two-stage questionnaire completed by participants
- Huskins's dependence–independence scale
- interviews with participants and their parents
- interviews with sports leaders
- interviews with YOT officers.

This meant that the research could examine case studies of individual clients, and these contributed to the case study at the programme level. The theoretical framework was provided by the model of personal growth directed by values, as outlined in Chapter Three, and the methods were designed to examine the same hypotheses derived from this model, as in the SportAction case study (see Chapter Eleven). So, again, research started from theory.

Similarly it was not possible to measure outcomes in terms of offending rates. Practical difficulties included: gaining access to YOT records; setting up a control group; the small number of clients involved; the short time period over which one could measure offending; and the very large proportion of youth offences that are not recorded.

Summit records of each meeting with each client, and clients' achievement of bronze, silver and gold awards, were used to plot clients' progress through the programme. It was also possible to plot the number of clients who were referred but who did not attend. The attendance records allowed identification of the critical cases for interview. As in the Sportaction programme, these were clients who had used the programme a significant number of times, and so would be likely to show how and why the programme had had an impact on them, if it did. If it had not had an impact on them, it was not likely to have had one on anyone else. Summit also made 10-hour action plans for work with each client that could be used to complement case study interviews.

A two-stage questionnaire strategy was adopted. Questionnaire 1 was completed by the client, but with the sports leaders' help if necessary, in the second sports counselling session. It was used at the second session so as to prove less daunting for the client. The second questionnaire was completed by the clients when they finished at silver level. Originally a three-stage questionnaire was planned, with a third for completion at the end of the gold award, or 12 weeks after the silver, if the client was not going on to gold, but this was not practical to administer. Each questionnaire asked the same question about sports participation and about self-esteem. The question about sports participation was to measure the extent to which independent participation in sport had changed while taking part in Summit – this being an objective of the programme. The question itself was adapted from the Allied Dunbar fitness survey (Sports Council/Health Education Authority, 1992), which asked about participation in the last 4 weeks and the degree of effort involved. This survey was designed to measure how much sport respondents did in relation to the amount that would have a positive impact on their fitness. To have a positive impact respondents would have to do sport for three 20-minute sessions per week at a level where they raised a sweat. The question could be used to see if such a level had been achieved including or excluding activities taken part in during Summit.

Rosenberg's (1965) measure of self-esteem was used because of its simplicity, successful use with a similar client group (WYSC), and because self-esteem was one of the dimensions of self-development suggested as important by the theoretical model outlined in Chapter Three.

The second questionnaire was designed to double as a review tool for the sports leaders, in that it asked not only if the client was taking part in any additional sport as a result of Summit, and what had helped them do this, but also if they would like any further assistance. The second questionnaire also asked about completion of the 10-hour action plan, and what had made this difficult or helped it. Thus it related to hypotheses about the success factors in the theoretical model outlined in Chapter Three. The pilot included a measure of locus of control that distinguished between three levels but this was not used in the final version as it was too complex for clients to complete.

Of a potential 70 clients who started the programme during the period of the research, 46 completed questionnaire 1; of the 70, 24 completed questionnaire 2, having finished at silver level. However, as some of those who completed questionnaire 2 had not completed questionnaire 1, this left only 18 cases in which clients had completed both questionnaires 1 and 2, and thus provided a matched pair. This was a poor response rate. The main sports leader was well motivated to administer the questionnaire, but it is possible that the other sports leaders were not.

At the same time that the first and second questionnaires were administered, the sports leaders placed the client at a point on the Huskins dependence–independence scale, which is a measure used in his curriculum development model for application in youth work (see Chapter Three). The scale was incorporated into a short structured recording sheet for the sports leader to complete at the same time as clients completed their questionnaires. This scale has been developed for evaluation of youth work. 'It describes young people's progressive involvement in decision making through seven stages from first contact to independence' (Huskins, 1996: 12). Huskins defines the stages as:

Stage 1   Initial contact when the young person is testing out the youth workers (What have these adults to offer me? Can they be trusted?).
Stage 2   Familiarisation (getting to know each other more, further testing, with the youth worker continuing the PR task of selling what the youth group has to offer).
Stage 3   Socialisation (the groups round the coffee bar, or watching TV) when the youth worker will be encouraging greater commitment and involvement in activities.
Stage 4   The activity level, taking part, for example, in a pool competition, and seeing it through to completion while being encouraged to move on to Stage 5.
Stage 5   When young people begin to take part in the planning and organising of the activities.
Stage 6   When young people run the activities themselves.
Stage 7   The leadership or peer education level, when they take responsibility for others as well as themselves.

A weakness of this tool was that the sports leaders were seeing the young person in only one setting so, while they may have developed to a higher level of independence while taking part in Summit, this does not necessarily mean that this level is replicated in the rest of their lives.

Several interviews with programme staff covered work with individual clients, but also the overall running of the programme. Case study clients were selected from those who had completed the gold award level, as these would give greatest insights into how the programme worked.

A method rejected – comparative ASSET scores

ASSET is a structured interview conducted by a YOT officer that covers a set of 'risk factors' and is designed to produce a 'risk' score as a measure of the client's degree of risk. The initial ASSET score is derived from the first interview between the client and YOT officer. This score might have been useful in showing whether the Summit clients were relatively high or low risk in relation to other YOT clients.

Some evaluations have used changes in ASSET scores as a measure of the impact of YOTs' work, and this is one reason for their design. However, this was not possible in Eastown: firstly because the YOT would not give access to the scores; and secondly because Easttown YOT completed second ASSET interviews for only a small percentage of clients. Even so, it is unlikely that a change in

ASSET score gives a valid picture of a change in a client as changes in score could be attributed as much to the development of the relationship between the YOT officer and the client, in knowing and trusting each other better, as it could to any real change. This was confirmed by an interview with one of the Easttown YOT officers, who, when asked if changes in ASSET score could be used as a research tool, replied:

> I'd find it hard to say that that would show anything really, there is too much discretion in the way you fill it out. You and me could do the form and might score a kid totally different ... . And they are more honest with you (at the end of supervision) as well; they get to know you more and they are actually giving a different, more open view about what they are doing. I mean a classic case of that is the drugs issue isn't it? The first time you start mentioning drugs he goes 'no I don't take them': when you get to know them, 'yes well actually I do, do a bit of whatever', because they are more relaxed with you and more open with you, or they trust you.

So changes in ASSET scores are as likely to measure a change in YOT officer–client relationship as they are a change in the client. Of course, it may be valuable to measure a change in this relationship if we think a greater relationship of trust is a positive outcome of the YOT supervision; however, the point is that we can't be sure that the changed ASSET score is measuring this either.

Results

Internal records

Records of attendance were divided into two periods, January 2000 to 5 March 2001; and 15 March 2001 to April 2002. These corresponded to a change in sports leader managing the project and to some degree a change of methods. The running of the programme was reviewed in April 2001, although the programme itself remained the same (see Table 12.1).

Data was collected up to November 2002 so all those starting in April of that year would have had time to complete at the gold level. From these figures have been excluded all those who were recorded by the sports leader as 'on hold' or 'referred'. It was presumed that these had not actually started the programme, perhaps because they had completed their period of referral to the YOT before they could be found a place on the programme. In the second period, two clients

Table 12.1 Summit participants who started January 2000 to April 2002

Start period	No shows	Started	Finished silver	Finished gold
1/00–5/3/01	4	34	15	7
15/3/01–4/02	10	38	21	7

were also recorded as 'terminated' before they had started; the reason for this is not clear. Compared with Sportaction the start rate was far higher, reflecting a better referral process and the lower risk level of participants.

Participant questionnaire

Change in sports participation (Table 12.2, column 2) – measured in reported times the clients had taken part in sport over the last 4 weeks, for 20 minutes or more, sufficient to get out of breath, and independent of Summit – shows no increase. Case studies of clients, discussed below, showed that one would expect the impact on sports participation to be small.

Column 3 shows net changes in the Rosenberg self-esteem score. Again there is no consistent change. Considering the problems of defining self-esteem (Emler, 2001), it is possible that even if there were an increase it might have just represented the respondent feeling more confident in the presence of the sports leader. As in the Sportaction case study, high self-esteem may not necessarily be associated with reduced offending, or other desired outcomes.

Column 4, the sports leader's perception of the stage of development of the client in terms of the Huskins's dependence–independence scale, shows an increase in 15 cases. In none is there a reduction. The care with which the sports leaders were using this scale is reflected in the attempts they made to make fine

Table 12.2 Summit questionnaire results

1. Client code	2. Sports activity	3. Self-esteem change	4. Development score	5. Development: Sports leader's comments	6. Client's reported problems/needs
C23	+2	+4	n/a	n/a	cost
4	n/a	+ 2	4 — 5	B	info on cost and venues
7	0	– 4	2 — 3/5	B	info
10	+1	0	1 — 3	C	
12	0	– 4	2 — 4/5	A	info
16	0	+ 5	1/2 – 1/2	A / B	leisure passport
17	0	– 5	3 — 4	A / B	info
26	0	– 3	2 — 4	B	
28	–3	– 2	2 — 3	B	
30	0	+ 4	2/3 — 5	B / A	info
53	0	+ 4	2 — 5	B /A	
57	0	– 2	2 — 4	B / A	info
61	–1	+ 8	1/2 — 5/6	B / A	info
62	+3	+ 6	2 — 3	B	
83	n/a	– 7	2/3 — 4	B	
107	–1	0	2 — 4	B	info
109	0	+ 9	2/3 — 2	B / C	
110	0	+ 1	2 — 5	B	info

distinctions between stages and is supported by the analysis of the sports leaders' comments, indicated in column 5. These were categorised as: A, primarily concerned with sports development; B, primarily concerned with personal development; and C, reporting an aspect of the client's lifestyle that was related to offending. However, it was not always easy to distinguish these categories, as illustrated by the following examples:

> Client 26 ... is at a stage where he is keen to set aside time for sport. He was also keen to have a structured project with which to complete a gold project. He has identified his own needs to get fitter and stronger and this has now been evident in his aims for the gold project. He needs to complete his gold project overall. More specifically, he needs to be able to motivate himself to take part in sport without encouragement from his counsellor. His programme for gold reflects this. He will attend the gym with a counsellor for the first five sessions ... the following five will be alone or with a friend.

This shows a goal of independent sports participation, but to achieve this the client needed to develop his own motivation and take responsibility to attend the sessions independently.

> Client 53 ... is quite able to trail around Easttown and into the town centre. His wish is to complete a climbing course with another Summit client. They are both at a stage where I feel confident they will be able to see through the course and continue participating independently. I think it is a case of ensuring they are clear about the climbing course and that ... he maintains a level of maturity. I will sit down with him to explain this and I feel that if he can understand this it will be a positive opportunity for him ...

Again this shows a concern with personal development as well as development of independent sports participation. The two overlap.

While the results appear to give evidence of personal development through sport they might also indicate the influence of the researcher on the work of the sports leaders. Through introducing the concepts of the personal development model, and through discussing how personal development was reflected in the progression from the bronze to gold awards in the succession of meetings with the sports leaders, the researcher might have altered the sports leader's understanding of his work in the same way as Pawson and Tilley describe a 'realist' interview as developing new understandings, for both researcher and interviewee (Pawson and Tilley, 1997: 165). The involvement of the researcher in data collection, sharing the rationale for that with the sports leaders, and gaining their commitment to it, will alter the way the sports leaders understand their work with clients.

Column 6 shows clients' reported needs and barriers to participation on their second questionnaire. It is interesting that the most frequent need is for more information on sports venues and opportunities to participate (info), indicating that Summit has developed this interest.

Case studies of individual participants

One can see how the quantitative results above give an impression of the programme, and they could have been collected by the programme staff themselves, with some help to design the measures. However, the final sample was small – only 18 paired responses. A much better understanding of how and why the programme had an impact was derived from the nine case studies of clients, four of which are reproduced below. Pseudonyms are used throughout – Charlie and George are sports leaders.

Colin

Colin lived in a rural location and was 15 at the time of interview. Charlie had an initial meeting in a café with him, having picked him up from his home. This was because she wanted to make sure he wanted to do the programme rather than it being his parents' wishes. However, she also talked to his parents, with whom she developed a good relationship. Colin felt he had a good relationship with Charlie:

> ... got on with Charlie all right, she was good with me and I was all right with her. I got on all right with Andy (another sports leader) as well.

Initially Colin did not want to do the programme, although he changed his mind after the first session, which was scuba diving.

Researcher: So at what point did you think, after not being sure, well I will do this then?
Colin: I don't know, I just felt like doing something instead of getting into trouble all the time so I thought I'd do it to keep me out of trouble.
Researcher: So after how many sessions into it did you think, this is all right then, I'll do this?
Colin: The first one, scuba diving.

He completed at gold level by organising a mountain bike trip for 4 Easttown Leisure Service staff and another client. The trip took an hour and a half to plan, although he did this with Charlie. Colin enjoyed this, in contrast to other non-active sessions which bored him.

Colin's YOT officer felt that Colin had been a 'major success of the programme'. In general he described the benefits of taking part in the programme and related these particularly to Colin:

> ... giving somebody hope again and something to work on. Long-term I'd say there is a major improvement in their health ... they are doing something that generally they enjoy doing and they are experiencing a different style of life because they are suddenly going to different places, different locations to

do whatever sport it is, and that's number one. It's a healthier vision. Number two, they are actually physically healthy ... And thirdly, really it's about broadening your outlook on life generally. It's giving them ... somebody to copy or aim for like your peer, your role model or whatever, it gives them something to look up to and to aim for.

... over the weeks and the months that he was involved with Charlie ... she motivated him to basically do things off his own bat, which he had never done before and he worked out a cycling route/map thing. Basically that was done, because over the weeks and the months she worked with him she raised his confidence up but she made him realise that he could do something down to himself rather than having everything done for him. The sport and the activity were allowing him to become independent really and produce something that he wanted to do ... before, when he was at home, he was still the lad who was being told what to do ... and it gave him the independence to do something I think.

However, at the time of interview, Colin had finished Summit and it had not led to any other activity. Charlie was aware that there were no more activities he wanted to do in his local area and had considered seeing if he could be re-referred to Summit to continue activities with her help. She had encouraged him to join the local football club (he had formerly won several trophies playing for a team coached by his father before moving to this area), and had offered to take him to the local school Duke of Edinburgh group, and to the local school gym, which could be used for weight training.

The fact that he was not doing anything was frustrating for his parents. They felt that he was not making the effort to get involved in things, such as the local football team, but that the things he said he wanted to do were not practical. His father said Colin was very good at motor mechanics. He would help his father maintain his car and was enthusiastic about the prospect of having his own motorbike. Colin said: 'Something to do with cars or motorbikes. That is what I want really.' His parents would have liked him to get involved in a well-supervised motorbike club, which taught maintenance and responsible driving. If there was one, they would have taken Colin to it, but they did not want to buy him an old bike he would restore then drive over the fields.

In many respects his parents were very supportive. This was confirmed by Charlie and the YOT officer. They would strongly encourage him to get involved with an activity they thought was right for him. Perhaps, as the comments by the YOT officer suggest, Colin's real need was to feel he had made independent choices about his leisure activity and therefore nothing his parents suggested, including the local football team, would be satisfactory. As his parents and Charlie acknowledged, the relative geographical isolation of where he lived meant that local opportunities were very limited and others would involve a long and costly bus journey. He was not interested in those that were available. So the programme had not led to independent sports participation. This was followed up in the interview with Colin's YOT officer:

But you could argue that, all right, to my knowledge, he hasn't re-offended but is he any further forward than what he was before he went on it? All right, we have done a bit of work because he hasn't offended since we've had him on it and that's good, but is he any further forward? I'm not sure.

So, for this YOT officer, while the experience Colin had had on Summit was excellent, a general problem was that it did not lead to anything else. The gold award did not appear to be a particular sense of satisfaction. Although there were several football trophies Colin had won displayed in a cabinet, there was no evidence of the gold Summit award certificate and he did not know where it was.

Thus Summit had motivated Colin to do things he had not done before, but all with the support of the sports leader. The initial scuba diving session had made him willing to take part in the programme and the range of activity had maintained his interest but the gold award was not seen as a major achievement. He developed good relationships with the sports leaders, which were important to him and contrasted with that with his parents, who although supportive also found Colin difficult to motivate. He had taken part in activities with the sports leader, but had not progressed to independent participation. One could argue that this reflected limited opportunities in a relatively rural environment. On the other hand, the local football team appeared an ideal opportunity, given his previous involvement in football.

Darren

Darren was 14 when he started the programme and 15 at the time of a second interview, conducted at a local climbing wall. He had been involved in a mass vandalism offence, along with two other Summit clients, but he, and his mother, said this was the first offence he had been involved in. Prior to involvement in Summit he had played regularly for a local football team, and had done so since he was eight. His mother was dissatisfied with his previous team and had hoped that a long-term result of Summit would be that Darren would join another local team. By the second interview Darren, or his mother, had found another local team themselves and he had started playing in it.

Darren's mother was keen for him to do Summit as it was 'something to do' and might lead to more sports participation. She was initially concerned: 'All sorts of kids would be there, all types of thieves, so I were a bit worried. But then when it started I saw it was just him and George, and I thought he needs to meet more people really.' She felt the YOT officer was 'really nice' when he visited. She was generally keen on Darren, and her other children, taking part in sport: 'They always go swimming, it keeps them off the streets.' The local pool was a close bus ride to their house; Easttown offered free swimming to children in the school holidays, and Darren was swimming the first time the researcher tried to interview him. Darren had also taken part in the summer sports activity sessions run by Easttown Recreation Department over the last four or five years.

Darren's bronze and silver sessions involved golf, snooker, climbing at an indoor wall, pool, badminton, a football competition and mountain biking. The sports leader's plan was for Darren to try a range of activities before settling on one for the gold award. After the last session Darren decided he would like to take a climbing course for the gold award, although he had to wait over a month before it started. The course ran for six weeks. Darren attended with another Summit client who lived close to him. The sports leader's aim was that they might continue to go together.

Darren passed the course, which gave him a card allowing him to attend a junior club by himself. The club meets two evenings a week from 5.30 to 6.30. Here he could borrow the necessary equipment. The sessions cost £1.50 and the centre is a short bus ride from Darren's house, at the same location as the swimming pool. Darren was aware of all these details and felt it was practical for him to attend. He had not done so at the time of interview, as the club had been closed for the previous 2 weeks. However, he was clearly enthusiastic about climbing, attempting difficult climbs and asking for details about equipment during the course of the second interview. He had also gained competence in the necessary basic techniques and was keen to use them. At the start of the second interview session he confidently used his own membership card to book himself and the researcher into the climbing wall. Darren reported that not everybody on the climbing course had passed and it appeared he had some pride in having passed it.

Darren's mother, when interviewed after the silver award but prior to the climbing course, said he had enjoyed the sessions: 'Every week he has looked forward to going.' George (the sports leader administering Summit) reported that 'he had improved his climbing skills such that he can do it himself'. He seemed more confident in himself, and in his climbing ability.

Darren, as the sports leader noted, 'knew from the beginning what he wanted to do and was well motivated.' He had a very supportive mother, had a history of active sports participation and, although only 15, had enough self-confidence to come to the climbing sessions by himself. When asked what he had done through Summit that he would not have done otherwise, he said he would have been interested in climbing anyway, as he had done it once before. However, Summit introduced him to this climbing wall and paid for him to do this course, allowing him to take part independently, so it is unlikely that he would have done this himself. On the other hand, he, or his mother, found the new football team he joined by themselves.

The overall impression is that Darren was a low-risk client, with a high chance of independent sports participation anyway. He had used his own initiative to join a football team and had maintained motivation for a month while waiting for the climbing course to start. Summit just gave him an extra set of opportunities. In particular, the climbing wall course was local, affordable and at a familiar venue. His mother was strongly supportive and thus further participation was likely. The Summit sessions covered the period over the summer school holidays, so this may have been fortuitous in giving him something else to do and to look forward to during this period.

Billy

Billy was only 12 when he started Summit. His YOT officer made a special case for him to attend as clients are supposed to be 14. He had been playing regularly for a local football team for 2 years. He lived with his parents and other siblings. At the second session George felt he was:

> ... quite able to think for himself and say honestly what he wants to do in terms of activities. He also realises some of the things he has done are wrong.

At the bronze and silver level Billy took part in snooker, canoeing, golf, climbing, mountain biking and squash. He was enthusiastic and his mother confirmed that he enjoyed the sessions and he had not missed any. For the gold award he took the same six week climbing course as Darren. Thus, as with other participants, the bronze/silver level acted as tasters for an activity he could concentrate on. He passed the climbing course, so could now attend the climbing wall by himself. After the first climbing session, he attended without the sports leader but with a friend who was not on Summit. He has since been to the climbing wall with this friend, who has his own equipment. He was also aware of the climbing club that he could attend. The programme led to a new sporting interest, although it was too early to say if it will be sustained. He did not mention any feeling of satisfaction at completing at the gold level.

Billy's mother felt strongly that the programme was too much of a reward and not balanced sufficiently by a punishment:

> He undoubtedly enjoyed it. For the crime that he committed, it's like he got rewarded, as it has to be a certain degree of crime for the YOT to do a report and to get a final caution. So it's like he is rewarded for the crime. Where is the punishment?

She felt that it could send the wrong message to other young people. They might see Billy being given a choice of sporting activities and being paid to go on a climbing course and think that this is what they will get if they offend. 'Kids who are good don't get that'. And: 'It has not taught him a lesson. That's not addressing his offending behaviour.'

Summit opened the practical opportunity for Billy to do a new sport he had not done before, and he may continue with his friend. He had the ability and confidence to go to the climbing wall sessions and borrow the necessary equipment, although he was only 13. This was partly because he went with a friend to the course. Although climbing looked a practical future activity, Billy could have chosen any of the other ones he did at silver level to continue at gold. There might have been less chance of him continuing independently in squash, canoeing or golf because of the cost and distance to travel. Both Billy and his mother thought the activity could be a diversion from offending, but the sessions were for only a relatively short period although, again by chance, they helped fill the summer holidays. This case again shows that Summit had the potential to lead to a long-term interest. The comments of Billy's mother indicated a potential negative impact of the programme in the message it gave to young people about the consequences of offending. However, it was not possible to confirm this with Billy or his peers.

Paul

Paul was one of the older clients, being 16. He had left school but was 'not doing anything particular' at the time of interview, although he had recently enrolled himself on a life skills course run by the local chamber of commerce. The sports leader reported that Paul had a difficult home life. His father lived away from home. His mother had five or six children to cope with. One reason for conducting the interview at a sports hall was because the sports leader thought it would be a better environment.

Paul took part in a local football team, playing on Sunday and training on Wednesdays. His initial questionnaire confirmed that he had done this in the previous 4 weeks. He had wanted to do Summit because of 'the different sports'. At the bronze and silver levels he had taken part in snooker/pool, badminton, tennis and mountain biking. At the gold level he did badminton. For two of the badminton sessions he was encouraged to bring a friend, which he did. This friend was very keen on badminton. They had been to the sports centre to play by themselves once since Paul had completed at gold level, 4 weeks before the interview. Paul thought this was practical as he could get the bus to the sports centre: 'It costs £1.50 to get in and a pound for the racket hire. It's not a lot.'

Paul reported that the difference between bronze, silver and gold levels was that at bronze he was picked up and dropped off. At silver, George picked him up for a bit, then expected him to make his own way there. At gold, he had to find his own way there. Clearly Paul enjoyed playing, as the researcher witnessed in a game of badminton prior to the interview. He also appeared to have a good relationship with the sports leader. From the interview he agreed that he would not have booked the badminton by himself before coming on Summit. He did not report any sense of achievement at completing at the gold level. 'Give you a bit of paper and a letter, didn't feel it was a big achievement, just felt it was all right.'

The sports leader felt that Paul was a good example of a client who had benefited from having a role model:

> His family is quite unstable, his officer says he struggles to get on with people ... he had nobody he can relate to. I've got to know him and he is really doing well at the moment. So, having a role model is quite important.

Paul felt the programme might have a diversion affect: 'Send you on it to keep you out of trouble. Keeps you out every day and stuff.' Summit had introduced Paul to a new sport he could do himself. This was helped by his ability to find a friend who was willing to do it with him. There was some progression of responsibility from bronze to gold, although limited to independently getting to the sessions. Paul had the confidence to book the badminton court himself, and he knew it was practical for him to do this in terms of the cost of admission, equipment hire and access. However, it is not clear that Summit had increased his confidence in general, as he had already demonstrated this by enrolling himself on the life skills course. The sports leader might have provided a role model, although he and Paul did not elaborate on the impact this might have had. Paul already played football twice a week, more times than he was likely to play badminton. So, while doing Summit may have provided him with an activity to keep him away from offending while he was doing this, future badminton participation is not likely to make a major impression.

To what extent do these case studies and other evidence indicate an impact on crime reduction?

The four sample case studies above were combined with other data collected at the level of the programme to examine the impact on participants in relation to crime reduction objectives.

Does Summit provide a diversion from offending?

In the short run there was some evidence for this. Colin and Paul both thought the programme would keep them 'out of trouble'. For Billy it gave him something to look forward to and his mother felt it was a diversion. However, Darren would have been involved in sport anyway and the amount of time clients are actually involved in the programme is minor. Summit might provide something to look forward to and (particularly for Darren and Billy) a structure, but that is only for 12 weeks as a maximum period.

Summit's greatest impact with respect to a diversion mechanism would be through a long-term influence on sports participation. However, there was evidence that only three of the nine case study participants were progressing to independent sports participation and one of these would probably have done so anyway. Records for Summit showed that, of the 45 clients who started the programme up to June 2000, only 12 completed at the gold level, so only about 25 per cent of those starting the programme could be expected to gain the maximum benefit from participation. This completion rate has, however, increased.

All three YOT officers supported the simple diversion mechanism. A YOT officer reported: 'I'm in favour of Summit because while they are on Summit generally they don't get involved with crime.' The three YOT officers interviewed also agreed that long-term involvement in sport was the ideal outcome:

> It's twelve weeks or twelve sessions and the thing about it is, or the way I view it is, it's there, it's a building block, it's a stepping stone for if they are keen enough and want to move on themselves then there are other avenues.

However, they also conceded that this might not be achieved:

> I think that's probably the weakness of any sports project, or any project, is that when you come to an end ... there are loads of expectations, loads of things been happening, then suddenly we say, right, for whatever reason we have come to an end ... what are we going to do now?

The sports leader estimated that 50–60 per cent of clients went on to independent sports participation, but this was based just on what clients said when they had finished, not any follow-up contact.

Thus, evidence for crime reduction through diversion was limited. The YOT officers had faith in this mechanism, but there is little concrete evidence. As discussed below, the potential of this mechanism in the long run is limited by the degree to which the programme can meet sports development objectives and overcome barriers to participation.

Does Summit have the characteristics of a programme designed to contribute to value-directed personal development?

The initial attractiveness of the activities had helped motivate clients. At the start of Summit they were presented with a very long list of activities they could try. All felt they had ample choice and this was confirmed by their parents. The case studies above confirm the importance of attractive activities; for example, Colin was attracted by scuba diving. The case studies also show how the range of activities could be used as far as possible to match the programme to clients' interests and lead them into ones where independent participation was practical. This was a conscious strategy of the sports leader and was done sensitively.

However, a progressive juxtaposition of challenging experiences with participants' needs and capabilities was both very limited and restricted to that directly related to the goal of independent sports participation. Typically this might involve the participant making their own way to the venue, attending a course or booking themselves into a session. Sport is not being used as the medium for a more general process of personal development; instead, as discussed in more detail later, the main purpose of the programme was to develop a commitment to further sports participation.

Although the bronze, silver and gold stages in Summit had been designed to maximise boosts to self-esteem from their achievement, the case study participants did not show that this had happened. Darren had gained some satisfaction from completing the climbing course. The mother of another client who had also completed the climbing course reported that 'it built up his confidence and self-esteem when he realised he could do it'. However, at the end of the gold award this client reported that, rather than a sense of achievement, 'it was a bit sad really, because it's the end really, it's over and done with'. Thus the gold award in itself did not provide a great sense of achievement; a greater sense was from actual achievement in the sport. This impression was supported by the sports leader:

... Some people do see it as a big thing, some [clients] recently have said their mum is going to frame the certificate and put it on the wall. [However], you get certificates for everything now; if they attend school they get certificates for various things, and all the exams and that sort of thing ... so they don't see it as a [major achievement] in comparison. Maybe we need to change the gold award to something a bit different.

As discussed above, the ability to offer long-term exit routes and support clients after the programme is limited. This was partly because the sports leader realised that he had to allocate his time carefully to meet the requirements of the YOT contract, in terms of achieving throughput. There was no additional time to give to clients after the programme, though in Colin's case the sports leader clearly felt he would benefit from a second programme. There is again little evidence of the programme offering a new set of pro-social peers. Colin's YOT officer suggested this was the case but an initial concern of parents was that Summit would involve their child mixing with offenders. For example, one parent reported that she was 'not keen on him mixing with the bad boys', and parents needed reassurance over this point. The extent to which the programme will change a peer group is limited to its ability to offer a long-term significant interest. Even so, one then has to assume that the new peer group is 'better' than the old, and there was no evidence of this.

The general relationships between the clients and the sports leaders were excellent, as one would expect from those who had maintained voluntary contact with the programme for its duration. The cases reported above, and others, also show the excellent relationship with clients' parents and the importance of this in gaining their confidence in the programme. However, to what extent did it extend beyond this to a mentor and role model relationship? The sports leader and the YOT officers felt that the provision of a positive role model was an important benefit. The sports leader reported:

It gives clients a chance to air their views with people other than those at home. I don't think they see me as part of the system, as I'm not part of the YOT or a teacher or anything, but they do see me as someone. They would not want to think I think bad of them. They will tell me things they have done, but they have a sort of reliance on me, so I don't think bad of them. Initially they all see you as someone who is from an organisation who is come to sort you out and whatever. Once they get past bronze [they] definitely see you not necessarily as someone to look up to, but someone they can talk to more openly. Perhaps they cannot talk to their parents; maybe it's the parent causing the problems.

YOT officers confirmed that a strength of Summit was 'building that other relationship that they might not have at home' and they all felt the Summit staff were very good at engaging young people.

The importance of the relationship with the sports leader as a mentor and role model will vary between clients. For Paul, it was probably more important because of his family circumstances, and Colin clearly felt it was an alternative to the strained relationship he had with his parents. The ability to go beyond this was limited by the length of the programme and the skills of the sports leaders, who realised they were not experts in dealing with offending. The quote below shows not only the sports leader's explicit acknowledgement of his limited scope to address the causes of offending, but also a recognition of the strengths and limitations of the programme in this respect:

> I think if you start looking at trying to reduce crime as being the main aim, you will fall down with Summit .... It is difficult to address all the issues there are for a young person starting to offend ... boredom, parenting, peer groups, funding drug habits; it's difficult to have an action plan which will work towards stopping you going out with your friends you have been involved in, being nice to your parents all the time, and making sure you are doing something all the time. So, ... to try and organise an action plan to stop offending, you would struggle. Yeah, it's easier to go through the sport avenue, but it is more effective, because you are offering alternatives, and they are deciding, 'I want to do this instead of being involved in crime'. And again, if you address it through crime, you are saying, you can't do crime, and you are making the decision for them, whereas you are offering an alternative and they are making the decision. They can go through the sport line, they may continue offending while they are doing the sport, but if you offer that sport, and it is positive, and they can get involved in something on a regular basis, it's something they can decide to do rather than being involved in crime.

For the sports leader, the relation between sport and crime was 'a bit iffy ... of course it's all speculation, but I think it's the alternative route that the young person can sort of travel down that addresses ... crime reduction'. So for the sports leader the major objective was sports development. He realised that, if he was to work systematically on crime reduction, the programme would be much more complex and beyond his capacity to deliver. But he believed that the link to crime reduction was that long-term sports participation offered an alternative.

Conclusion on the programme and evaluation methods

With regard to crime reduction, the programme had a limited diversion effect, both for the duration of participation and afterwards, to the extent that this will be achieved by independent sports participation. Barriers to further sports participation included income, transport, geographical proximity to facilities, parental support and the attitude of the young person themselves. Apart from the attitude of the individual involved, all these are aspects of social exclusion relevant to young people taking part in sport (Collins, 2003: 26). The case studies indicate that these are all significant. They also illustrate ways in which these constraints have been overcome: largely by the availability of cheap, easily accessible activities; through supportive parents; and possibly by attending the facilities with a friend. However, to overcome all these would be a considerable achievement for a programme working with 14–17-year-olds over a relatively short period.

Summit's clients could be considered at the low end of 'medium risk' in terms of Table 6.1 (see page 51) – they did not just live in areas subject to risk, but they had actually entered the criminal justice system through being referred to the YOT. So was there evidence of value-directed personal development and the programme characteristics that would facilitate this? Again, evidence of this impact was limited. There was not a great sense of achievement at completion – perhaps it did not represent such a contrast with the greater experience of failure felt by clients on WYSC or Hafotty Wen. Work with the sports leader helped build up a good relationship – but it did not become a significant mentoring one, again as in WYSC. This may be because the contact was not so significant, and again because the relationship with the sports leader was not so important as a substitute for other relationships that were lacking.

The main objective of the Summit sports leader was sports development, in the sense that he aimed to progress participants towards independent sports participation and structured the programme to achieve this. This objective was shared by the YOT officers. So, although the programme was being used by the YOT and its officers supported it, its main focus was on achieving sports development objectives, on the assumption that these would then contribute to crime reduction.

The simple mechanism of providing a diversion from alternative activity, or something to look forward to during the week, may reduce crime. If the programme succeeded in generating long-term independent sports participation (and some fine tuning would have helped to improve this), it could lead to a major life interest that could give an alternative to offending, as suggested by the sports leader. This helps explain why the YOT bought the Summit programme – officers believed the synergy with sports development was sufficient to justify its use. In addition, if the target group is relatively low risk, an explicit focus on crime reduction may deter some clients and their parents; for example, Darren's mother was concerned he would be mixing with criminals. This is important where participation is voluntary.

Thus an implication is that the lower the target group of the programme is on the risk continuum in Table 6.1 (see page 51), the less focused the programme is likely to be on crime reduction and the more indirect will be the impact of the programme on this objective. Synergy with other objectives, such as sports development, may well become more important. Some may say this challenges 'programme integrity' as there are now at least two objectives, to which one might add a third – reduction of social exclusion. This criticism is unrealistic, firstly because the provision of sport within local authorities has always had several objectives and, secondly, the relative importance of different objectives changes, and especially in response to changed funding sources. Thus programmes may evolve, in the same way that Summit evolved as a result of changed partnerships with the probation service and YOT, and then the ISSP.

Rather than criticising a lack of programme integrity, a better way to look at the programme is how it achieves synergy between different objectives. The question then becomes, how well can it do this? In the case of Summit, more acknowledgement of the sports development objective might have led to some extra follow-up work with clients to try to boost independent participation in sport. And an officer skilled in sports development work has to recognise his limitations in dealing with the causes of crime.

However, this leads to another important aspect of the programme – its need to meet its contracted targets of dealing with a specific number of clients. To do this the programme had to be tighter than WYSC or Sportaction, in that it had a clearly defined end. A client would receive a set number of hours of contact time. Clients and sports leaders knew this. It may conflict with sports leaders' desire to do 'just a little more' for any one client, but it means the contract with the YOT can be met.

The evaluation approach showed how a case study could triangulate various sources of evidence. One could measure some intermediate outcomes, as represented in Tables 12.1 and 12.2 (see pages 141 and 142). Most of these could be collected by the programme staff themselves, with some help. However, the further one moves from the high-risk level of clients, the harder it becomes to gather any meaningful data on offending. And, for all of the outcome measures, sample sizes were small.

The case studies were valuable in showing how and why the programme had an impact – but they were labour-intensive to conduct. One could argue that their thoroughness compensated for the lack of ability to collect and analyse quantitative data in a way that would provide positivists with what they regard as 'robust measures of intermediate outcomes' (Coalter, 2002: 53). The combination of case study methods were thorough enough to provide a convincing story at an academic level (Nichols, 2004b), but programmes don't usually have these resources to devote to evaluation.

13 Splash

Summary

This case study is of a local authority-run summer holiday activity programme, Westtown Splash, targeted at 8–18-year-olds. This programme had been running for several years previous to 2001, at which time the Youth Justice Board (YJB) decided to fund a set of programmes nationally that were essentially the same thing. Thus Westtown received YJB funding to extend its programme. In relation to Table 6.1 (see page 51) it was targeted at low-risk participants and the main mechanism by which it might reduce crime was by a simple diversion from boredom. This is a very common type of programme, run by many local authorities (Nichols and Booth, 1999a). However, it is particularly difficult to evaluate, mainly because the programmes are usually open access – participants can drop in and out at any time, so it is difficult to keep a record of who is attending. Further, it is targeting low-risk participants – normally just through the location of the sessions. These characteristics make it hard to implement methods that focus on the individual participants – and the impact on any one participant may not be that great. However, it is also not easy to show an impact on crime at a local area level. These difficulties in showing a causal relationship between the programme and crime reduction highlight the general dilemma, especially relevant to this type of programme, of the extent to which policy can be led by evidence, and how much evidence is considered enough.

This case study shows how a combination of methods could be used to evaluate such a programme – but the considerable resources used to do this are not normally available. Conclusions consider what are the most useful evaluation methods such a programme can implement by itself.

Introduction to the programme

The local programme

Splash was an open-access sports activity programme, aimed at 8–18-year-olds, targeted on the areas of Westtown (pseudonyms are used throughout this case study), which were most socially and economically disadvantaged. The sites used by Splash were playing fields, parks and fields or hard surface areas adjacent to leisure and community centres. The programme had been run by a partnership of Westshire Police and Westtown Leisure Services for over 10 years. Up until 2002 the programme had been offered on each site for 1 week of the school summer holidays. From 2001 the sports development section, which was responsible for the programme, had been relocated into Westtown Young Peoples Services. Apart from its long-term continuity, as a consequence of core funding being established within the local authority budget, Westtown Splash was typical of many local authority-run programmes.

A combination of a small core of full-time staff from the sports development section and temporary staff employed for the summer offered a range of sports and games. Participation was free. On-site activities were complemented by a set of off-site trips. Over the previous 10 years there had been a degree of continuity in that the majority of sites had had Splash provided on them for 1 week of each summer holiday. At some sites activities had also been offered at Easter and the rest of the year, mainly by the permanent sports development workers. This provided the potential for long-term relationships to be built up between participants on particular sites and the worker allocated to that site. In addition, Splash Forums had been run in three areas of Westtown. These were sports-related youth groups, the members of which were drawn from the regular Splash sites. These groups offered additional activities throughout the year and through them the young participants were encouraged to take roles of responsibility in organising and raising funds for the activities.

In 2001 the Youth Justice Board (YJB) provided extra funding to expand the programme to run it on three additional sites. As before, Splash was run on each site for only 1 week, but the number of sites was expanded and the funding enabled a 3-day residential course to be offered at the end of the summer. In 2002 the programme was again extended, using YJB funds, enabling 10 clusters of sites to each offer the Splash programme over 5 weeks of the summer holiday. Some sites were used for only 1 week, and some for 2, but the geographical clustering of sites meant that young people could travel relatively easily from one to another. This opened the possibility that young people might attend for all 5 weeks of the summer. As in 2001, a 3-day residential course was provided at the end of the summer at a local education authority outdoor pursuits centre.

The YJB insisted that all the programmes it funded nationally were also called Splash. This was convenient, as the established Westtown Splash scheme had built up considerable brand loyalty over its years of operation and a forced change of name to obtain the YJB funding could have caused confusion. A limitation of the additional YJB funding was that it was confirmed only a few weeks before the programme was due to start. This led to difficulties in recruiting additional staff, buying and storing additional equipment, and arranging transport between sessions in a very short time period. In fact it appeared that the YJB had to dispense a large amount of funds in a short period of time, so were concerned to direct them to credible projects (very similar to the distribution of the Positive Futures funds by Sport England – see Chapter Eleven).

In terms of Table 6.1 (see page 51), Westtown Splash was 'primary prevention', working with low-risk clients. It aimed to prevent people at risk of becoming involved in crime actually committing it by targeting times and places where it was considered the risks were relatively high – during school holidays and in areas of higher relative deprivation.

Evaluation

The evaluation of this programme took a case study approach, triangulating a set of methods, including:

- questionnaires completed by participants in 2000 and 2001
- questionnaires completed by parents in 2000 and 2001
- pilot interviews with participants in 2001, interviews with individual participants in 2002 combined with a brief questionnaire
- interviews with Splash staff
- observation of Splash sites
- use of local crime data.

The methods were designed to address hypotheses around the model of personal growth in Chapter Three, but were modified as it was found that a simple mechanism of diversion from boredom was more relevant.

Questionnaires to parents

Questionnaires were distributed to participants' parents via their children, on the fourth day of a week's session at any one site. It was not possible to control distribution and there is always the risk that children in higher-risk households may have been less likely to have returned a questionnaire. A chaotic home life might mean they did not actually return home between sessions!

In 2000, parents' questionnaires asked open questions about why they thought it was a good idea for their child to attend Splash, the perceived benefits of their child attending Splash and other questions to give Splash feedback on the popularity of its sessions and its marketing. Thus the questionnaire was designed to help the research, but also to provide useful practical information for the programme. The response rate was 19 per cent.

The 2001 parents' questionnaire also asked why they thought Splash was a good idea. It changed open questions about the benefits of Splash to closed ones, and new questions asked specifically about parents' perception of the impact on crime. These questions and responses are reproduced on the next page.

Table 13.1 Splash questionnaire – excerpts

What were the main reasons why you thought it was a good idea for your child to attend the Splash sessions? Tick any that apply.

	%
To relieve boredom/something to do in the holidays	89
Because they enjoy it	74
To gain benefits of mixing with other children	45
To keep out of trouble	39
To learn sporting skills	66
To keep them off the streets	43
Because it is a safe environment	56
To learn skills of playing with other children	40
Other. Please specify ...	6

[the 'other' category included parents who said a benefit was so they could go to work or did not need child care]

Of the reasons above, which were the **two most important ones** for your child attending Splash?

i)..

ii)..

Both responses added up below.

	%
To relieve boredom/something to do in the holidays	56
Because they enjoy it	40
To gain benefits of mixing with other children	15
To keep out of trouble	12
To learn sporting skills	31
To keep them off the streets	14
Because it is a safe environment	21
To learn skills of playing with other children	8
Other. Please specify ...	2

What have been the **main benefits** of your child attending Splash this year? *First two responses of 70 respondents added up below.*

	%
They enjoyed it	23
To mix with other children/make new friends	13
Learning new sports/trying new activities	10
Not bored/something to do in the holidays/kept busy	9
Gives parents free time/allows parents to work or do other things	7
Getting them out of the house	6
Because it is a safe environment	6
Learn to play/work with others	4
To keep them out of trouble	3
Something to look forward to	3
Improved skills/learn skills	3
Keeps them out of trouble	3
Doing the activities/sports	2

Splash is supported by Westshire Police. Do you think Splash has an impact on crime in the local area? Please tick **one**.

	%
It has no impact	22
It reduces crime while Splash is on	61
It reduces crime in the long term	19

In view of the results from the previous year's research, the question on the impact on crime distinguished between an immediate impact on crime while Splash was on, a diversion effect, and a long-term impact that might be associated with pro-social personal growth, the main initial focus of the research. There was also scope for parents to add qualitative responses, which provided valuable data. This questionnaire had a 12 per cent response rate, 97 being returned.

A slightly modified version of the 2002 questionnaire was distributed to parents again in 2003 but the response rate was so poor that results were not used. This was due to the expansion of Splash in 2003 funded by the YJB. Its monitoring required completion of so many questionnaires by participants that this severely limited the capacity or willingness of the sports leaders and the programme to distribute any more. Staff and participants were suffering from 'evaluation overload'.

Questionnaires to participants

Questionnaires were completed by 207 participants in 2000 and 280 (20 per cent) in 2001. The questionnaires were administered by two work-experience students who were working for Splash over the summer. Sample selection was not systematic (for example, every nth child). This would have been difficult to achieve given the open-access nature of the programmes. Instead the sports leaders asked participants if they would like to leave the sports sessions briefly to take part in the survey. From observation on 2 days there were very few refusals and the work experience students, who had both taken part in Splash when they were younger, were sensitive in asking the questions. However, there is always the possibility that sports leaders allocated the most enthusiastic participants to take part.

Questions asked about previous participation to see if they attended regularly – year to year. In 2000 this asked for several previous years, but this was answered poorly, so in 2001 participants were asked just about the previous year. A set of questions asked about best and worst sessions and how participants had heard about Splash, for purposes of giving feedback to the programme. A question asking what participants liked best about Splash was asked to see if it related to the characteristics of a good programme, as defined in the model in Chapter Three. As in the questionnaire to parents, the 2000 version acted as a pilot for the 2001 version.

Interviews with participants

At the end of the summer programme in 2001, individual interviews were conducted with six participants, and another five were included in a focus group. The interviews acted as a pilot for research during 2002 in which interviews were conducted with 63 Splash participants at eight sites and at a residential course, held during the last week of the school summer holidays. These participants were selected by sports leaders on the basis that they had greatest involvement in the programme, and ideally had attended for two or three consecutive years. This may have biased responses, but it meant that those interviewed had most to report about their experience of the programme. In practice only 23 out of the 63 interviewed had attended Splash for three summers or more.

The interviews took about 10 minutes each. Usually participants were interviewed in pairs to give each other support. The pilot in 2001 showed that it was hard for an interviewer to maintain direction of a larger focus group of young people. The restricted length of interviews meant that they lacked depth; however, the skills of the interviewer in building up a quick rapport meant that interviewees were often frank about issues, such as their involvement in crime. Interviews were conducted in a place away from the other participants so they would not be overheard or interrupted. Good weather meant that they could nearly always be conducted in the open air, within sight of sports leaders and other participants, though out of hearing. This was important because it removed potential security issues concerning being alone with interviewees where they were interviewed individually.

Interviews were not recorded. In the first interview this was attempted, but it stultified responses and the tape recorder was a distraction. As in similar research with this age group into Street-Sport in Stoke-on-Trent (McCormack, 2000; 2001), it was found more effective to take notes corresponding to the interview structure, and then write them up as soon as possible after the interview. In studying the Sport Solent project McCormack had used a 'life history' method, in which participants recalled significant events in their lives in relation to risk and protection factors, and involvement in crime. This was not possible in the Splash research as, although an attempt was being made to discover the long-term impact of Splash, participants were younger and might have had no involvement with crime.

Although the interviewees were selected as critical cases in terms of the mechanism by which Splash might reduce crime through long-term pro-social development, the interviews could build on the questionnaire results from participants and parents over the summers of 2000 and 2001, indicating that the main impact of the programme on crime reduction was through giving young people 'something to do' to alleviate boredom in the school holidays.

Before being interviewed, the 32 participants who had attended for 2 years or more were asked to complete a questionnaire. This asked for details of attendance and introduced topics that were to be covered in the open discussion. It ensured that basic factual information was collected, such as length of participation, but also meant that all interviewees had written initial responses to the more open discussion questions, making it easier to bring them into active participation in the discussion by referring to the written responses they had already made.

This method was labour-intensive, but it gave the researcher a good 'feel' for the research situation through combining the interviews with observation of the sessions. One exception to the interview procedure above was an interview with a long-term participant who had become a volunteer. This was conducted individually and tape recorded as the interview was longer and there was more detail.

Interviews with sports leaders and programme managers

Several interviews were held over the three years of the study, covering the general management of the programme and work with individual participants.

Use of local crime data

As in the national evaluation of Splash (see below) it was possible to collect local crime data based on police basic command units corresponding to the geographical areas in which Splash was operating. It was possible to compare rates for some crimes before and after Splash was run. Access to this data was made easier by the close relationship between the leisure department of the local authority and the local police, who had been partners in running Splash since it was set up.

Methods that were rejected

Use of Youth Offending Team and school records

The open-access nature of the programme (one of its strengths from participants' point of view) meant there were not accurate records of who attended and for how long. This also presented problems in defining a participant – how many sessions would someone need to have attended to be classified as a participant?

If one had accurate records of attendance one could relate these to Youth Offending Team (YOT) records to see if participants were known offenders. If they were, it would indicate that the programme had managed to target known offenders, and this increases the possibility that it might be diverting them from crime. In this case study it was not possible to gain access to the YOT records. Even if it had been possible, one would ideally want to show that YOT clients were over-represented among programme participants. For example, if 3 per cent of people aged 8–16 in the area the programme was running were YOT clients, one would have wanted a significantly higher percentage to be represented amongst Splash participants. Of course, one might not get this 'positive result' because the catchment areas of the programmes did not correspond to the geographical area in which the YOTs operated. Further, this method assumes that a YOT record is an accurate reflection of offending.

Had accurate records of attendance been practical to keep it might have been possible to relate attendance at Splash to attendance at school. However, apart from similar problems to the ones described above in relation to the use of YOT records, there would still be difficulty interpreting any relationship. If Splash participants had a poor record of attendance at school, was this good, as it showed that Splash had engaged young people who had themselves rejected school? Or was it bad if it showed that regular attendance at Splash did not lead to improved attendance at school?

Measurement of protection factors

In the initial questionnaires to parents and participants, administered in 2000, an attempt was made to apply a method used in evaluating the UK Communities That Care (CTC) programmes (Crow *et al.*, 2004). CTC is a community-based risk prevention programme established in the USA and piloted in three neighbourhoods in the UK. Its design is based on the risk protection factor paradigm discussed in Chapter Three. The idea is that risk factors can be identified, risks reduced and protection factors applied early in young people's lives. Local communities will be actively involved in this process. The CTC evaluation included a two-stage questionnaire to school children, administered before and after the introduction of CTC with a $2^1/_2$ year gap between surveys. (This is part of a classic experimental and control group design – see Chapter Four.) This asked about risk and protection factors. An attempt was made to replicate these questions in the questionnaires to Splash participants and their parents. Specifically, a 13-statement question, each scored on a 4-point Likert scale, was used to ask if the programme provided protection factors corresponding to those that the theoretical model in Chapter Three suggested would lead to pro-social personal growth.

The response rate to this complex question was not high (the CTC research applied it to a 'captive audience' in schools) and it also suffered from set response – that is, respondents were not discriminating enough in their answers. In the 2001 surveys this question was replaced with an open one, asking what participants and parents felt were the best things about Splash. This was more useful.

The impracticality of before-and-after measures

We have seen that some of the more intense programmes with higher-risk participants used before-and-after measures – for example, West Yorkshire Sports Counselling and Fairbridge. It was not possible to use any before-and-after measures to attempt to measure change in Splash participants for several reasons. First, as noted above, it was difficult to record and define participation. Second, one might make a set of measurements in year 1, but be unable to measure the same set of participants in year 2 as different people attended and were captured by the survey – a lot of measurements would be wasted. Third, one has to consider how valid any measures might have been: will a questionnaire administered to a

10-year-old, by a work experience student, in a field, give a valid measure of self-esteem, or any other personal characteristic, even if the measuring tool has been previously validated? And finally, how reasonable is it to use this type of measure to attribute any change to the experience of the programme? If a 10-year-old attends a week-long summer activity session it is not such a major event in their lives such that one might expect it to have a significant impact on some measurable character trait or skill. It might be a nudge in the right direction – but would not be of the same significance as, say, the West Yorkshire Sports Counselling programme might have been to long-term probationers.

Use of records of vandalism on Splash sites

A further mechanism by which Splash might reduce crime was by simple deterrence – for example, if Splash is being run on a school site it is less likely that someone will throw a brick through one of the school windows at the same time. It would have been possible to collect information on insurance claims from schools where Splash had been run to see if a reduction in claims related to damage and theft had been reduced during the period of the summer holidays in which Splash used the school site. These could have been supplemented by asking school caretakers to keep a record of minor vandalism which would not have been recorded in insurance claims.

Evaluation of the national programme

The YJB asked programmes they had supported in 2000 and 2001 to compare police records of crime and incident data of the categories most associated with youth offending in an area where a scheme has been provided with the previous year when it was not. One difficulty with this method is that the geographical areas used in the collection of police records, called police basic command units (BCU), may not match the areas covered by the Splash scheme. Second, collating the evidence requires considerable additional time and effort for the police. Third, small numbers may make any change insignificant – a small change in any one area could be due to just one or two persistent offenders moving in or out of the area. It might be possible to identify this if one also had accurate records of the movement of known offenders.

These difficulties are illustrated by reports on the YJB-funded programmes in 2000 and 2001. The Cap Gemmini Ernst and Young (2001) report on the 2000 YJB-funded schemes reported that of 102 schemes only 73 had provided 'final reports', and of these only 43 had provided comparative crime statistics – although producing such evidence was a condition of funding. Cap Gemmini Ernst and Young was the 'national supporter' (2001: 1) of the YJB programme. According to a separate commentary by Gaber (2002), they ran the scheme as well as producing the evaluation report, and their main business is as a computer consultancy. The report on the 2000 schemes says that, 'comparing August 2000 with August 1999, figures where we have a large enough sample to be confident in the results show: a reduction in domestic burglary of 36 per cent, a reduction in "youth crime" of 18 per cent' (Cap Gemmini Ernst and Young, 2001: 3, 8). However it is not clear how many of the 43 schemes that were able to produce crime data also showed a large enough sample to be 'confident in the results'.

In monitoring the 2001 programme, the 2002 Cap Gemmini Ernst and Young report (2002) compared changes in reported crime in seven categories of offence between the increased number of Splash scheme areas and high-crime BCUs (Table 13.2).

Table 13.2 shows how many of the 145 schemes were able to provide data for these categories of crime. This ranges from 76 for drug offences to 46 for juvenile nuisance (one of the categories we might be most interested in), but for three other categories of crime it does not report the number of schemes that provided data. The commentary implies that the data in bold is that which is statistically significant. From this we can deduce that the number of schemes providing data on burglary, robbery and criminal damage were too small to produce significant findings. It notes that 'as expected, schemes which ran in 2001 for the first time, achieved even greater reduction in two of the three statistically significant categories: motor crime, 13%; juvenile nuisance, 22%; and drug offences, 24%' (Cap Gemmini Ernst and Young, 2002: 21). However, it goes on to say that 'the sample size of schemes running in both 2000 and 2001 and variations in data reported by schemes each year, rendered the results statistically insignificant' (2002: 21). So, it is not clear which data in Table 13.2 is significant. This finding is not related back to the previous year's report, which, as noted above, commented on a significant reduction in two types of crime.

Thus, the reports by the organisation that ran the national Splash scheme in 2000 and 2001 show the difficulties of obtaining local crime data, which may reflect the problem of matching it to Splash areas, and the problems of small numbers, either of schemes with data or of crime figures in individual schemes.

Table 13.2 Changes in crime 2000–2001, by BCU areas

Crime/incident category and sample	High-crime BCUs % change 2000–2001	Splash BCUs % change 2000–2001	Differential – Splash BCUs vs high-crime BCUs
Motor crime (70 schemes)	**39%**	**–11%**	**–50%**
Burglary	16%	4%	–12%
Robbery	19%	16%	–3%
Criminal Damage	N/A	4%	N/A
Juvenile nuisance (46 schemes)	N/A	**–16%**	N/A
Drug offences (76 schemes)	N/A	**–25%**	N/A

Source: Cap Gemmini Ernst and Young (2002) *Splash 2001: Final report*, London: Cap Gemmini Ernst and Young, 21

Interestingly, a Home Office Briefing Note on the 2000 Summer Splash Schemes (Loxley *et al.*, 2002) (although including a disclaimer that the views in it were not necessarily those of the Home Office, nor did they reflect government policy) reported that, of the six schemes the researchers examined, only three were able to produce detailed crime and disorder incident data. Of these, one showed a decline in incidents from 1999 to 2002. This was on a site where there had been little provision in 1999. In the other two there was 'no impact on crime and disorder'. This report questioned the need to target crime reduction resources in August as in only two of the three areas that provided crime data was there an increase in crime in August, and this was very slight. Thus this report also confirms the difficulty of collecting crime data and that, even when it is available, changes in individual areas may be very small. As noted below, these problems were apparent in Westtown where figures comparing crime in 2000 and 2001 for the three sites funded by the YJB in 2001 were small.

It is interesting that the research reports on Splash nationally could be seen to reflect the pressure for policy to be led and justified by evidence, but the value of the evidence produced appears to have been inflated by those who wish to promote the projects. The attempt to compare changes in categories of crime between BCUs, with and without Splash, reflects policy makers' preference for the classic experimental design (see Figure 4.1, page 32).

Results

Was Splash associated with crime reduction? – results from questionnaires and interviews

In 2001, responding to a closed question, 56 per cent of parents thought a major benefit of Splash for their children was 'to relieve boredom/something to do in the holidays'; 12 per cent 'to keep out of trouble'; and 14 per cent to 'to keep them off the streets'. This closed question was designed from the most common open responses in the 2000 parents' survey. Asking specifically about the relation to crime reduction, in the 2001 survey 22 per cent of parents felt Splash had no impact on crime in the local area; 61 per cent that it reduced crime while Splash is on; and 19 per cent that it reduced crime in the long run. These responses suggest that at least 61 per cent of parents believed that Splash had an impact on crime by reducing boredom and keeping children 'out of trouble'.

This was supported by interviews with participants. Thirty of the 63 participants interviewed in 2002 reported that Splash reduced crime either at exactly the same time as it was on or generally over the period of its provision. The major problem during the holidays was boredom. A participant commented:

> I think it just like helps people get out more. The only reason they did stuff what's bad 'cos they didn't have 'owt else to do. And that's like last resort, it's like they wanted attention and did something wrong, and then they got it, so they got chased ... Get out of the house when bored, it was boring at home.

When you're at school its, yea!, it's the holidays, but after a while you get bored. But when they have been doing Splash, there is something to do in the 6 week holidays. It's maybe only for a week, or two, but it's something to do.

Thirteen participants from those interviewed in 2002 made remarks that implied that they themselves had been prevented from getting in trouble. For example: 'We used to go out twocing cars (taking cars without owner's consent) and bricking windows. Other kids would ask us if we wanted to do it. Splash prevents us getting involved.'

When asked if Splash reduced crime they responded: 'Definitely, 'cos it's exciting.' It was 'summat to do instead of doing mischief'. It was 'better than chasing'. (Chasing is when you break a window and see if someone will chase you.) The impact on crime, as implied by these interviews, varied between sites. The following responses, from six different respondents, were all from one site:

> ... think it does [reduce crime] 'cos it gets them away from doing bad things by doing sports and things.

> [It does not reduce crime because] older kids, when doing crime and that, don't do it till late.

> [It would be better] if more kids who were not young offenders came. That has put off some of my friends. Yea, I think it does [reduce crime]. Before this summer a series of cars were set on fire here and since then its been better, there has not been one.

> Does it keep kids out of trouble? ... Yeah, it gives us something to do.

> Does it reduce crime? No, all the trouble starts at night.

> Would it make a difference if Splash went on longer? It would have to go on till 1.30 at night. Half the troublemakers don't come anyway.

So at this site some offenders have been involved in the programme – it was a diversion, but only when they were attending. A difficulty this poses for the sports leaders is in both leading the activities for these young people who are more disruptive and maintaining the interest of the other children. Two younger children at this site said that 'when we play with the older ones they swear' and 'sometimes the big ones spoil our games'.

Over the whole sample of 63, only 12 respondents did not think that Splash reduced crime while it was on. This might be because those involved in crime do not come to Splash or, as suggested by some of the quotes above, because Splash is not on long enough during the day: 'Makes no difference really ... [They] can still do crime when they leave here.' Overall, the interviews confirmed the impressions from the parents' questionnaires of 2000 and 2001 – that Splash does provide a diversion from crime when it is on.

Was Splash associated with crime reduction? – results from local crime data

Analysis of local crime data did not show a significant reduction in youth-related crime. Figures comparing crime in 2000 and 2001 for the three sites funded by the YJB in 2001 were too small, even if there had been a positive change, to show anything significant. Any change could have been due to one or two regular offenders moving in or out of the area.

Table 13.3 shows changes in recorded crime between August 2001 and August 2002 for the eight Splash areas that received additional YJB funding in 2002. This enabled them to offer a 5-week programme rather than 1 week, and thus would have been expected to increase a diversionary effect. August is used as this is the month in which the impact would have been expected to be most significant.

'All crime' is that recorded in the Home Office categories. Youth crime is 'other youth-related incidents'. In April 2001 a new standard for recording crime was introduced to achieve national consistency, but this should not have affected comparisons between August 2001 and 2002.

Table 13.3 allows a comparison of the areas in which Splash operations were expanded in 2002, with the trend for Westtown overall. The Westtown totals show an overall crime increase, expressed as a percentage. Overall this shows that in five out of eight areas youth-related incidents increased by a higher per centage than the Westtown total by between 7 per cent and 63 per cent more. Thus the recorded crime statistics did not support a diversion effect – unless one can argue that the increase is less than the increase in 'all crime' and Splash may have helped keep the youth increase from being even greater! The evidence above could suggest that without Splash the youth-related incidents would be higher than they are but this is masked by several other factors. As a sports leader reported, '... there are too many other factors within the young persons' lives to

Table 13.3 Changes in recorded crime between August 2001 and August 2002 for the eight Splash areas that received additional YJB funding in 2002

Area	All crime 2001	All crime 2002	% change	Youth incidents 2001	Youth incidents 2002	% change
Site 18	87	47	−50	77	81	+5
Site M	108	98	−9	117	120	+2
Site 17	69	101	+46	79	135	+70
Site D	76	81	+6	81	89	+10
Site DM	72	142	+97	111	162	+46
Site 12	109	129	+18	92	116	+26
Site B and 5	103	149	+45	114	142	+24
Site CM	66	87	+31	124	78	−63
Westtown Total	13,191	14,464	+10	2,335	2,494	+7

Source: Westshire Police

take into account which may have an impact on their criminal make up and pro-file, we are just one part of it'. So, Splash is only one influence on their lives; there may be others predisposing them towards crime, and possibly other local initiatives that reduce it. So attributing an impact of Splash on the statistics is very difficult, as it would be at a national level.

How and why might Splash be related to crime reduction?

Apart from the simple diversion mechanism discussed above, analysis of results was structured to examine if the factors one would expect to contribute to pro-social development were present. Generally these were in place for only a small minority of participants who were involved throughout the year.

The programme was attractive enough for young people to participate voluntarily, to want to attend again, and to want more of it. The 2000 and 2001 surveys of parents showed that in 85 per cent and 74 per cent of cases respectively it was the child who had made the decision to attend. In 2001, 91 per cent of children intended to come again the following year. When the children were asked the three best things about Splash the first was that it was fun (52 per cent); second, to meet new friends/new people (45 per cent); third, playing the games/activities; fourth, meet my friends; and fifth, off-site trips or a specific trip. Parents' major suggestion for improvement was extending the period Splash was run over the summer, or the length of individual sessions. Thus Splash was attractive to young people, they participated voluntarily, and their parents wanted more of it. Parents had confidence in the way Splash was run. There were very few negative comments and the vast majority were complimentary of the service. In 2001, 53 per cent of young people said they had attended Splash sessions in the previous year – confirming not only the popularity of Splash but also that there was some repeat involvement from one year to the next. In 2002 additional off-site trips – including climbing, canoeing, go-karting, mini motor bikes and a DJ workshop – were made possible through the YJB funding. These trips were very popular and valuable in keeping participants' interest. So parents and children enjoyed Splash and wanted more of it. For participants the major attraction was that it was fun, and particular activities were important to them.

The sports leaders had good relationships with the participants. The questionnaire completed by participants prior to the interviews in 2002 asked if they thought of their favourite sports leader as like a teacher, parent, friend or policeman. Of the 40 who responded 30 regarded the sports leader as a friend.

The long-term impact

There was no evidence that the summer Splash programmes by themselves contributed to long-term pro-social development; however, unlike many other similar programmes, Splash could have a long-term impact through the Splash Forums, in which young people could participate throughout the year, and through some of the related sports development sessions, also run during the year at a few sites. This was also possible because regular participants at the summer sessions might be able to become voluntary leaders, and this was the way many of the summer paid staff were recruited. This was so as summer staff would have a good feel for the ethos of the programme.

Interviews with some long-term participants and the full-time sports leaders showed how for a few young people Splash had become a very significant part of their lives. It had led to opportunities to take sports leadership awards, volunteer in the summer programme, and possibly choose a career in sports leadership. There was evidence of strong mentor relationships with individual sports leaders who would guide participants through a series of challenges. However, it was also recognised by sports leaders that it was hard to know 'when to let go'. One could spend a lot of time with just one or two participants, outside of one's work time. As in WYSC, there was a conflict between commitment to wanting to do a good job and knowing when one could reasonably stop.

Conclusion on the programme and evaluation method

Evaluation

As noted above, this type of summer activity, open-access programme, is very common, but is also difficult to evaluate. The case study approach, using a triangulation of methods, started from theory – in that methods were designed to test for a mechanism of pro-social development linking the programme with crime reduction – although it moved to a focus on diversion. The evaluation methods were extensive – beyond the scope of any programme to reasonably implement itself. Yet they also produced contradictory results. What is more convincing – the crime statistics in Table 13.3 (see page 168), which show a rise in crime in areas where Splash was introduced, or interviews with young people who say that Splash prevented them getting involved in petty crime? This takes us back to the debates in Chapter Four around what constitutes evidence. My conclusion was that the programme did have an impact on crime reduction through the diversion mechanism. There could be many reasons why the local crime data did not support this view.

Of the methods above, the most useful was the interviews with participants conducted on the sites in 2002. These allowed the researcher to not only find out from young people what the programme meant to them, but also to get a feel for how it was run. However, this was intensive work and required particular interview skills to quickly build a rapport with young people. For an internal evaluation the simplest tool would be the questionnaire to parents, including questions on why they used the programme, what was good about it, how it could be improved, and a direct question about a relation to crime via a diversion or a long-term personal development mechanism. In addition, as a minimum, programmes should keep the best record they can of how many children are using them, and ideally who is attending. During the period of the research Splash was attempting to set up a database of participants. This would also be very useful for marketing.

Whatever evaluation methods are used, they should start from a plausible story linking programme inputs, process and outputs, which they then set out to test. For most programmes, which operate only in the school holidays, this is probably that they provide either a direct diversion from offending or a diversion from boredom that may lead to offending. Methods need to be simple enough to be practical, and not get in the way of the process of the programme.

Similarly to the theory of change approach that seeks to influence policy (Chapter Four), as a programme manager it is worth thinking about who the key policy makers are and what type of evidence will impress them. The evidence may have to respond to a changing political agenda and priorities. For example, does the programme reduce crime, increase social exclusion, reduce drug use, or keep the residents of a particular marginal ward happy in the knowledge that something is being done to reduce minor vandalism? It must be sufficient to convince key politicians. If there is external funding, such as from the YJB, one may be obliged to produce specific types of evidence, such as the local crime data or a mass of participant evaluation forms. In this case the important thing appeared to be to actually produce some evidence, as much as what it actually appeared to show.

The programme

Westtown Splash had been successful in mainstreaming its basic budget. This was very important as managers did not have to worry about if they had funds to run next year's programme and it meant that Splash's continuity from year to year allowed for participants to develop into voluntary and paid leaders, and for parents to be familiar with the programme and look for it every year. Marketing and establishing the trust of parents was so much easier. The continuity is a major advantage over any Splash programme that relied entirely on YJB funding.

Focusing on the summer programme, key success factors were the quality of the staff, the attractiveness of the activities (including the extra off-site sessions put on in 2002 with the additional funds from the YJB), and the ease of access to the physical locations. Not only were the sessions within walking distance for the large majority of participants but they were also free. Participants commented that even a small charge would soon add up to a significant sum over a set of sessions. And the ability to drop in and out of sessions was a positive feature for participants – not least because people don't want to commit themselves to an outdoor session if the weather is miserable! (However, some very loyal participants braved all conditions.) Of course, the sessions also had to be well planned: staff and equipment had to be at the right place and at the right time.

The long-term work with young people had the characteristics of good youth work, in that a good relationship with a sports leader allowed him or her to lead the participant through a set of experiences involving greater challenge and responsibility. But as there were only a small number of sports leaders employed throughout the year, and they could only deliver a few sessions, the scope for this work was limited.

Balancing crime reduction and sports development objectives

While one objective of the Westtown programme was crime reduction, another was sports development. Initially Splash was set up as a crime prevention programme using sport, and was called Youth Against Crime. However, over time, objectives changed to sports development and reducing social exclusion. Thus encouraging socially disadvantaged young people to take part in sport was just as important as crime reduction. The programme was run by staff from the sports development section of the leisure department, though this had been moved to within the Young Peoples Services. This is not to say that in this case the crime reduction objective had been tacked on again to gain funding, in response to the YJB funding. However a sports leader explained: 'Sports development has always been key to me. ... when we were in Leisure, sports development was our main focus, but it's quite easy to see that the steering group's main focus was crime reduction. You never go out with one single focus.'

This illustrates not only the overlap between objectives but also that they change in response to funding sources. The balance of objectives needs to be recognized. Thus, while Loxley *et al.* (2002), in their review of Splash programmes, make recommendations for improving the programme from a crime reduction perspective, there may be some conflict with maximising the sports participation of disadvantaged young people. If the programme focused more on offenders it would deter more non-offenders, and thus reduce its ability to prevent young people getting involved in offending in the first place. This was illustrated on one site where participants were interviewed (quoted above); participant would be put off attending if the programme was focused on offenders and parents would not see it as the sort of programme they wanted to send their children to.

Similarly, Loxley *et al.* (2002: 2) suggested a pragmatic pricing policy, tailored to 'need, capacity to pay, and supply and demand'. This is considering efficiency – the need to achieve crime reduction at the lowest cost. But it is difficult to see how this could be applied in the Westtown situation, where participation was free, without significantly reducing involvement of those the scheme wishes to target the most; so it would reduce the effectiveness of both the crime reduction and sports development objectives. In any case, it is not practical in an open-access programme.

Given the sports development objectives, Westtown Splash had attempted to invite local sports clubs to run introductory sessions linked to the Splash programme. However only one had done this. This is an area where links to sports development could have been improved. Another was where a Splash site was adjacent to a leisure centre, which the Splash participants were not able to use as it had not been possible to negotiate an affordable rate with the contractor managing the centre. This gave a negative impression – that the centre was not for the young people using Splash. This reflects a general difficulty of building sports development objectives into contracts for facility management.

14 Northtown Parks for All

Summary

Parks for All was a policy, rather than a programme, directed towards improving use, and changing perceptions, of public parks. The parks had been in a spiral of neglect and under-use. Local residents were concerned about vandalism and anti-social behaviour by young people. A 'presence' in the parks was provided by leasing disused park buildings to martial arts centres (dojos) at a peppercorn rent and thus providing a deterrent to vandalism. The dojo operators' contract included patrolling the park. Simple recording systems for vandalism were set up, which showed a reduction coinciding with the establishment of the dojos. Just as important were changes in perception by local user groups. The scheme appeared to work in the short term, but in the long term it was asking too much of the partnerships with the dojo operators.

Introduction to the programme

Northtown Borough Council (this is an anonymous case study) introduced the Parks for All scheme in public parks in response to concerns of local residents. Residents were concerned about the run-down state of the parks and the removal of local park keepers in the early 1990s. In common with other local authorities, this was probably the result of a combination of financial constraint and the application of compulsory competitive tendering at the time. These were sensitive issues to local residents – some 'friends' groups had advocated fencing off and locking up parks to keep young people out and had objected to proposed schemes to develop a skateboard facility for young people.

Local political power in the Council was finely balanced, and this may also have contributed to the need to address the problem as a sensitive local issue. In 1996 the Council received a report commissioned from a consultant to identify the role of parks on the life of local young people of about 10–18 years of age, and their needs, with a view to increasing leisure opportunity for them: and to identify the role of parks in the life of local people and the attitude of adults and parents of the needs of young people in relation to parks and outdoor recreation. The consultation work included meetings with local groups (youth groups, teachers, youth service, residents' associations, police etc.), visits to facilities, a borough-wide self-completion questionnaire to households, and a survey of pupils in two schools. The conclusions were that there was a potential conflict of interests between adults and teenagers as they used the parks to meet different, although legitimate, needs. Both groups shared some views on the shortcomings of the parks, such as litter, graffiti, unruly gangs and dirty toilets. A recommendation was that the Council should 'not concentrate on large capital schemes but should encourage greater use by means of programming, enabling and experimental low-cost projects'. Private sector partnership and better use of existing facilities, such as pavilions, was recommended.

Presumably these recommendations were mindful of the financial constraints that had led to a run down of the parks in the first place, but an interesting conclusion is that the conflict between older and younger users might be as much perceptual as anything else. While some older residents might have a fear of crime, and the assumption is that this can be attributable to young people, many young people shared concerns about crime and the consequences of it. Hence the new policy was called Parks for All. The aim was to break out of a situation where a small number of young people engaged in anti-social behaviour, leading to a large number of young people being influenced by this, and local residents feeling threatened.

The key to achieving this was seen as a greater presence in the parks through an opportunistic use of disused facilities. This was first developed in Hill Recreation Ground, a large traditional park with a wide range of facilities, a year before the production of the consultant's report, noted above. Two martial arts exponents wanted a facility in which to run a 'dojo' – a martial arts training centre. An ideal facility was the unused cricket pavilion in this park. In exchange for the use of the pavilion at a peppercorn rent the dojo operators were required to provide a 'presence' in the park by patrolling it at intervals and reporting on vandalism. Another dimension to the initiative was that the martial arts training would be offered to local young people who might be considered to be 'at risk' – the training itself being assumed to lead to increased self-respect, respect for others and self-discipline. It was also planned to use the dojo as a drop-in centre for young people for 5 hours a week and to develop a youth forum, led by an officer from the youth service.

It is not known if the dojo had a means of targeting young people 'at risk'; however, it quickly became very successful in attracting a large number of participants who regularly practised martial arts, and attained high levels of performance. This was very likely due to the enthusiasm and personal qualities of the dojo operator, who combined an infectious enthusiasm for his martial art with an ability to develop an excellent relationship with the participants and public in the park. For example, if a member of the public needed a drink for their dog he would provide it. This was more an attitude of mind than a strict application of the conditions of the dojo rent. The operator was a former martial arts champion, with many years' experience in the sport. His partner in the dojo also had many years' experience in martial arts, and was chairman of the local youth action group. Both were very popular. The impressions local residents had of the dojo were further enhanced by publicity given to one of the operator's enforcement of a 'citizen's arrest' on a burglar who was attempting to escape from a local house by climbing over a garden fence into the park.

Originally, at the same time that the dojo was established, a contract was made with a commercial gym operator to run a gymnasium and manage the playing courts in the park from the same building as housed the dojo. This achieved the objective of developing use of the facilities, but the gym operator's objectives were purely commercial and did not extend to providing a general presence in the park. Thus the success of the dojo in achieving the Council objectives owed a lot to the personalities of the dojo operators.

The success of the dojo led a 'friends' group at a second park, Mound Recreation Ground, to approach the Council to ask if a similar facility could be developed. This friends group had previously been strongly critical of Council policy; it had opposed suggestions to develop facilities for young people, and in contrast had proposed restricting access to the park. Council officers supported the introduction of a dojo but, rather than suggest it directly, they suggested that the friends of this park contact the friends of the Hill Recreation Ground for advice and this led to enthusiasm for a similar solution.

A Chinese martial arts centre was opened in this park in 1998. In this case it was housed in a former lodge and then in pre-fabricated buildings, which were erected for the purpose in the park. The same peppercorn rent arrangement applied, but with a more formal contract to patrol the park at specific times. This included up to midnight on Friday nights – the time at which local residents perceived most anti-social behaviour took place. The work with young people was developed more formally; a youth forum was established in the martial arts centre, facilitated by the operator. This was part of a youth strategy for Northtown, which in turn was part of a county youth strategy. Thus, the work in the park could be presented to Council members as part of this broader youth strategy, which had a certain political credence. The operator was a former teacher so he had skills of working with young people.

After the martial arts centre opened the Mound park operator moved into the park lodge, so he was there for a longer period than just when the centre was open. Now friends groups, instead of reporting disturbances to the police, reported them directly to the rangers or to the dojo operator. They could then investigate them and involve the police only if that was strictly necessary. They would meet the young people directly. This role of engagement was considered more effective than using the police in an enforcement role. The friends group also perceived that they had a direct link to someone who would do something about the problems.

By 1999 the first dojo, in Hill Recreation Ground, was well established. The second, in Mound Recreation Ground, had yet to build up sufficient income to become viable in the long term. Both facilities depended on being able to generate sufficient income to operate as a viable business.

So, in terms of mechanisms of crime prevention, one might regard the scheme as mainly one of deterrent, to the extent that it reduced vandalism in the park.

The young people attracted to participate in the dojo and martial arts centre might experience some long-term pro-social development, though no evidence of this was collected, and it is not known if the same young people were responsible for any of the previous vandalism. However, just as important as either of these was the change in perception of the park by local residents, as somewhere they felt comfortable using, and that they felt they could take action to reduce vandalism. Ideally this would lead to greater use of the parks by all groups, which in turn would lead to reduced vandalism.

Evaluation and results

Evaluation methods were conducted internally by the Council, using reports of the park ranger service, reports of the martial arts instructor in Mound Recreation Ground, and local police incident reports.

The park ranger service developed a systematic record of vandalism in the parks from 1995. This was supplemented by records of youth disturbances reported to the rangers. In Hill Recreation Ground incidents of vandalism recorded by the park ranger service were 14, 10, 9 and 5 in 1995, 1996, 1997 and 1998 respectively. This fall coincided with the development of the dojo in 1995. The park ranger records were able to show the specific types of vandalism and comparisons with other parks over the same time period. From this one could see that the main drop was in vandalism related to buildings, probably because the buildings were now occupied for much of the time. The comparisons showed that Hill Recreation Ground had relatively low levels of vandalism compared with similar parks, and had dropped down a rank order of vandalism over this period. So, although the figures were relatively small, they supported the view that the dojo had acted as a deterrent. These figures were used in reports to councillors. It would also have been possible to translate them into the costs saved by the reduced need for repairs. The figures also showed a marked decline at Mound Recreation Ground for the 2 years after the introduction of the martial arts centre.

The ranger recording system could also be used to show general patterns of vandalism and disturbances, which were as expected: a peak in the summer months; most disturbances at weekends; greatest damage to buildings, followed by damage to park furniture.

An interesting observation in the ranger report for the period 1995–1999 was that, while public perception, as far as it could be gauged, appeared to be generally equal to reality, in 1999 vandalism in Hill Recreation Ground had increased to 18 instances from 5 the previous year. Yet user groups had not noticed this. This may have been because the overall change was not great, or because the pro-active efforts of the martial arts centre staff had such a strong impact on public perceptions of safety. It was also recognised that vandalism figures may appear to increase as the recording process became more sophisticated, so they needed to be treated with caution.

In Mound Recreation Ground the operator kept a record of youth disturbances, which could be complemented by those of the ranger service and of the friends of the park group. The ranger service reports only covered the period between 6 pm and 8.45 pm, while the operator's reports covered the period up to 1 am. These reports were useful because, in the first few weeks the operator was making them (May to July 1998), they showed that the main problem was groups of about 30 youths drinking between 11 pm and 12 pm, who committed minor vandalism. A police presence was effective only when the police were on the site; after they left the youths would return. There were few problems when the ranger service, or the martial arts instructor, were actually present, though it was difficult to engage the youths to work with them as they were there only late at night. Temporary reductions in late-night gatherings of drunken youths were associated with bad weather or alternative parties rather than the presence of the martial arts instructor. Initial reports indicated that building up a relationship with the youths would take more than a few weeks.

A third source of data was provided by police records of incidents in the parks. These need to be interpreted with care because many incidents, such as 'suspicious person', 'false alarm', 'collapse/illness' and 'disturbance' were not related to any crime. Actual crimes fell in Hill Recreation Ground from 19, to 2, to 4 from 1997 to 1999. Again, although the overall figures are small, this supports the view that the dojo was a deterrent. Similarly to the ranger data, incidents were more common in the summer and more when the park was closed. At Mound Recreation Ground recorded crimes were none in 1997, 1 in 1998, and 3 in 1999. But these changes were far too small to show anything significant.

A fourth source of information was from meetings with the friends groups – who were enthusiastic about the scheme. As the discontinuity between friends' perceptions and incidents recorded by the rangers in Hill Recreation Ground in 1999 showed, the friends' perceptions were probably the most important thing. Potentially further monitoring could have been through surveys of those occupying houses surrounding the parks to compare perceptions over time. This was not conducted and would have been expensive.

Conclusion on the programme and evaluation method

The chief recreation officer viewed the park as a valuable asset that needed to be used to its full potential. Innovative partnerships with the commercial sector, in the form of the dojo operators, allowed a presence to be provided in the park at no additional cost to the Council. It was crucial to gain the support of the local residents, and this could be done by the physical presence of the dojos, the positive relationships with the dojo operators, and the knowledge that something would be done soon if they made a complaint. The 'theory of change' was that a presence would deter vandalism and encourage more use of the park, which in turn would reduce vandalism further. A second aspect of this was that youths involved in vandalism might otherwise be diverted into martial arts – although there was no evidence that this was the case. The simple but systematic recording systems for vandalism allowed evidence to be collected and presented to councillors and residents. However, figures were small and could easily be distorted by specific factors, or the way they were collected. If the main mechanism was deterrence, one could argue that figures for the areas around the parks would be required to show if vandalism had merely relocated. However, the recording systems were practical for a local authority to implement without specialist input.

So how much of this was by design, and how much by chance, and to what extent is this approach replicable? In the case of Hill Recreation Ground, much of the benefit of the scheme was due to the personality of the dojo operator. The contract to patrol the park was relatively under-developed, but the dojo operator's personality meant that local residents had a very favourable impression. In Mound Recreation Ground the contract was more specific and involved patrols by the dojo operator at times associated with youth disturbances. However, this, and the possibility of being called out at other times, was an onerous obligation. The long-term presence of both dojos depended on them being financially viable.

To what extent was martial arts itself a significant factor? The chief recreation officer stressed its positive attributes in developing young people, but there is no indication whether participation acted as a direct diversion for those who might otherwise have been involved in vandalism. The dojos had the advantage of operating in the evenings – when vandalism might otherwise have occurred. The skills of the dojo operators in working with young people and, to a point, their own physical presence, may also have been a factor.

The Parks for All policy had potential for developing in many different ways and work with young people was only part of it. A family festival in Mound park and involving local friends groups in planting trees and shrubs were others. These innovations reflected the approach of the chief recreation officer at the time.

Postscript

The case study above was completed in 1999 and subsequent events showed that the scheme was not viable in the long term. The dojo operators were small contractors and it was asking them to do too much to both run a sustainable business and patrol the park, and conduct youth work with difficult groups of young people. The most they could do was provide a presence in the park just by running the dojos in previously unused buildings. The ranger service was expanded, and youth development officers were employed to work with the young people in the parks. Thus, the principle of letting private sector operators use vacant buildings in the parks so at least someone was there, was valid. The recording systems used by the ranger service were also a useful monitor of vandalism.

15 Modelling programmes and balancing objectives

Starting programme design from theory

Programme design should be based on informed theory about how and why the programme might reduce crime. This should be made as explicit as possible in terms of who the programme will work with, how they are involved, the process of the programme, intermediate effects/outcomes and long-term outcomes – as in Figure 15.1.

Making this 'theory of change' explicit, however simple it is, is the first step towards a coherent programme design, and communicating this between stakeholders and programme staff, and is a general principle of sports development work (Coalter, 2002). Programme design can be broadly informed by the combination of target group risk level and the mechanism by which the programme might reduce crime – as in Table 15.1.

Thus, the theory of change – how and why the programme achieves its objectives – has implications for programme design. For example, if the prime mechanism is simple diversion from boredom, and if the target group is low-risk participants, it is a good idea to deliver the programme in areas of relatively high crime and high socio-economic deprivation. The activities have to be attractive to divert the target group from whatever else they might have been doing. Further, if one of the results of boredom is vandalism of properties during the

1	2	3	4	5
Type of participant	Process of getting involved	Programme content and process	Intermediate effects	Main objective – reduced propensity to take part in crime

Figure 15.1 The elements of the process of a crime reduction programme in sequence

Source: author

Table 15.1 A typology of programmes and mechanisms

Risk level/ mechanism	Tertiary – high risk	Secondary – medium risk	Primary – low risk
Pro-social development	Positive Futures/ Sportaction	Fairbridge	Splash (long term)
		Clontarf	
	WYSC Hafotty Wen 14 Peaks		
Deterrence			Northtown Parks for All scheme Splash on-school sites
Diversion		Summit	Splash Many local authority holiday schemes

school holidays, then it makes sense to site the programme at these properties to take advantage of a deterrent effect mechanism as well. Thus, the Splash programme described in Chapter Thirteen was targeted at such sites – combining mechanisms of diversion and deterrence. Cunning programme design can capitalise on a synergy between mechanisms.

Of course, one would expect this theory of change to develop as a result of programme evaluation and review. Hence, the Parks for All policy (Chapter Fourteen) was initially based on an assumption that young people involved in vandalism would be recruited to the marshal arts dojos and benefit from a process of pro-social personal development. In practice there was no evidence that this happened, so either the theory of change would need to be modified or the programme changed to achieve it. Changes are more likely to be refinements to improve existing mechanisms; for example, the WYSC programme introduced follow-up sessions for participants to keep their interest in the activities and maintain a diversion effect.

Table 15.1 and the outline of theory in Chapter Three are, of course, only one starting point in understanding how and why sports programmes might reduce youth crime. This starting point depends on the breadth of theory that can be crystallised into one model. For example, Pawson (2006) reviews in much greater depth an understanding of mentoring than is covered in Chapter Three. And theory will evolve with more research.

Starting programme evaluation from theory

I concur with Pawson and Tilley (1997) that evaluation, as well as programme design, should start from theory – whether evaluation is conducted by the programme itself, or by external consultants. Ideally evaluation should be built into

programme design. Theory may be from textbooks, such as this, or from the programme staff's theory of change as in the Fairbridge evaluation. In practice there
will not be a clear distinction between the two, and it would have been interesting
to have researched where Fairbridge staff's theory of change came from. From an
academic point of view it is easier to add to academic theory if that is one's starting
point (and much easier to then produce academic papers – a key performance indicator in the academic world). However, an advantage of the approach in Fairbridge
was that the staff felt engaged and motivated in the research process through this,
and through their further involvement in design of the research tools.

A compromise between the two positions (starting from 'academic' theory or
programme staff's theory of change) is offered by Pawson and Tilley's (1997:
164–5) description of the interview process in realistic evaluation. Rather than
the researcher coming to the interview with a completely blank page, the interview is a process through which the researcher tests out and refines their own
theory through first sharing it with the interviewee, then learning how the interviewee understands the situation, and this results in a refined theory. Thus the
interview is a process of theory sharing and refinement. In the Fairbridge case
this might have worked by the researcher coming to the Fairbridge staff, presenting them with the ideas in Chapter Three, and then exploring the degree to
which they corresponded to the staff's experience. This would need to be treated
with care as Pawson and Tilley's account does not acknowledge the implications
of the asymmetric relationship between researcher and interviewee in terms of
existing knowledge and status. If I were to interview Fairbridge staff in this way
to elicit a theory of change, which we then shared, I would have to be very careful to emphasise that the theory I brought with me was just one perspective and I
really valued their own views, which might well be different because of their own
particular experience.

Dangers of starting evaluation from theory

If the research is focused on only one mechanism, one might overlook another
which the research instruments are not designed to explore. One needs to be
aware of this possibility. Thus an evaluation of Splash could start with methods
designed to explore the mechanism of long-term pro-social development but
find out that the mechanism of simple diversion was more important. In the
case study of Splash the focus was able to change because the research was conducted over 3 years. However, other mechanisms such as the ability to offer
employment to long-term participants and, through this, income and a stake in
society, might also have been important. More generally, one can't assume that
every possible mechanism is covered by the models in Chapters Three and Six
above. The criticism of research findings being limited by the perspective one
comes from can be generally applied to a realist or deductive evaluation. For
example, Pawson's review of research into mentoring programmes (Pawson,
2006: 125) starts from his own model of the process and views other studies
through this 'lens'. I'd agree that it is reasonable to start from the researcher's

synthesis of theory (as demonstrated by the structure of this book), and make this explicit, but one has to be wary of this precluding other interpretations.

A further difficulty is that research might be led to explore the mechanism it is easiest to research. For example, the national research into Splash concentrated on the diversion mechanism because it could do this using secondary data on local crime statistics, which the programmes were obliged to collect as a condition of funding. There were not the resources to conduct the depth of research, as in the Splash case study reported here. The focus on local crime statistics would miss any impact a long-running programme, such as the Splash case study, might have had on long-term pro-social development.

Choosing to measure outputs and outcomes, and the assumptions linking them

In common with any sports development programme (Coalter, 2002: 38), the choice of outputs and outcomes to measure will be determined by the theory of change. Outcomes are usually thought of as an indication that the objectives of the programme have been achieved (has crime been reduced by this programme?), and outputs as an indication of the process (how many people were on the crime reduction programme and for how long?). It may be easy to build output measurement into the programme administration. For example, the Summit programme measured attendance of participants and how many gained gold, silver and bronze awards. Clontarff measured retention rates at school. WYSC could measure programme completion rates and Hafotty Wen could measure the numbers who completed the 14 Peaks expedition.

It is harder to measure outcomes – the long-term objectives of the programme. This is partly because one wants to measure change over a longer period of time. It is easier to do this with high-risk participants who are monitored more intensively and where resources are more likely to be available. So it was possible to measure reconviction rates of WYSC and Hafotty Wen participants, partly because the data was already collected on these higher-risk participants. However, one could still argue that this was over only a 2-year period. Clontarff was able to monitor the number of its students who moved into employment, although it is not known how long it was possible to monitor this after they left the academy. The Fairbridge study was exceptional in having the resources to track down participants a year after the initial programme, but no longer than that. However, in all these cases it could be argued that ideally one would want to examine outcomes over several years, and the longer the time period involved, the harder it is to show a causal relationship to the programme.

One might also measure intermediate outcomes. For example, from the model of pro-social development in Chapter Three, if this was the ultimate outcome, then intermediate outcomes might be increases in self-confidence, social skills, new peers, and a progression in responsibility.

Outcomes are not easily split into intermediate and final categories. So rather than thinking of them as in Figure 15.1 (see page 180), as discrete stages, where the intermediate outcomes correspond to box 4 and the final outcomes to box 5, really we are looking at a process where there is a sequence of outcomes, which our theory of change suggests will have a causal relationship to each other, in a chain reaction. For example, our theory may suggest that increased social skills and self-esteem might lead to greater employability and hence reduced offending. Thinking of change as a process is consistent with the notion of generative causality – the interaction between the participant and the programme. Breaking this down into discrete stages is a conceptual tool, useful to describe the process and inform evaluation. This means that the distinction between outputs and outcomes can become unclear – either can be a measure of part of a causal chain of events. For example, the Fairbridge programme aimed at long-term behavioural improvements in young people. These included better performance in jobs and education, stable housing arrangements and having a positive attitude towards self and others. These, it was claimed, were facilitated by gains in personal skills – which in turn were a result of the good relationship between participants and Fairbridge staff, and the activities that gained initial commitment to the programme, and were an effective medium for the process.

So what exactly are outputs, intermediate outcomes and long-term outcomes in this chain of events? In the Fairbridge case one could argue that the outcomes were the long-term behavioural changes in participants, the intermediate outcomes were the short-term changes, and the outputs were how many people attended the programme and what they did on it. However, an output might also have been the number of people who took part in a canoeing session – and persuading people to take part in such a session could be seen as an intermediate outcome. What is more important is that a logical chain of events is being measured at different points.

While in many cases it will not be possible to measure the final outcome corresponding to the objective of the programme, if we settle for measuring an intermediate outcome, this is only as valid an indication of the final outcome as is our theory linking the two together. For example, in the Summit programme a two-stage questionnaire attempted to measure changes in self-esteem and personal fitness. The sports leader was also recording changes in the amount of responsibility taken by participants, and the researcher was also exploring, through interviews, independent sports participation. The assumption was that these intermediate outcomes would lead to pro-social personal development, which would reduce potential to be involved in crime. The validity of positive changes in any of these intermediate outcomes as an indication of long-term crime reduction were only as valid as the assumptions linking them to pro-social personal development and to crime reduction. So, at some points in the chain of causality one is still going to have to rely on theory rather than evidence.

Similarly, even if one can distinguish between outputs and outcomes, there is only any point measuring outputs if they are related to long-term outcomes. For example, one might measure the number of times the sports leader met a client in the Sportaction programme, but this is useful only to the extent that the amount of contact is positively related to the outcome of behavioural changes: perhaps the quality of contact is more important.

So, overall, what one decides to measure in evaluation will be determined by the theory of change of the programme, but at some point one may have to settle for not being able to measure the final outcomes, and acting in the faith that our theory of change provides a valid link to these outcomes. The difficulties of not being able to measure the final outcome offer particular problems to scientific realism, which seeks to test outcome/mechanism/context configurations.

Limits of 'evidence-led' policy

There are technical and practical reasons why it is harder to produce 'evidence' linking programmes working with clients low on the risk scale, and using the mechanism of diversion, to crime reduction.

As noted in Chapter Thirteen, discussing national evaluation of the Splash programme, comparing police records of crime and incident data of the categories most associated with youth offending in an area where a scheme had been provided with the previous year when it was not, is limited because the geographical areas used in the collection of police records may not match the areas covered by the scheme. Further, collating the evidence requires considerable resources beyond the capacity of most schemes, and requires a well-funded research programme with guaranteed access to relevant data. Third, small numbers may make any change insignificant. Fourth, a small change in any one area could be due to just one or two persistent offenders moving in or out of the area. In the Splash programme, self-completion questionnaires sent to parents of participants were used and interviews were conducted with participants, but these methods, especially the interviews, required considerable resources. However, this chapter explains why several other methods were not practical, including: comparison of attendance with YOT records; use of school records; and before-and-after measures – including those attempting to measure development of social skills and protection factors.

In the Splash programme, looking for a mechanism of pro-social development, parents' questionnaires and interviews with participants could go a little way towards this but, the less intense the programme, the harder it is to explore generative causality. In the Splash case the experience of just one summer holiday week might have nudged a participant in the right direction – and the possibility of long-term involvement through the Splash Forums and volunteering on the programme might have been significant. But one can't get a long way towards understanding changing perceptions of the participant through the programme (generative causality) if the programme is only 1 week on a field (Splash), and the means of gaining this understanding is limited to a 10-minute interview on the side of the same field. This does not rule out the possibility of a mechanism of pro-social development in programmes such as Splash: it is just harder to detect it, and it won't be very significant.

So a general implication for 'evidence-led' policy is that a programme such as Splash, working with low-risk participants, where the primary mechanism is diversion, but where there may be some deterrent and pro-social development too, and where there is an open-access policy, has inherent difficulties showing a causal relationship to crime reduction. However, such programmes are the most common type run by local authorities and touch the lives of many young people. Having a little impact on a lot of people (although it is hard to measure it) may be better than having more impact on a few people (programmes such as Hafotty Wen and WYSC). So some programmes are disadvantaged if policy is led entirely by evidence. However, Chapter Sixteen will argue that evidence is only one thing that leads policy.

Responses to changing funding sources

The objectives of programmes may be malleable in response to funding opportunities and political priorities. A major objective of programme managers, especially in local authorities, is to obtain external funding to allow them to continue running (Nichols and Booth, 1999a); a consequence of short-term funding is that this objective of programme survival can easily overtake the one of what the programme is actually supposed to achieve. This applies to a wide range of local authority programmes (Long *et al.*, 2002). While a criticism of many programmes has been that they have been short term, some of the case study programmes showed how they bid for new funding sources, and were successful in obtaining them, and as a consequence experienced a changed focus of objectives.

This was best illustrated by the Splash programme. Splash was initially set up as a crime prevention programme using sport, called Youth Against Crime, as a partnership between Westshire Police and Westtown Sports Development. At the time it was easier to obtain funds for a programme that had a stated objective of crime reduction than it was to obtain funds for developing sport. However, its position in the sports development section of the local authority leisure department meant that sports development objectives had equal importance. Later, as social inclusion became a broad political agenda at the local level, it was fitted into this. In the summer of 2001, in response to national concerns over racial crime, additional funding was received from the Youth Justice Board (YJB) to run Splash on additional sites, targeted at reducing racial tension. These were sites where there were significant concentrations of ethnic minority groups in relation to the general population. In 2002 further funding was also given from the YJB, focused on general crime reduction. Westtown Splash was targeted by the YJB as a recipient of funds only a few weeks before the summer programme was due to start in 2002. Westtown was told to accept the additional funding for 2002, or they believed that the extra funding they had received in 2001 would be withdrawn. This reflected the YJB's need to allocate funding in a short period of time to organisations they trusted to deliver the programmes. Thus this Splash programme had had successive objectives of sports development, crime reduction, achieving social inclusion and reducing racial tension. The balance between these had changed in response to political imperatives and the objectives of funders.

This example also shows that a funding organisation may have a short period of time in which to distribute funds. There is a concern to make sure that the funds will be well spent but, on the other hand, it is not practical to research in detail the quality of work of each organisation the funds are allocated to (the opposite of the National Lottery, where there is an extensive application process). Funds may be allocated more on reputation than extensive evidence of an organisation's work. This was also apparent in the Sportaction case, where funds were distributed by Sport England under the Positive Futures programme.

While the Summit programme's objectives – crime reduction through sport – remained constant, its client group changed as the work of the organisations it sold its programme to within the youth justice system changed. The Summit programme changed its client group from probationers, to YOT clients, to the higher-risk ISSP clients. When YOTs were introduced, Summit was in a good position to gain work from them as there were few alternative programmes they could buy. Easttown Leisure Department had substantial credibility with the YOT due to its previous work on a Splash-type programme with the local police; several YOT officers had been involved in this Splash programme; and the Easttown sports development manager knew the YOT manager personally. The main need for Easttown YOT was to find a credible programme deliverer: a YOT officer reported that the programme's strength was that it would take youngsters referred to it within 2 weeks – other programmes were not run so effectively. This confidence in delivery was at least as important as evidence of effectiveness, in terms of outcomes.

Thus programme objectives and participants may change with funding sources and political priorities. This can happen at short notice because funders have short periods in which to allocate funds. As a consequence, funds may be allocated on the basis of reputation rather than extensive evidence of effectiveness. Multiple and changing objectives are a practical necessity in ensuring funding. This can lead to a criticism of unclear programme objectives (McCormack, 2001; Witt and Crompton, 1996) although this fails to recognise the programmes' development.

Balancing programme objectives

A further complication is that local authorities may have multiple objectives for programmes – crime reduction, sports development, social inclusion and community development may all be relevant. Examples are Summit, Splash, Parks for All and WYSC. This is one reason why planning and evaluation may be more difficult than in the private sector. But does this necessarily lead to a lack of programme integrity – a mismatch of objectives, resources and delivery methods – or is it a demonstration of synergy? There may be a synergy between objectives of sports development and crime reduction through either diversion or pro-social development mechanisms. In the short run a programme such as Splash can both introduce socially disadvantaged young people to new sports opportunities and contribute to crime reduction through diversion. To the extent that programmes target the socially disadvantaged, there is also an overlap with objectives of reducing social exclusion. In the long run, if any of the programmes lead to long-term independent sports participation, this may also contribute to a diversionary effect. The potential for developing sports leadership skills and responsibilities contribute to pro-social development through increasing self-esteem, social skills and locus of control. Thus, there is a further overlap between sports development and crime reduction via the pro-social development mechanism. So, there will be synergy between objectives in any one programme. This has implications for programme design and evaluation.

Where a programme has both sports development and crime reduction objectives, although they overlap, one would expect the emphasis to be on crime reduction with high-risk participants and on sports development with low-risk ones. Thus Splash had a greater emphasis on sports development and WYSC more on crime reduction.

To the extent that there is an overlap of sports development and crime reduction objectives, based on the assumption that sports participation will provide a long-term alternative to crime, the barriers to overcome include all those associated with social exclusion and low sports participation (Collins and Kay, 2003). These were recognised by the sports leaders in the Summit programme as: lack of transport; lack of parental support; cultural barriers preventing young people becoming involved in organisations that are dominated by middle-class participants; and funding for kit. Of these, cultural barriers were especially significant. These are more likely to apply disproportionately to those involved in offending, where offending is related to social disadvantage. Thus, if an objective is sports development, one will need to design the programme to overcome the barriers to sports participation.

Careful planning can maximise the synergy between sports development and crime reduction objectives. The Westtown Splash programme had a site in a field next to a local authority leisure centre, but was not able to use this centre because the management contract for the centre did not include use by the Splash programme. Even when there was heavy rain, the Splash sessions remained outside in a field, while the centre was under-used. The was counter to sports development objectives and ideally the programme would have included at least an introduction to use of the centre.

Balancing sports development and crime reduction

Splash illustrated a potential conflict between sports development objectives and crime reduction. Loxley *et al.* (2002), in concluding a review of Splash programmes, recommended increasing effectiveness in crime reduction through using police records of youth-related disturbances to show the times and places at which most took place, and therefore when and where programmes should be delivered. However, if programmes were targeted more effectively at offenders, as appears to have happened at one Splash site in the case study, it will present greater problems for the sports leaders in managing the sessions. It may also deter non-offenders and the parents of non-offenders, who want to send their children to a 'safe' environment rather than to mix with the youngsters whom they know are involved in offending. Thus, a more precise targeting of Splash on crime reduction would conflict with sports development objectives and probably be beyond the capability of sports development officers to deliver. The balance between sports development objectives and crime reduction will determine if one employs workers with the skills for predominantly one role or the other. One can always argue that a sports development worker will be limited in what they can do for crime reduction – as discussed in the Sportaction and Splash case studies.

Balancing financial and crime reduction objectives

A difficulty faced especially by more intensive programmes is balancing the needs of participants, and the motivation of staff to meet them, with the allocation of resources to run the programme. The WYSC programme had an ill-defined duration, in that after the basic course sports leaders might keep in touch with participants to help them take part in further activities. This had a positive impact – but probably relied on the part-time sports leaders putting in more time than they were paid for. A similar problem with Fairbridge was knowing when to stop work with any one client. Again, in the Splash programme, for example, a sports leader's commitment to helping a participant who was involved in the Splash Forums meant they spent a very large amount of time with just one person. In the Sportaction programme a very large proportion of the sports leader's time was spent with just two clients. The concentration of resources is a reflection of the sports leaders' commitment to their work, but may not be seen as effective in terms of costs or time. The Summit programme evolved to take a more 'hard-headed' approach to this in that its contract was to deliver a specific number of programmes to YOT clients in a specific time. Therefore the sports leader had to give clients only what was defined in the contract with the YOT – 12 sessions – and then move on to the next client. This enabled the sports leader to manage his resources effectively in terms of achieving the outputs that had been sold to the YOT. However, a little extra work with clients, paid for from the sports development budget, could have enhanced their chances of long-term sports participation.

Loxley *et al.*'s (2002: 2) review of Splash programmes suggested a pragmatic pricing policy, tailored to 'need, capacity to pay, and supply and demand'. It is difficult to see how this could have been applied in the Westtown situation, where participation was free, without significantly reducing the involvement of those the scheme most wished to target. It would conflict with the objective of reducing social exclusion, and it would probably deter offenders from attending. As Splash is an open-access programme, charging could be applied only to the off-site trips participants had to register for. This would alienate children whose parents could not afford to pay for them. It could even increase crime if some offenders stole to gain money to pay for the trips!

16 The approach to evaluation, the values of key policy stakeholders, and what is practical

An academic perspective – the role of methodology

Chapter Four outlined four different research approaches: the classic experimental design; qualitative methods; critical realism; and the 'theory of change' – in two different forms. These are not definitive, but they show how the choice of approach can be justified by methodological assumptions about how we generate knowledge about the world (epistemology) and the nature of reality (ontology). Such a justification is required if one is preparing a PhD or an academic paper. It is important to be clear and consistent about these assumptions so one's approach to the creation of knowledge can be justified. Others may not share the same assumptions, but as their position is based on different ones they can't argue that your position is wrong – just incommensurable. (Such was the debate between Pawson and Tilley, and Farrington, described in Chapter Four.) So one reason for choosing a particular research approach is because it is based on methodological beliefs, and thus is academically credible. Of course, another might be that one actually happens to believe those 'beliefs' and has a degree of intellectual integrity! However, the world is not inhabited solely by philosophers, so other factors come into play.

A pragmatic perspective – the role of value judgements of research sponsors, policy makers, local politicians and gatekeepers

The influence of research sponsors

Research sponsors may have a preference for a particular research approach, whether based on a philosophical position or value judgements, and this will determine the methods used. This is particularly significant in contract research – where research is contracted to a research company/consultancy/academic department, which then has to conduct it in the way the sponsor wants.

It appears that the UK Home Office and Youth Justice Board has in the past had a preference for the classic experimental design. For example, the Cap Gemmini Ernst and Young (2002) report on Splash 2001 (reviewed in Chapter Thirteen) was based on this design, in that crime statistics for areas where Splash was run were compared before and after the Splash programme was operating. Similarly, the report for the UK Department for Education and Employment on their summer activities scheme for 16-year-olds used a simple before-and-after questionnaire (Hutchinson *et al.*, 2001; Nichols, 2001b). This programme aimed to help the transition from secondary school to adult life, and to enhance a range of personal and social skills among young people who might otherwise lose contact with education, employment and training. This was to be achieved through programmes varying in length between 3 and 21 days, predominantly using outdoor adventure activities. The evaluation attempted to measure changes in eight sets of personal skills, using 20 statements in total, each measured on a four-point Likert scale. Questionnaires were administered before and after the courses. To give a specific example: self-esteem was measured by responses to the statements:

- I feel good about myself most of the time.
- I sometimes feel that I cannot cope with things.

Of course one can question these methods. How valid a picture of an individual's self-esteem do these two statements give? How valid will be a measure of change over a 3-day period? To what extent will responses be a reflection of the participants' immediate circumstances – starting a new course in a new setting with new people, or immediately at the end of the course – rather than a longer-term change? The report itself noted that project managers dealing with 'young people with low academic ambition' (Hutchinson, *et al.*, 2001: 57), who are the target group of the programme anyway, thought the questionnaire should be simplified. However, this before and after questionnaire was either the approach favoured by the Department for Education and Employment, or the one that the evaluators employed by them thought they would favour, despite the fact that from its own perspective of the 'classical experimental design' this type of evaluation virtually never meets its own 'gold standard' (see Chapter Four).

The influence of policy makers

If the purpose of evaluation is to influence policy, the methods used have to be regarded as valid by key stakeholders in the policy community. This was exactly the approach taken by the Fairbridge evaluation, in which key stakeholders in the policy community were invited on to an advisory group. This group met several times during the period of the evaluation – which took over three years. Members included representatives of the government Connexions Service for young people, Her Majesty's Inspectorate of Education in Scotland, the government Social Exclusion Unit, the Joseph Rowntree Foundation (a foundation that supports research to influence policy with objectives of social justice), an academic, a representative of the Department for Education and Science, and a former Chief Probation Officer. Crucially this group agreed at the start of the research the standard of evidence that would convince them that the Fairbridge programme had particular outcomes. Clearly members of this group were influential members of the policy community, relevant to Fairbridge's work. The consultants managing the research made a considerable effort to keep the members of the advisory committee involved. The length of the evaluation meant that new members were invited to join as new organisations became important in youth policy. It is in this sense that the theory of change refers not only to the change in participants brought about by the programme, but also the change in policy brought about by the research.

The influence of local politicians

Local politicians are one set of policy makers – of particular importance to the many programmes run through local government. This was confirmed by a survey of such programmes in the UK (Nichols and Booth, 1999a) and in the USA (Schultz *et al.*, 1995). Given the difficulties of conducting evaluation at a local level, the views of local politicians on what is valid and adequate evidence of programme success are crucial.

Of course, this does not mean that all a programme has to do is invite key politicians to photo opportunities with groups of young people enthusiastically taking part in the programme – although this helps! The collection of evidence is still important and one has to make the most of what can be obtained. Thus the Splash programme reported here had at one time collected information on insurance claims for school property at sites where the programme was operating in the school holidays. Over the corresponding 16-week period the year before the programme was operating, insurance claims were £40,000: when the programme was operating these were reduced to £5–6,000. Similarly, the Northtown Parks for All programme had set up a system whereby the park ranger service collected records of vandalism – and these simple measures were used in council reports. However, the officer managing the Northtown scheme was aware that the interpretation of these records was not straightforward – an apparent increase in vandalism might reflect an improved recording system.

The Parks for All programme also illustrates the political importance of local pressure groups. In this case the parks' 'friends' groups were more important because of the delicate political balance on the council. The favourable impression the friends group had of the dojo in Hill Recreation Ground was more important than the recorded rise in vandalism in 1999. In both parks local residents were impressed by the scheme because they felt they now had a chance to do something directly about disturbances in the parks by reporting them to the dojo operators. So, the management of public opinion is also important. If the public think a programme works and are enthusiastic about it, it will be hard for councillors to cut it.

More generally, Crompton (2004), in the USA, has argued that if one is going to convince key policy makers of the value of leisure and recreation, one must convince them that it achieves some policy objective they value. His starting points are: he values leisure for its own sake but, to justify it, he has to understand which objectives policy makers value, and produce evidence that convinces them that leisure achieves these.

The influence of academic gatekeepers and a sociology of 'adequate' explanation

Academic gatekeepers' views on the validity of evidence are more relevant when one attempts to publish the findings rather than when one is designing the research. Journals have methodological preferences. For example, the American *Journal of Applied Recreation Research* and *Journal of Park and Recreation* favour a positivist approach and the 'classical experimental design'. So an account of the Fairbridge research appeared in the second of these. On the other hand, *Leisure Studies*, a UK journal, features more qualitative work – and an account of the Summit programme appeared in this. Of course, journals obtain a reputation for accepting certain types of work so, while what they publish is partly a reflection of the methodological preferences of the editorial board, it also reflects what academics choose to send them. (Ideally a journal will have a policy that accepts equally all methodological positions.)

Given the difficulties of conducting evaluation research that is beyond academic criticism, one might consider that, to a point, the judgement of research validity is if it tells a convincing story – does it appear to build on theory and draw logical conclusions from justified methods? And does it do a reasonable job, given the circumstances? For example, within a framework of scientific realism it may not be possible to measure outcomes, and thus test outcome/mechanism/context configurations. So one may be left having to adopt a case study approach that merely seeks to answer questions of how and why something happens, but not how much of it happens. One might bombard the case study with methods in a way that tests 'how' and 'why' hypotheses, in a convincing manner (as in the local Splash and Sportaction evaluations above), but in the end one may still not be able to quantify the programme's effect. So, one judgment of validity is if one has done the best one could, given the circumstances.

This would apply as well to those coming from the ideal of the classical experimental design. While one might aspire to the exacting criteria – the 'gold standard' – of such research design (Chapter Four), an acknowledgement that this is virtually unattainable may lead one to accept research with limitations. For example, the use of the comparative conviction rate score analysis in West Yorkshire Sports Counselling could be criticised in that it is very difficult to disentangle the effect of characteristics of participants that volunteer for a programme and that sustain participation in it; and the impact of the programme itself. But the research was frank about these difficulties (Chapter Seven) and it was generally acknowledged that it did the best job it could to overcome them.

The same point is illustrated by Coalter's (2002: 53) discussion of evaluation in sports development programmes in general. Coalter would favour the classical experimental design if at all possible; however, he has to acknowledge that 'it is extremely difficult to prove categorically that any changes in broader indicators [social outcomes] are related directly to a sports development programme' (i.e. a reduction in crime to one of the case study programmes), and goes on to assert that evidence will be required to argue that 'on the balance of probabilities' positive changes are indicated. Even this does not give categorical guidance though, as the quality of this evidence is itself unclear, defined by ambiguous phrases such as 'theoretically strong', 'systematic', 'robust' and 'relative contribution of other factors'. In other words, even if the project can, and does, collect a lot of data, the 'on the balance' evaluation of impact still rests on a set of judgements – presumably in Coalter's case, his own – of what is adequate.

The lack of a shared definitive criteria in the academic world for valid knowledge and 'theoretically strong', 'systematic' and 'robust' evidence means that disputes between academics may be as much about contesting academic status as they are about technical questions of validity. Such was the exchange between Farrington (1998) and Pawson and Tilley (1998a) in the journal *Evaluation*. This was about more than who might win a significant contract to evaluate the Communities That Care programme; it was also about dominance in the world of criminological research.

A sociology of 'adequate' explanation is also apparent within scientific realism in that it is not clear how different from the hypothesised context/mechanism/outcome configuration a result has to be to challenge the original theory (Nichols, 2005). This appears to be analogous to a paradigm shift in Kuhn's analysis of the development of scientific thought. Kuhn used the word 'paradigm' (Kuhn, 1962; 1970) to describe the activity of 'normal science' in which theory represents a framework 'within which scientists do their day-to-day work of refining observation and measurements, and constructing a detailed and precise representation of the physical world' (O'Hear, 1989: 65). A paradigm is replaced when a critical number of observations are found to be unexplainable within it (Kuhn gives the example of Newtonian science being replaced by Einstein's relativity). However, the shift to a new paradigm is dependent on more than its superior explanatory power. It is also dependent on 'the social effect of authority in the scientific community: the way publication and preferment, and research money will be distributed by those at the top of the community and in accordance with their favoured paradigm' (O'Hear, 1989: 72). Or, as Kuhn put it (Lakatos and Musgrave, 1970; back page), 'whatever scientific progress may be, we must account for it by examining the nature of the scientific group, discovering what it values, what it tolerates, and what it disdains'. So this implies that the decision to continue to accept, or to reject, a particular context/mechanism/outcome configuration will also depend on the distribution of power and influence in the academic community.

So, research sponsors, policy makers and academic gatekeepers may all inform the selection of evaluation research methods.

Practical limitations on evaluation – given resources and capability

Any research project is a compromise between what one might ideally like to do and the resources available – and this is certainly the case in programme evaluations. Table 16.1 illustrates a considerable variation in methods across the case studies.

Table 16.1 Evaluation methods used in the case study programmes

West Yorkshire Sports Counselling	Use of programme records Offender Group Reconviction Score analysis Comparative reconviction rates Before-and-after questionnaires Interviews with participants, probation officers and sports leaders Case studies of participants
Hafotty Wen	Offender Group Reconviction Score analysis Interviews with participants, probation officers and sports leaders Case studies of participants
Fairbridge	Use of programme records Interviews with programme staff and managers A questionnaire for participants measuring personal characteristics A questionnaire for participants measuring self-perception of personal skills, administered at three times Interviews with participants three months, and a year, after the initial course
Clontarf Foundation's Football Academies	Internal records of school retention rates and post-school employment, compared to national statistics Testimonials from stakeholders
Positive Futures/Sportaction	Internal records of participation Sports leader's structured records of sessions Interviews with sports leaders and participants
Positive Futures/Sportaction (national evaluation)	Interviews with programme managers – face-to-face and by telephone
Summit	Records of participation kept by the programme A two-stage questionnaire completed by participants Huskins' dependence–independence scale Interviews with participants and their parents Interviews with sports leaders Interviews with YOT officers
Splash (local evaluation)	Questionnaires completed by participants Questionnaires completed by parents Interviews with participants Interviews with Splash staff Observation of Splash sites Use of local crime data Use of insurance claim records Residents' survey (not reported here)
Splash (national evaluation)	Use of local crime data
Parks for All	Ranger service records of vandalism (could have been costed) Dojo operator records of contact with young people Police incident reports Meetings with 'friends' groups

The Fairbridge evaluation was the most comprehensive – funded by an anonymous donor. So, unusually, it was able to include follow-up interviews 2 years after the basic programme. Evaluation of West Yorkshire Sports Counselling cost £16,000 in consultants' fees in 1995, although the true cost in time given to the research was far more than this. The research reported here into Hafotty Wen, Summit, Sportaction and the local Splash programme were all conducted at no cost to the organisation, as part of academic research projects. It is very unlikely that this breadth and depth of research by an outside organisation could have been afforded by the programmes themselves. Methods such as analysis of offending records, and in-depth interviews of participants, take a great deal of time. This shows the benefits of being able to use student research, where the student is working for a dissertation or a thesis, although the quality of research may be less reliable. On the other hand, if commercial consultants are employed they will work to the budget given them, so the national evaluation of Positive Futures involved only one interview per programme with staff, and half of these were done by telephone.

A key is to build simple evaluation measures into the design of the programme so that basic information is collected automatically. For example, the Parks for All programme built in record keeping by the park ranger service and by the dojo operator in one of the parks. Summit built in records of who had attended sessions and how many they had attended. It is generally easier to record outputs rather than outcomes – who attended, rather than how they changed as a result of attending. However, with reference to a theory of change, this can be done. Summit also used the Huskins dependence–independence scale (Huskins, 1998) to measure the extent to which participants were taking greater responsibility. An advantage of the theory of change approach is that evaluation measures can be developed with programme staff, such as the 'who are you' quiz used by Fairbridge.

Sometimes one can take advantage of data already collected by other agencies. Clontarf was able to compare its student retention rates between years with national averages. The Splash programme was able to use records of insurance claims made for school premises during the school holidays – records that were kept anyway by another council department. The Splash programmes' use of local police data in the national evaluation is another example, though in this case it did require extra effort by local police to produce the data in the required form and someone had to analyse it. In Chapter Thirteen it was noted that of the 102 Splash schemes funded by the Youth Justice Board in 2000, only 43 had provided comparative crime statistics, though producing such evidence was a condition of funding. This is an indication of the difficulties of providing the evidence.

Whatever methods are used they still need to be based on a theory of how the programme might reduce crime. When policy makers consider the evidence of programme performance they need to remember the practical difficulties of gaining such evidence – how much evidence is it reasonable to ask for? This is part of a much wider debate about the rationale for public intervention in leisure and the extent to which this can be justified by the achievement of social objectives (see, for example, Gratton and Taylor, 2000).

... And events

I believe it was Harold Macmillan who, as prime minister, responded to a question about what influenced his ability to implement policies with the reply 'events dear boy, events'. However thorough the evaluation, it is possible that some unforeseen events will have a major impact on the programme. West Yorkshire Sports Counselling was unusual in investing a significant proportion of its budget in evaluation research. The results showed both a positive result from the reconviction analysis, as long as participants were in the programme for 8 weeks or more, and an understanding of why these occurred. However, the programme still lost its contract with the probation service. Contributory factors were the introduction of competitive tendering and the inexperience of both the probation service and West Yorkshire Sports Counselling Association in dealing with this. The contracting process emphasised the conflicts within the relationship rather than the shared objectives.

Hafotty Wen also closed shortly after the evaluation work reported here. Merseyside Probation Service cut funding for the centre as part of a round of budget cuts. In general all local authority programmes are vulnerable to budget cuts. In a survey of such programmes (Nichols and Booth, 1999a) it was found that of 26 programmes funded by a grant and that were able to give an indication of that grant's duration, 18 of the grants were annual. This shows how insecure many programmes are. Similarly, Long et al. (2002: 82), in their review of programmes to reduce social exclusion, found that managers were 'often preoccupied with organising and managing current activities and planning for the future, particularly securing funding', thus preventing them evaluating what they were doing. The conclusion of the 1999 report is applicable to all programmes: 'in the end political support at the local level is likely to be the factor that determines a programme's future, but in line with other public services, there will be an increasing emphasis on the production of evidence of effectiveness, however imperfect' (Nichols and Booth, 1999a: 24). The fragility of funding emphasises the value of core funding for Westtown Splash being built into a leisure department's budgets.

17 Key success factors and the role of sport

This book started with the role of sport, then looked in detail at a mechanism of pro-social development, and then placed this in a model juxtaposing different mechanisms and participants. This was the right way round for building the argument in this book, but the wrong way round for considering the role of sport. It is useful to understand the value judgements wrapped up in the use of sport, but, as in programme design and evaluation, the more fruitful starting point is theory – theory about how and why the programme might reduce crime. So at this point it is useful to revisit the main mechanisms by which programmes might impact on crime, the success factors involved, and consider the role of sport in them.

Diversion

Sport as a hook

Specific sports can attract young people to the programmes to gain their involvement. However, a limitation of concluding that sport is an attractive activity from the case studies here is that the programme participants are not likely to be those who have joined despite an aversion to sport! Attitudes towards sport are strongly linked to gender stereotypes, and there is much evidence that girls and young women are negatively affected by these (for example, Scraton and Flintoff, 2002). On the other hand, sport might reinforce a certain image of masculinity for some young men. Do programmes want to capitalise on this, or is this something not to be encouraged? The growing number of obese young people are unlikely to be attracted to an activity they find difficult. The Splash programme showed how a wide range of off-site activities could be used to maintain interest once the programme was extended from 1 week. These included non-sporting activities, such as a disco workshop and art work, so variety may be important to appeal to a wide range of participants. So this is a proviso to McGuire and Priestly's conclusion (1995: 3–34) that 'on balance the learning styles of most offenders require active, participatory methods'. Active participation is needed, but not necessarily great levels of physical activity. The important thing is that the activities attract the target group of participants.

Sport as long-term diversion through participation

In the long run, sports participation might provide a diversion from crime. In the same way that it seems obvious that someone can't be committing crime at the same time as they are on a summer Splash programme, the same long-term effect would be achieved by long-term sports participation. In this respect crime reduction and sports development objectives coincide. This mechanism is a rationale behind many programmes. For example, a YOT officer interviewed in the Summit programme felt that if participants developed an interest in sport it would reduce offending, and implied this was a long-term commitment, in the sense of Stebbins's (1997) serious leisure – a major life interest. This would prevent them getting involved in anything else. It was part of the rationale behind all the programmes that shared sports development objectives.

While this sounds plausible, there was limited evidence for this effect in the case studies. In the Summit programme, after 12 weeks of sessions there was evidence that only three out of nine case study participants were progressing to independent sports participation and one of these would probably have done so anyway. Of the 45 clients who started the programme up to June 2000, only 12 completed at the gold level, so this restricts the potential for independent sports participation. This does not mean that the mechanism of developing a commitment to sports participation, which will then act as a long-term diversion from crime, is invalid. It just means that the programme has not succeeded in achieving this by overcoming all the barriers.

So, in the long run, good practice in crime prevention through sport as a diverison becomes the same as in sports development work – enthusing participants, identifying barriers, overcoming them, and providing viable 'exit routes' for independent participation. One then has to ask, why should sport be any better an exit route than any other activity? Why not promote interest in voluntary work around other interest groups – such as youth groups or conservation volunteers? Or in religion, car maintenance, artistic expression and so on? Chapter Two reviewed potential benefits of sport, but are these better than benefits from any alternative activity, and is sport the best activity for all participants? The answer is no – at least not in all cases. In fact there are examples of programmes built around car or motor bike maintenance, fishing, or art work (Eccelstone, 1999; Spurdle, 1997; Manby, 2000). However, if programmes share sports development and crime reduction programmes, they will want to do both. An advantage of sport is that it offers a wide range of viable exit routes, through many different sports and many different providers. It also contributes to a public health policy agenda.

Pro-social development

Sport as a hook

Again, in long-term programmes, sport can be important as a hook to gain involvement – apparent in the WYSC, Hafotty Wen, Fairbridge and Clontarf programmes. Clontarf was an excellent example, where a passion for Australian Rules Football built a bridge between the Indigenous young people and the rest of Australian society. It was a major motivation in Indigenous young people joining the programme. Fairbridge found that activities such as canoeing attracted young people to the initial programme – one had to attract participants before one could engage their commitment to the longer-term programme. In WYSC the idea of sports counselling attracted probationers who were not enthused by other programmes. In Hafotty Wen the 14 Peaks expedition, and other outdoor activities, attracted certain participants – although others were deterred by not wanting to be shown to be relatively physically inept.

On the other hand, some activities might be seen as challenging to participants and may deter them. Hafotty Wen was a good example, where a bail hostel warden described the trepidation with which violent criminals might approach horse-riding. In some cases the warden might not mention the horse-riding before the participants went on the course, but would review how they felt about it afterwards. This was part of skilfully managing participants' apprehensions to achieve an experience through which they could come to terms with expressing their emotions and seek constructive ways out of difficulties rather than resorting to violence. Drug rehabilitation clients might have fears of how they might perform physically, and of how their physical condition might affect their ability to live in a new residential environment.

So sport is attractive to some participants in some circumstances. In others it fulfils a different function.

Success and self-image/self-esteem

Sport offers a medium for personal achievement – though in any competitive sports activity there are inevitably winners and losers. The case studies did not reveal particular boosts to self-esteem from sports participation – though this may occur. However, they showed that the greater the challenge of the activity, in terms of the subjective perception of challenge and capability (see Figure 3.1, page 22), the greater the reward.

Thus achieving the 14 Peaks expedition was a major achievement for the Hafotty Wen participants, and so was completing the WYSC programme for probationers who had not achieved anything similar. The certificate of completion became a valued possession for participants who had never had official recognition of any previous achievement and had generally been labelled as failures. However, this was not nearly as significant for participants who completed the Summit programme, broken down into bronze, silver and gold awards. These participants had not experienced as much failure before. This can be explained by Barry's (2006) understanding of young people's need to accumulate capital, in Bourdieu's (1986) sense. Completing the WYSC programme or the 14 Peaks programme was a very significant contribution to the participants' cultural capital, as they started from such a low base. Their socially recognised achievements had been so few and they had been much more familiar with being labelled as a failure. Perhaps, before achievement on the programme was able to occur, the participants had to 'buy into' the value system within which the certificate of completion was considered to be valuable – the value system of the sports leaders as mentors.

Managing risk

If the greatest risk is that to self-identity, sport offers the opportunity to match the participant to a risk level that will challenge them just enough, but not too much for them to fail completely. This could be in the physical sense, as in Hafotty Wen's 14 Peak expedition – and failure to finish the expedition had to be dealt with sensitively. However, more significant is the opportunity to put a participant in a situation that will stretch them in other ways. A new activity, such as horse-riding, challenged the Hafotty Wen participants emotionally, as discussed above. They had to come to terms with their fears. Sometimes this may occur by chance, and the leaders have to make the most of the opportunity. The description of how a chance situation between a female bail hostel worker officer and a male client on a Hafotty Wen course – she needed help crossing a river and he provided it (Chapter Eight) – shows how this allowed the client to take a risk in the way he related to the opposite sex. So, sport may be a medium for far more than physical risk-taking and it can be used as a tool to set up a wide range of emotional and social risks sensitively. Sometimes it will allow situations to arise where such risk-taking is unpredictable but, in these instances, staff need to review the outcome sensitively. Programme staff need the skills to do this. This supports the view expressed in Chapter Three, that a pre-occupation with physical risk may obscure the understanding of psychological risk, and the appreciation of personal develop-ment as a risk in self-concept.

Developing responsibility

Sport also offers a very suitable medium for helping clients take responsibility: within the Summit programme the sports leader could gradually give the partici-pants more responsibility for aspects of the activity, such as finding their own way there and booking the court; within Splash those who had participated for a few years could assume roles as voluntary leaders; within Sportaction participants could take roles in coaching sessions for other children. So sports-related con-texts offer many opportunities to develop participants through a structured progression of taking greater responsibility.

Related qualifications and paid work

Sportaction and WYSC showed how participants could take sports leadership qualifications and these could lead to paid employment, either within the pro-gramme or with another organisation. This was significant for participants with poor job prospects. As noted in Chapter Three, gaining employment could be very important.

A catalyst for mentor relationships – the qualities and skills of programme staff

Within Fairbridge the most important factor associated with positive long-term behavioural change was its staff. The second was the activities. In the Summit, Sportaction, Splash and WYSC programmes the participants and sports leaders sharing the activities was a catalyst for developing a good relationship of mutual respect. This was especially so when it was clear that the sports leader was not an expert but 'on a level playing field' with the participant: the Sportaction leader survived three rounds of boxing with a client who had considerable boxing experience – perhaps not a wise choice!; the Summit sports leader described playing badminton on equal terms with a client; a sports leader on Splash described how she tried hard to lose a pool game with a client to help build up a relationship; probation officers described how sharing the Hafotty Wen 14 Peaks expedition with clients changed their relationship with them.

Of course, the quality of the resulting relationship between sports leader and client depends on the qualities of the sports leader. None of the studies above examined this specifically. Pawson (2006), based on a review of studies of mentoring, encapsulated the process as accomplishing functions of befriending, direction-setting, coaching and advocacy. The mentee's trust may be hard to gain and may not develop smoothly. Mentors will need to help the mentee through relationships with a range of other agencies (as in the Sportaction leader's assistance with housing agencies, social services, etc.) and this implies that mentoring works better if it is embedded in a programme offering further support (though this is rather idealistic – see Sportaction and Summit). Remarkably, Pawson's summary focuses just on the process of mentoring and avoids saying anything about the type of person the mentor is, or should be. Perhaps this is because, consistent with a realist approach, the synthesis of previous studies is 'selective and theory-driven', but it could be a good example of the theory one starts with desensitising one to what is important. If one is to believe the former warden of Hafotty Wen, the key characteristic of leaders on his programmes were that they must set an atmosphere and expectations of mutual respect, and never respond aggressively to aggression. Staff had to be role models in the values required to live together harmoniously. Staff had to be humble enough to admit their own mistakes, respectful, understanding and have integrity. The manager of Clontarf also put prime importance on staff qualities. He aimed to employ staff who wanted to 'make a difference – not a dollar'. As noted in Chapter Three, in a survey of probation service programmes (Taylor *et al.*, 1999) managers consistently reported that high-quality staff were essential, and in assessing the quality of staff they put much more emphasis on the values they portrayed than technical skills. Given that staff will need to be dealing with young people who are in a transition in their own sense of self, as described by Barry (2006) and Hendry *et al.* (1993), the staff themselves must have a depth of maturity.

One could extend this to identify the importance of the motives, values and drive of key people in making programmes happen. There is a lot to be said for the role of 'charismatic nuts' (Pitts, 2006) whose individual flair can mould the character of a programme and defy the application of an 'off the shelf' answer. The managers/leaders of Haffoty Wen and Clontarf might both be considered to fit this label.

Values

The discussion of mentors helps put the values of sport in perspective, which, as noted, may be positive, negative, or neutral – but are not inherently 'good'. The important values are those of the sports leaders themselves, especially if they are to aspire to a mentoring relationship. Again, if the programme is in a residential setting, such as Hafotty Wen or Clontarf, these values have to permeate every-thing that happens. The centre manager at Hafotty Wen stressed that the centre environment was the opportunity for participants to experience a new way of behaving and living together.

> I make them as much aware that they are the future society; and how they function in that society, that's the society they are going to have. We could not function without their respect for us and our respect for them. That respect goes right across the whole spectrum of what we do. This is also about respecting the environment, not leaving litter around, and respecting the centre. The centre is their responsibility, there is no one cleaning up after them. The centre is their home ... We are dealing about behaviour now, whatever we are doing. [The climate of responsibility] ... starts with respect: there is no other way for it.

So the values permeating the centre are linked to the ability to allow young peo-ple to take responsibility for their own actions in a residential setting and experience the consequences of this. As a probation officer remarked, living through this was intensive for staff too!

New peers

There was little evidence that sport itself offered new peers and that these peers were any less likely to be involved in offending. This would have relied on long-term sports participation being established, and the case studies did not illustrate this. However, at the higher-risk end of the spectrum, new peers were very important to participants in Hafotty Wen and WYSC as they allowed them to maintain a new sense of self-identity and values. To stay off drugs, Hafotty Wen clients found they had to move to a new area with a new network of friends. One described how he had developed an interest in conservation work but:

> I could not tell my friends and [old] associates, 'that is a robin redbreast there, and that does stay here in the winter, and that is a blackbird and that is a song thrush' ... me street cred would have gone, so it was all suppressed ...

He could do this only when he moved to a new environment. This was very important for drug addicts coming out of rehabilitation, and who needed to establish a new life – a home, a job and social networks.

Similarly, one of the WYSC clients reported:

> To get out of [crime] you have to first get away from friends who are committing crimes and then move to a new area. When you have little money it is very tempting to commit crime when you see friends walking down the road with new clothes and things they have got as a result of crime the previous night.

So new peers who support the new sense of self identity and a new life-style are important. As for most people, sport is only a minor part of their lives, the new peers with which people are in daily contact are more significant.

Sport as offering an alternative excitement to acts of crime

There was little evidence that sport offered a direct alternative to a sense of excitement derived from crime. Some Splash participants reported that Splash reduced crime because 'it is exciting'. It was 'summat to do instead of doing mischief'. It was 'better than chasing' (chasing is breaking a window and seeing if someone will chase you). So in this sense Splash was an alternative excitement to crime, and acted as a direct diversion. There was no evidence that sport provided a long-term alternative to excitement derived from crime, in the sense of Lyng's (1993) concept of 'edgework', or in the sense of Csikszentmihalyi and Csikszentmihalyi's (1992) sense of flow. This remains an unproven possibility.

Other benefits of sport

Of course, inherent benefits of sport are that it improves personal fitness (Department for Culture, Media and Sport, 2002) if one does enough of it, and if one avoids injury. It is also associated with good mental health. But, as noted in Chapter Two, this still leaves the question of how this is related to crime reduction.

Conclusion – sport as a tool

This chapter has aimed to put the use of sport in perspective, and untangle it from the value judgements surrounding it. In the context of programmes to reduce youth crime, sport is a tool to facilitate a process, much more than an end in its own right, and needs to be used with sensitivity. So its value rests very much on the ability of programme staff to use it in that way. This will require an awareness of the process and an ability to match the needs of the participant with the experience sport offers. It may also require an awareness of how perceptions of sport (for example, associations with masculine physical prowess and physical risk) may get in the way of what a programme is trying to achieve.

18 Conclusions

This book started by stating it was aimed at programme managers, researchers, policy makers and students. The conclusions are structured according to these audiences.

From the perspective of programme managers

For programme managers, programme design must start from a plausible 'theory of change' – a chain of events linking the type of participant, the process of getting involved, programme content and process, intermediate effects, and the long-term objectives. Chapter Six suggested three main mechanisms: diversion, deterrence and long-term pro-social development. Chapter Three discussed details of this last mechanism and the role of sport was discussed both initially in Chapter Two and, drawing on the case studies, in Chapter Seventeen. The most relevant mechanism for long-term offenders is a redefinition of self-identity consistent with not offending – to achieve which they will need a lot of support. Of course, an alternative mechanism might be incarceration, so there is no chance of offending; however, incarceration is a very good predictor of further offending. The case studies have not included any programmes run in prison, although some Hafotty Wen participants were in drug rehabilitation centres or borstal. However, the potential for long-term pro-social development to occur in confinement is bound to be limited as there is little chance to develop new peers and a new reference group to support a new sense of self-identity. Cunning programme design may try to capitalise on more than one mechanism, and in local authorities can maximise synergy between crime reduction and other objectives such as sports development.

The design of a programme and the resources one can justify allocating to it per participant will reflect the seriousness of the 'risk' of the participant, in the sense of the risk they present to society. The model in Chapter Six puts Hafotty Wen and WYSC clients at the top end of this risk scale, but this scale would be extended if one included all the offending population. The higher up the risk scale participants are, the more they are likely to be experiencing multiple and related 'risk factors' – such as problems with income, housing, health and lack of qualifications. Thus sports leaders in the Sportaction and Summit programmes recognised the limitations of what could be achieved by offering just sports activities, and what they felt able to offer. The Clontarf programme recognised the importance of establishing participants in stable employment to help them overcome the multiple disadvantages of the Indigenous community in Australian society. Hafotty Wen participants described the problems of establishing new lives – finding a flat and paying the bills, and, especially for those on drug rehabilitation, a new social life. So the role of sport has to be kept in perspective.

Programme design is complicated by the fact that programmes may have more than one objective and may also evolve, and thus the emphasis on any one objective may change in response to changing funding sources and political priorities. This can be seen as an opportunity for synergy between objectives, as much as it might appear to be a challenge to programme integrity.

Success factors in programme design include activities that will attract the target participants. A programme has to attract participants to join before it can do anything else with them – assuming participation is voluntary. The quality of programme staff is critical. Staff will have to have different levels of skills for dealing with different types of clients and if a programme has shared objectives, for example sports development and crime reduction, staff will need a balance of skills to deal with both. If a programme aims to work through long-term prosocial development of participants, it needs enough time to be able to guide participants sensitively through a progression of opportunities to take responsibility and challenge their perceptions of themselves. On the other hand, to use resources effectively it will need to decide a cut-off point beyond which a participant will have to have achieved independence. The more serious the offender the longer this will be, but another factor is how much work per participant the funding of the programme will allow.

For many programmes, especially those run by local authorities, a critical factor is ensuring continued funding. If at all possible, it is desirable to build core funding into a mainstream budget so one does not have to re-justify it every year. Specific grants can then be added to this as they become available. Programme managers have to convince sponsors, policy makers and politicians that their programmes are worth funding in a climate of 'evidence-led policy' where proof of effectiveness is required. As many simple evaluation measures need to be built into the day-to-day running of the programme as possible, based on the relevant theory of change, but not to the extent that they get in the way of achieving the programme objectives. (No participant on a 5-day course wants to spend the first 30 minutes completing a complicated questionnaire they have to be talked through – and then have the task repeated on day 5.) Programme managers need to bear in mind the evaluation audience – what will convince key politicians (local or national) and local residents; and what evidence is required as a condition of any grant. Given this, especially in local government, managing publicity to maintain positive public opinion is also crucial. The strong value judgements surrounding youth crime and sport make any programme very susceptible to the 'rewarding criminals' story, which the media may always be tempted to develop. 'Good news' is harder to sell.

From the perspective of researchers

In research or evaluation the choice of methods should start from a theory of change. This may be based on academic theory, or on the programme staffs' views of how the programme works. If based in academic theory it must be plausible to the programme staff and lead to evaluation tools that are accepted as practical to implement. The exception to this is if one starts from an interpretivist perspective and believes that the social world is purely a social construction, in which case one might start from a theoretical blank sheet. I would argue that this is never the case, as one's research topic will always have been determined to some extent by one's own interests and preconceptions. The 'blank sheet' does not exist.

So, the extent to which one starts from theory will depend on one's methodological assumptions, which will also determine the way in which one approaches research and the methods one chooses. These assumptions are more important if one is researching for a PhD or to produce a top-quality academic paper targeted at an academic journal (the editors of which are more likely to share this methodological disposition). However, other important stakeholders are policy makers, and their views of what is valid knowledge may also influence the researcher's choice.

My own preference is for a methodology based on scientific realism, because the notion of generative, rather than secessionist causality (as in positivism), more accurately represents the experience of a participant on a programme – and more generally the relationship between the individual and society. There is an interaction between participant and programme (between agent and structure). Scientific realism also holds that knowledge gradually creeps towards a more accurate understanding of an external reality. Bryman (2001) quotes Bhaskar, the philosopher who founded this approach (1975: 250): 'science then is the systematic attempt to express in thought the structures and ways of acting of things that exist and act independently of thought'. Bhaskar's position is that the researcher can move towards a more complete understanding of an external reality, but, as in the natural sciences, we are dealing with probabilities. We will never be able to say with absolute certainty that 'a' causes 'b': we can say that understanding is moving towards reality, but we must recognise that reality, which exists independently of our knowledge, always has unexplored depths to it (Collier, 1998). In other words, 'we know we can't know everything, but we do know we are moving in the right direction because we have a systematic approach to knowledge generation' (Nichols, 2005: 23). However, within scientific realism there are still difficulties of how exactly one defines a context/mechanism/regularity configuration, and when the evidence is sufficient to support or modify it. As in a deductive approach, one needs to be aware that the theoretical framework one starts from might determine where one goes, at the expense of what is actually happening.

I also sympathise with Tilley's (2000: 110) personal academic agenda.

> In my particular case, realistic evaluation has provided a way of dealing with two sources of contemporary unease: about that aspect of postmodernism

which casts doubt on the possibility of objective knowledge; and about that aspect of modernism that promises universal unconditional truths. Realistic evaluation ... seems to me to steer a course between the Scylla of relativism and the Charybdis of absolutism.

A further consideration in the choice of methods is what is practical, both with reference to the resources available, and the research situation. Ideally programme managers and researchers might work together at the design of a programme to maximise the benefit of simple measures. The summary table in Chapter Sixteen gives examples of these.

From the perspective of policy makers

Policy makers need to look for a programme that can articulate a convincing theory of change. It is able to justify who it works with, what it does, and how it achieves its objectives. As far as possible a systematic collection of evidence will have been built into programme design, and any external evaluation will both have been designed to test, and will be based on, this theory of change. However policy makers must be reasonable in the expectations of evidence. They must bear in mind the inherent difficulties of producing evidence of outcomes, especially over any period over 2 years, and the greater difficulties of demonstrating a link to crime reduction for programmes working with low-risk participants and where this is only one of the objectives. Be realistic about the limitations of evidence-led policy.

In allocating resources between programmes, there may be a difficult decision to make between programmes that work intensively with a few participants (Hafotty Wen, WYSC) and those that work less intensively with a large number of low-risk participants (Splash). It is tempting to direct resources towards the first type of programme but this is to ignore the less tangible, but possibly significant, impact of the second. In practice this trade-off does not normally occur, as different types of programme tend to be funded by different agencies.

From the perspective of students

This book has hopefully given an insight into the practical issues in programme design, management and evaluation, placed in a broad theoretical context of the role of sport, programme mechanisms, the political environment and methodological debates. It is not the complete picture – and never will be. This book started from particular concerns: understanding the role of sport, and other activities, in the personal development of young people; the need to justify the subsidy of leisure to achieve social objectives; and a need to find a methodology that made sense of the world and could also lead to policy implications. A different starting point would have led on a different journey, so treat this critically, as a starting point of your own.

References

Altschuler, D. and Armstrong, T. (1984) 'Intervening with serious juvenile offenders'. In Mathias, R. and Demuro, P. (eds) *Violent Juvenile Offenders*, San Francisco: National Council on Crime and Delinquency. In Bateman, T. and Pitts, J. (eds) (2005) *The RHP Companion to Youth Justice*, Lyme Regis: Russell House Publishing, 248–58.

Astbury, R. and Knight, B. (2003) *Fairbridge Research Project – Final report*, London: Charities Evaluation Services.

Audit Commission (1996) *Misspent Youth*, Abingdon: Audit Commission.

Bacon, S. (1983) *The Conscious Use of Metaphor in Outward Bound*, Denver: Colorado Outward Bound School.

Barry, M. (2006) *Youth Offending in Transition: The search for social recognition*, London: Routledge.

Bateman, T. and Pitts, J. (2005) 'Conclusion: what the evidence tells us'. In Bateman, T. and Pitts, J. (eds) *The RHP Companion to Youth Justice*, Lyme Regis: Russell House Publishing, 248–58.

Beck, U. (1992) *Risk Society: Towards a new modernity*, London: Sage.

Bhaskar, R. (1975) *A Realist Theory of Science*, Leeds: Leeds Books.

Bourdieu, P. (1986) 'The forms of capital'. In Richardson, J.G. (ed.) *Handbook of theory and research for the sociology of education*, Westport, CT: Greenwood Press. In Barry, M. (2006) *Youth Offending in Transition: The search for social recognition*, London: Routledge.

Brantingham, P. and Faust, F. (1976) A conceptual model of crime prevention, *Crime and Delinquency*, 22 (3), 284–96.

Brookes, A. (2003) 'Adventure programming and the fundamental attribution error. A critique of neo-Hahnian outdoor education theory'. In Humberstone, B., Brown, H. and Richards, K. (eds) *Whose Journeys? The outdoors and adventure as social and cultural phenomena*, Penrith: The Institute for Outdoor Learning, 403–22.

Brown, H. and Humberstone, B. (2003) 'Researching youth transitions and summer activity initiative: problems and possibilities'. In Humberstone, B., Brown, H. and Richards K. (eds) *Whose Journeys? The outdoors and adventure as social and cultural phenomena*, Cumbria: Institute for Outdoor Learning, 261–72.

Bryman, A. (2001) *Social Research Methods*, Oxford: Oxford University Press.

Bryman, A. and Bell, E. (2003) *Business Research Methods*, Oxford University Press: Oxford.

Cap Gemmini Ernst and Young (2001) *Summer Splash 2000: Final report*, London: Cap Gemmini Ernst and Young. At: http://www.youth-justice-board.gov.uk/policy/summer_splash_ 2000_final_report.pdf accessed 12/02.

Cap Gemmini Ernst and Young (2002) *Splash 2001: Final report*, London: Cap Gemmini Ernst and Young. At: http://www.youth-justice-board.gov.uk/policy/splash_2001.pdf accessed 12/02.

Cassell, C. and Synon, G. (eds) (2004) *Essential Guide to Qualitative Methods in Organisational Research*, London: Sage.

Catalano, R. and Hawkins, J.D. (1996) 'The social development model: a theory of antisocial behaviour'. In Hawkins, J.D. (ed.) *Delinquency and Crime*, Cambridge: Cambridge University Press, 149–97.

Coalter, F. (1996) *Sport and Anti-social Behaviour: A policy-related review*, Research Digest no. 41, Edinburgh: The Scottish Sports Council.

Coalter, F. (1999) Sport and recreation in the United Kingdom: Flow with the flow or buck the trends? *Managing Leisure*, 4 (1), 24–39.

Coalter, F. (2002) *Sport and Community Development: A manual*, Edinburgh: Sportscotland.

Coalter, F. (2006) 'The duality of leisure policy'. In Rojek, Chris, Shaw, Susan and Veal, A.J. (eds) *A Handbook of Leisure Studies*, Basingstoke: Palgrave, 162–81.

Collier, A. (1998) 'Critical realism'. In *Routledge Encyclopedia of Philosophy*, London: Routledge.

Collins, M. and Kay, T. (2003) *Sport and Social Exclusion*, London: Routledge.

Collison, M. (1996) 'In search of the high life', *British Journal of Criminology*, 36 (3), 428–44.

Commission on Social Justice (1994) *Social Justice, Strategies for National Renewal*, London: Vintage.

Communities That Care (1997) *Communities That Care*, London: CTC (UK).

Connell, J.P. and Kubish, A.C. (1998) 'Applying a theories of change approach to the evaluation of comprehensive community initiatives: progress, prospects and problems'. In Fullbright-Anderson, K., Connell, J.P. and Kubish, A.C. (eds) *New Approaches to Evaluating Community Initiatives: Theory, measurement and analysis*, Washington, DC: Aspen Institute.

Coopers and Lybrand (1994) *Preventative Strategy for Young People in Trouble*, London: ITV Telethon/The Prince's Trust.

Copas, J. and Marshall, P. (1998) 'The offender group reconviction scale: a statistical reconviction score for use by probation officers', *Applied Statistics*, 47 (1), 159–71.

Copas, J., Ditchfield, J. and Marshall, P. (1994) 'Development of a new reconviction prediction score', *Home Office Research and Statistics Department Research Bulletin No. 36: Prisons and prisoners*, London: Home Office Research and Planning Unit.

Craine, S. and Coles, B. (1995) 'Alternative careers; youth transitions and young people's involvement in crime', *Youth and Policy*, 48, 6–26.

Critcher, C. (2000) 'Sport is damaging to your health', *Recreation*, December 2000, 17–20.

Crompton, J. (2004) 'Why leisure matters'. Unpublished plenary presentation to the 8th World Leisure Congress, Brisbane, 2004.

Crow, I. (2001) *The Treatment and Rehabilitation of Offenders*, London: Sage.

Crow, I., France, A., Hacking, S. and Hart, M. (2004) *Does Communites That Care Work?*, York: Joseph Rowntree Foundation.

Csikszentmihalyi, M. and Csikszentmihalyi, I. (1991) 'Adventure and the flow experience'. In Miles, J. and Priest, S. (eds) *Adventure Education*, Pennsylvania: Venture Publishing.

Csikszentmihalyi, M. and Csikszentmihalyi, I. (1992) *Optimal Experience: Psychological studies of flow in consciousness*, Cambridge: Cambridge University Press.

Department for Culture, Media and Sport (1999) *Policy Action Team 10: A report to the Social Exclusion Unit*, London: DCMS.

Department of Culture, Media and Sport (DCMS)/Strategy Unit (2002) *Game Plan: A strategy for delivering Government's sport and physical activity objectives*, London: Cabinet Office.

Eccelstone, V. (1999) 'Breaking barriers', *Leisure Manager*, 17 (12), 16–19.

Emler, N. (2001) *Self-esteem, the Costs and Causes of Low Self-worth*, York: Joseph Rowntree Foundation.

Farrall, S. (2002) *Rethinking What Works with Offenders: Probation, social context and desistance from crime*, Devon: William Publishing.

Farrington, D. (1994) 'Early developmental prevention of juvenile delinquency', *RSA Journal*, November 1994.

Farrington, D. (1996) 'The explanation and prevention of youthful offending'. In Hawkins, J.D. (ed.) *Delinquency and Crime*, Cambridge: Cambridge University Press, 68–148.

Farrington, D. (1997a) 'Human development and criminal careers'. In Maguire, M., Morgan, R., and Reiner, R. (eds) *The Oxford Handbook of Criminology*, Oxford: Oxford University Press, 361–408.

Farrington, D. (1997b) 'Evaluating a community crime prevention program', *Evaluation*, 3(2), 157–73.

Farrington, D. (1998) 'Evaluating "Communities That Care"', *Evaluation*, 4 (2), 204–10.

Farrington, D. (2000) 'Explaining and preventing crime: the globalisation of knowledge – the American Society of Criminology 1999 Presidential Address', *Criminology*, 38 (1), 1–24.

Fletcher, M. (1992) *An Investigation into Participation in Amateur Boxing*. Dissertation submitted in part requirement for the degree of MSc in Sport and Recreation Management, University of Sheffield.

Flick, U. (2002) *An Introduction to Qualitative Research*, London: Sage.

Gaber, I. (2002) 'Every picture', *Guardian*, 31 July 2002.

Gibson, B. (ed.) (2000) *Introduction to Youth Justice*, Winchester: Waterside Press.

Gibson, M. (1979) 'Therapeutic aspects of wilderness programs: a comprehensive literature review', *Therapeutic Recreation Journal*, second quarter 1979, 21–33.

Giddens, A. (1991) *Modernity and Self-identity*, Cambridge: Polity.

Glass, G.V., McGaw, B. and Smith, M.L. (1981) *Meta-analysis in Social Research*, London: Sage.

Glyptis, S. (1989) *Leisure and Unemployment*, Milton Keynes: Open University Press.

Gordon, W., Cuddy, P., and Black, J. (1999) *Introduction to Youth Justice*, Winchester: Waterside Press.

Graham, J. and Bowling, B. (1995) *Young People and Crime*, Home Office Research Study 145, London: Home Office.

Gratton, C. and Taylor, P. (2000) *Economics of Sport and Recreation*, London: E.&F.N. Spon.

Greenaway, R. (1995) 'Powerful learning experiences in management learning and development'. PhD thesis, University of Lancaster.

Hattie, J., Marsh, H.W., Neill, J. and Richards, G. (1997) 'Adventure education and outward bound: out-of-class experiences that make a lasting difference', *Review of Educational Research*, 67 (1), 43–87.

Hedderman, C. and Sugg, D. (1997) *Changing Offenders' Attitudes and Behaviour: What works? Part II: The influence of cognitive approaches: A survey of probation programmes*, Home Office Research Study 171, London: Home Office.

Hendry, L.B., Shucksmith, J., Love, J.G. and Glendinning, A. (1993) *Young People's Leisure and Lifestyles*, London: Routledge.

Holt, R. (1990) *Sport and the British*, Oxford: Oxford University Press.

Hopkins, D. and Putnam, R. (1993) *Personal Growth Through Adventure*, London: David Fulton.

Howell, J., Krisberg, B., Hawkins, D. and Wilson. J. (eds) (1995) *Serious Violent and Chronic Juvenile Offenders: A sourcebook*, London: Sage. In Bateman, T. and Pitts, J. (eds) *The RHP Companion to Youth Justice*, Lyme Regis: Russell House Publishing, 248–58.

Huskins, J. (1996) *Quality Work with Young People*, Kingsdown: Huskins.

Huskins, J. (1998) *From Disaffection to Social Inclusion: A social skills preparation for active citizenship and employment*, Kingsdown: Huskins.

Hutchinson, J., Henderson, D. and Francis, S. (2001) *Evaluation of Pilot Summer Activities for 16-Year-Olds: Summer 2000. DfEE Research Report No. 260*, London: Department for Education and Employment.

Jupp. V. (1995) 'The crime and sport equation: sport's contribution to crime reduction'. Unpublished address to the ILAM national conference.

Katz, J. (1988) *Seductions of Crime: Moral and sensual attractions in doing evil*, New York: Basic Books. In Lyng, S. 'Dysfunctional risk taking: criminal behaviour as edgework'. In Bell, B. and Bell, W. (eds) (1993) *Adolescent Risk Taking*, London: Sage.

Kuhn, T. (1962) *The Structure of Scientific Revolutions*, 2nd edn, London: University of Chicago Press.

Kuhn, T. (1970) 'Logic of discovery or psychology of research'. In Lakatos, I. and Musgrave, A. (eds) (1970) *Criticism and the Growth of Knowledge*, London: Cambridge University Press, 1–24.

Lakatos, I. and Musgrave, A. (eds) (1970) *Criticism and the Growth of Knowledge*, London: Cambridge Unviersity Press.

Lloyd, C., Mair, G. and Hough, M. (1994) *Explaining Re-conviction Rates: A critical analysis, Home Office Research Study 136*, London: HMSO.

Long, J., Welch, M., Bramham, P., Butterfield, H. and Lloyd, E. (2002) *Count Me In*, Department for Culture Media and Sport. At: http://www.lmu.ac.uk/ces/lss/research/countmein.pdf accessed 2/03.

Loxley, C., Curtin, L. and Brown, R. (2002) *Summer Splash Schemes 2000: Findings from six case studies. Crime Reduction Research Series Paper 12*, London: Home Office.

Lyng, S. (1993) 'Dysfunctional risk taking: criminal behaviour as edgework'. In Bell, B. and Bell, W. (eds) (1993) *Adolescent Risk Taking*, London: Sage.

Manby, M. (2000) *Evaluation of Moving Ahead Project*, Huddersfield: Nationwide Children's Research Centre.

Maruna, S. (2001) *Making Good*, Washington: American Psychological Association.

Mason, S. (1999) 'Feminist ethics of leisure', *Leisure Studies*, 18 (3), 233–48.

Martinson, R. (1974) 'What works? Questions and answers about prison reform. The public interest', 35, 22–54. In Crow, I. (2001) *The Treatment and Rehabilitation of Offenders*, London: Sage.

Martinson, R. (1979) 'New findings, new views: a note of caution regarding sentencing reform', Hofstra Law Review, 7 (2), 243–58. In Crow, I. (2001) *The Treatment and Rehabilitation of Offenders*, London: Sage.

McCormack, F. (2000) *Leisure Exclusion? Analysing Interventions Using Active Leisure with Young People Offending or at Risk*. Thesis submitted in fulfilment for the degree of Doctor of Philosophy, University of Loughborough.

McCormack, F. (2001) 'The potential of outreach sports interventions for young people to achieve community development and social inclusion through leisure'. In McPherson, G. and Reid, G. (eds) *Leisure and Social Inclusion*, Publication 73, Eastbourne: Leisure Studies Association, 7–22.

McGuire, J. and Priestley, P. (1995) 'Reviewing what works: past, present and future'. In McGuire, J. (ed.) *What Works: Reducing offending*, Chichester: Wiley.

Merrington, S. and Hine, J. (2001) *A Handbook for Evaluating Probation Work with Offenders*, London: Home Office.

Mortlock, C. (1984) *The Adventure Alternative*, Milnthorpe: Cicerone Press.

Muncie, J. (1999) *Youth and Crime*, London: Sage.

Nicholl, J., Coleman, P. and Brazier, J. (1994) 'Health and healthcare costs and benefits of exercise', *PharmacoEconomics*, 5 (2), 109–22.

Nichols, G. (1998) 'Would you like to step outside for a moment? – a consideration of the place of outdoor adventurous activities in programmes to change offending behaviour', *Vista*, 4 (1), 37–49.

Nichols, G. (1999a) 'Developing a rationale for sports counselling projects', *Howard Journal of Criminal Justice*, 38 (2), 198–208.

Nichols, G. (1999b) 'Is risk a valuable component of outdoor adventure programmes for young offenders undergoing drug rehabilitation?', *Journal of Youth Studies*, 2 (1), 101–16.

Nichols, G. (2000a) 'A research agenda for adventure education', *Australian Journal of Outdoor Education*, 4 (2), 22–31.

Nichols, G. (2000b) 'Risk and adventure education', *Journal of Risk Research*, 3 (2), 121–34.

Nichols, G. (2000c) 'What is development training?'. In Barnes. P. (ed.) *Values and Outdoor Learning*, Penrith: Association for Outdoor Learning, 10–12.

Nichols, G. (2001a) 'The use and limitations of reconviction rate analysis to evaluate an outdoor pursuits programme for probationers', *Vista*, 6 (3), 280–8.

Nichols, G. (2001b) 'Review of: Evaluation of pilot summer activities for 16-year-olds: Summer 2000', *Horizons*, 14, 23–5.

Nichols, G. (2004a) 'The impact of sports programmes on youth crime'. Thesis submitted to the University of Sheffield in fulfilment for the degree of Doctor of Philosophy.

Nichols, G. (2004b) 'Crime and punishment and sports development', *Leisure Studies*, 23 (2), 177–94.

Nichols, G. (2005) 'Reflections on researching a causal relationship between sport and youth crime – the hope of scientific realism'. In Hylton, K., Long, J. and Flintoff, A. (eds) *Evaluating Sport and Active Leisure for Young People*, Eastbourne: Leisure Studies Association Publication No. 88, 23–44.

Nichols, G. and Booth, P. (1999a) *Programmes to Reduce Crime and which are Supported by Local Authority Leisure Departments*, Melton Mowbray: Institute of Sport and Recreation Management.

Nichols, G. and Booth, P. (1999b) 'Crime reduction programmes supported by local authority leisure departments', *Local Governance*, 25 (4), 227–36.

Nichols, G. and Crow, I. (2004) 'Measuring the impact of crime reduction interventions involving sports activities for young people', *Howard Journal*, 43 (3), 267–83.

Nichols, G. and Taylor, P. (1996) *West Yorkshire Sports Counselling, Final Evaluation Report*, Halifax: West Yorkshire Sports Counselling Association.

Nichols, G. and Taylor, P. (1997) 'A case study of competitive tendering of sports counselling services', *Vista*, 3 (1), 36–46.

Nichols, G., Taylor, P., Crow, I. and Irvine, D. (2000) 'Methodological considerations in evaluating physical activity programmes for young offenders', *World Leisure and Recreation*, 42 (1), 10–17.

O'Hear, A. (1989) *An Introduction to the Philosophy of Science*, Oxford: Clarendon Press.

Paulus, D. (1983) 'Sphere-specific measures of perceived control', *Journal of Personality and Social Psychology*, 44 (6), 1253–65.

Pawson, N. (2006) *Evidence-based Policy: A realist perspective*, London: Sage.

Pawson, R. and Tilley, N. (1997) *Realistic Evaluation*, London: Sage.

Pawson, R. and Tilley, N. (1998a) 'Caring communities, paradigms polemics, design debates', *Evaluation*, 4 (1), 73–90.

Pawson, R. and Tilley, N. (1998b) 'Cook book methods and disastrous recipes: a rejoinder to Farrington', *Evaluation*, 4 (2), 211–13.

Pitts, J. (2003) *The New Politics of Youth Crime: Discipline or solidarity?*, Lyme Regis: Russell House Publishing.

Pitts, J. (2006) Unpublished conference presentation. Doing Youth Justice Conference, April 2006.

Priest, S. (1991) 'The adventure experience paradigm'. In Miles, J. and Priest, S. (eds) *Adventure Education*, Pennsylvania: Venture Publishing.

Priest, S. and Gass, M. (1997) *Effective Leadership in Adventure Programming*, New Hampshire: Human Kinetics.

Purdy, D.A. and Richards, S.F. (1983) 'Sport and juvenile delinquency: an examination and assessment of four major theories', *Journal of Sport Behaviour*, 6 (4), 179–93.

Putnam, R. (1985) *A Rationale for Outward Bound*, Rugby: Outward Bound Trust.

Rapoport, R. (1982) 'Unemployment and the family. The Loch Memorial Lecture 1981'. London, The Family Welfare Association. In S. Glyptis (1989) *Leisure and Unemployment*, Milton Keynes: Open University Press.

Raynor, P. and Vanstone, M. (1994) *Straight Thinking on Probation, Third Interim Evaluation Report*, Bridgend: Mid Glamorgan Probation Service.

Ringer, M. and Gillis, H.L. (1995) 'Managing psychological depth in adventure programming', *Journal of Experiential Education*, 18 (1), 41–51.

Ringer, M. and Spanoghe, F. (1997) 'Can't he see me crying inside? – managing psychological risk in adventure programs', *Zip Lines*, summer 1997, 41–5.

Roberts, K. (1992) 'Leisure responses to urban ills in Great Britain and Northern Ireland'. In Sugden, J. and Knox, C. (eds) *Leisure in the 1990s: Rolling back the welfare state*, Eastbourne: Leisure Studies Association.

Roberts, K. and Brodie, D. (1992) *Inner-city Sport: Who pays and what are the benefits?*, Voorthhuizen: Goirano Bruno Culemborg.

Robins, D. (1996) 'Sport and crime prevention; the evidence of research', *Criminal Justice Matters*, 23, spring 1996.

Rose, D. (2002) 'It's official – prison does work after all', *Observer*, 5 May 2002, 20–1.

Rosenberg, M. (1965) *Society and the Adolescent Self Image*, Princeton, NJ: Princeton University Press.

Rosenthal, S.R. (1982) 'The fear factor', *Sport and Leisure*, 23, 61.

Ross, R. and Fabiano, E. (1985) *Time to Think: A cognitive model of delinquency prevention and offender rehabilitation*, Ottawa: T3 Associates.

Schultz, L., Crompton, J. and Witt, P. (1995) 'A national profile of the status of public recreation services for at-risk children and youth', *Journal of Park and Recreation Administration*, 13 (3), 1–25.

Scraton, S. and Flintoff, A. (2002) *Gender and Sport: A reader*, London: Routledge.

Smith, M.K. (2003) 'From youth work to youth development: the new government framework for English youth services', *Youth and Policy*, 79, 46–59.

Sport England (2001) *General Household Survey: Participation in sport – past trends and future prospects*, Wetherby: Sport England.

Sport England (2002a) *Positive Futures: A review of impact and good practice, Summary report*. At: http://www.sportengland.org/index/get_resources/research/learning_lessons/postive_futures_review2002.htm accessed 21/4/06.

Sport England (2002b) *Positive Futures: A review of impact and good practice. Individual project reports*. At: http://www.sportengland.org/resources/pdfs/publicat_pdfs/PF_Site_Reports.pdf accessed 4/04.

Sport England (2002c) *Sport is Getting Youngsters Away from Crime and Helping Fight Drug Abuse, New findings reveal*. At: http://www.sportengland.org/news/press_releases/sport_is_getting_youngsters_away_from_crime_and_helping_fight_drug_abuse,new_findings_reveal.htm accessed 21/4/06.

Sports Council/Health Education Authority (1992) *Allied Dunbar National Fitness Survey*, London: Sports Council.

Sports Council Research Unit, North West (1990) *Solent Sports Counselling Project Final Evaluation Report*, Sports Council: London.

Spurdle, L.S. (1997) 'An evaluation of the Artskills project for young people at risk from drugs'. Dissertation in part requirement for the MA in Arts and Heritage Management of the University of Sheffield.

Stebbins, R. (1997) 'Serious leisure and well-being'. In Haworth, J. (ed.) *Work, Leisure and Well-being*, London: Routledge, 117–30.

Steering Committee for the Review of Commonwealth/State Service Provision (2005) 'Overcoming indigenous disadvantage – key indicators 2005'. At: http://www.pc.gov.au/gsp/reports/indigenous/keyindicators2005/overview/index.html accessed 21/4/06.

Stewart, B., Nicholson, M., Smith, A. and Westerbeek, H. (2004) *Australian Sport: Better by design?*, London: Routledge.

Tashakkori, A. and Teddlie, C. (1998) *Mixed Methodology*, London: Sage.

Taylor, P., Crow, I., Nichols, G. and Irvine, D. (1999) *Demanding Physical Activity Programmes for Young Offenders under Probation Supervision*, London: The Home Office.

Thurston, P. (1997) 'A case study of competitive tendering of sports counselling: foul play or sour grapes!', *Vista*, 3 (1), 47–51.

Tilley, N. (2000) 'Doing realistic evaluation of criminal justice'. In Jupp, V., Davies, P. and Francis, P. (eds) *Doing Criminological Research*, London: Sage, 97–113.

Torkildsen, G. (2000) *Leisure and Recreation Management*, London: E & FN Spon.

Trujillo, C.M. (1983) 'The effect of weight training and running exercise intervention programs on the self-esteem of college women', *International Journal of Sports Psychology*, 14, 162–73.

Vanstone, M. (2000) 'Cognitive behavioral work with offenders in the UK', *Howard Journal of Criminal Justice*, 39 (2), 171–83.

Vennard, J., Sugg, D. and Hedderman, C. (1997) *Changing Offenders' Attitudes and Behaviour: What works? Part 1: The use of cognitive-behavioral approaches with offenders: Messages from the research*, Home Office Research Study 171, London: Home Office.

Warr, P. and Jackson, P. (1983) 'Self-esteem and unemployment among young workers', *Le Travail Human*, 46 (2), 355–64.

Weiss, C. (1998) *Evaluation*, New Jersey: Prentice Hall.

Witt, P. (2000) 'Positioning, protection and proof'. In Morgan, D. (ed.) *Sport Versus Youth Crime*, Bolton: Bolton Institute.

Witt. P. and Crompton, J. (1996) *Recreation Programs that Work for At-risk Youth*, Pennsylvania: Venture Publishing.

Witt, P. and Crompton, J. (2003) 'Positive youth development practices in recreational settings in the United States', *World Leisure Journal*, 45, 4–11.

Yin, R. (1994) *Case Study Research*, London: Sage.

Yin, R. (2003) *Case Study Research: Design and methods*, London: Sage.

Index